ROYAL HISTORICAL SOCIETY
STUDIES IN HISTORY

THE POLITICS OF STABILITY
A Portrait of the Rulers in Elizabethan London

For Don Black,

Best wishes to a

fellow anglophile.

"Mike" Foster

THE POLITICS OF STABILITY
A Portrait of the Rulers in Elizabethan London

Frank Freeman Foster

LONDON
ROYAL HISTORICAL SOCIETY
1977

The Society records its gratitude to the following, whose generosity made possible the initiation of this series: The British Academy; The Pilgrim Trust; The Twenty-Seven Foundation; The United States Embassy's Bicentennial funds; The Wolfson Trust; several private donors.

Printed in England
by Swift Printers Ltd
London, E.C.1.

IN MEMORIAM HENRY LITHGOW ROBERTS

CONTENTS

TABLES

ACKNOWLEDGEMENTS

Eugene F. Rice, Jr., Orest A. Ranum, the late T.F. Reddaway, Philip E. Jones, Wallace T. MacCaffrey, Robert Ashton, and Anne Firth Murray all read part or the whole of an earlier version of the book and made valuable suggestions. I especially appreciate the careful attention of Mr. Jones, who pointed out several errors, and the omnivorous curiosity of Professor Ashton, who forced me to think about economic connections. Professor G.R. Elton read the entire work in its penultimate form and provided the kind of criticisms that led to my final revisions. Robert A. Wijsman, Department of Mathematics at the University of Illinois, pointed out what I could and could not do with the modest statistical illustrations I had in mind.

A number of others have made my memories of the time spent on this project the more pleasant. I am most grateful to the masters and wardens of the following livery companies of London for permission to visit their halls and consult their records: the Mercers, Drapers, Goldsmiths, Skinners, Merchant Taylors, Haberdashers, Ironmongers, and Clothworkers. Many kindnesses were received in the livery companies, especially from Miss Jean Imray of the Mercers Company and Mr. Frank Keefe of the Clothworkers. English archivists and their assistants are among the most undervalued ambassadors of goodwill. Dr. Albert E.J. Hollaender opened to me the many treasures of the Guildhall Library. Mr. Jones did the same for those in the London Records Office. His former assistant, Miss Betty Masters, now his successor as Deputy Keeper, deserves special mention for her cheerfulness and unceasing patience in the face of innumerable queries. The Research Board of the University of Illinois helped with a grant during the summer of 1971, and the Department of History underwrote some of the typing costs.

Abbreviated parts of chapters 4 and 6 appeared earlier in "Politics and Community in Elizabethan London', *The Rich, The Well Born, and The Powerful: Elites and Upper Classes in History,* ed. Frederic C. Jaher (1973), pp. 110-38.

Punctuation and spelling have been modernized, except in personal names and in a few quotations which will be obvious. Dating is New Style, but the days of the week remain the same. Unless noted otherwise, all books mentioned in the footnotes were published in London.

ABBREVIATIONS

Add. MSS	British Library Additional Manuscripts
APC	*Acts of the Privy Council*
BL	British Library
CA	Churchwardens' account book
Cal. Let.-Book	*Calendar of Letter-Books Preserved among the Archives of the Corporation of the City of London at the Guildhall,* ed. Reginald R. Sharpe (1899-1912)
CLRO	Corporation of London Records Office
CPR	*Calendar of Patent Rolls*
CSPD	*Calendar of State Papers Domestic*
DNB	*Dictionary of National Biography*
GLMR	Guildhall Library Muniment Room
HMC	Historical Manuscripts Commission
Jour.	Journal of the Court of Common Council
PCC	Prerogative Court of Canterbury
PRO	Public Record Office
Rep.	Repertory of the Court of Aldermen
VM	Vestry minute book
WIM	Wardmote inquest minute book

1

INTRODUCTION

Probably every student of early modern England has been struck by the prominence of London in the kingdom, yet just as noticeable, but harder to explain, is the absence of anything like a proportionate share for London in the historical writing on the Tudor-Stuart period. The work of Professor Valerie Pearl[1] is the only lengthy and critical study which takes London as its main focal point, yet her book serves to underline how much is still not known. Thanks to a number of recent local studies, government and society are probably better understood in the counties during the early seventeenth century than in London.

In a way, of course, it is absurd to bemoan the deficiencies of London historiography, since, from the fifteenth century to the present day, a number of chronicles, histories and intimate portraits of one sort or another have been appearing in order to satisfy the apparently insatiable hunger for London miscellany. The antiquarian's loving attention, prompted and sponsored by civic pride, has given London a physical exposure that perhaps takes second place to no other city in the world. And who does not still marvel at the industry and curiosity of John Stow, or stand humbly before the erudition of William Maitland[2] or John Strype?[3] Because they are the best of the older historians, their works continue to be useful to the modern student of London history, even though they conform to a traditional and limited format. The older historians offered a conglomerate of biographical sketch, aphorism, fact and myth, all loosely joined in a chronological narrative that was structured around a number of topics: topography, geography, architecture, parish churches, guilds, prominent citizens, leading events, and occasionally — but really incidentally — political development.[4] One could not discuss the mayor without

1 *London and the Outbreak of the Puritan Revolution: City Government and National Politics, 1625-43* (1964).
2 *The History of London*, 2 vols. (1756).
3 *A Survey of the Cities of London and Westminster*, 2 vols. (1720).
4 For guides to the vast body of traditional literature, consult John Parker Anderson, *The Book of British Topography* (1881); *Catalogue of the Guildhall Library of the City of London, with Additions to June 1889* (1889); Charles Gross, *A Bibliography of British Municipal History*, with preface and revisions by G. H. Martin, 2nd ed. (Leicester, 1966). The traditional literature has received a warm but uncritical appreciation in Stanley Rubinstein's *Historians of London* (Hamden, Conn., 1968). Those who are curious to sample the literature on London since 1900 should refer to the catalogues of the British Library and the Guildhall Library. Among the useful printed guides are Marjorie Plant, *A London Biblio-*

describing his many ceremonial activities, or elaborate upon economic regulation without discoursing on markets, the Steelyard, the assize of bread, or the Thames watermen. The aldermen were seen against a background of ancient customs and pageants, watches, orphans, hospitals, and law courts. This traditional emphasis on a broad survey, though useful for general orientation, has helped to delay more fundamental understanding of the political process in London.

But to explain the dearth of political analysis it is not enough to point to the ponderous irrelevancies of the conglomerate historians. Side by side with them legal digests and constitutional summaries have been appearing with some frequency.[1] Although some were issued irregularly in the sixteenth century, they multiplied during the 1640s and continued to appear through the rest of the century. The flow receded somewhat during the eighteenth century and the first part of the nineteenth but gushed again over the last half of the nineteenth century. Not surprisingly, the volume of this literature grew during periods of constitutional crisis: the Civil War years when the traditional manner of ruling London was challenged, the *quo warranto* proceedings of Charles II against the City, and later the basic reforms brought about by the Metropolitan Board of Works in 1855 and by the formation of the London County Council in 1888. Despite the occasional value of these works for the political historian, their existence has had a distorting effect upon historical understanding. The tenor of some of this literature, especially that of the nineteenth century, is frankly polemical and biased, arguing for or against continuing the City's privileges. But there is a less obvious and greater distortion than bias. The sheer volume of books on various legal aspects of the City's history, particularly the collection of charters, the citing of court precedents and the tiresome reference to ancient custom, has made the constitutional history of London resemble nothing so much as the triumphal growth of the common law. If this obfuscation has been mostly the work of lawyers, it might be remembered that that venerable and revered compiler of London's most famous customal, John Carpenter, town clerk in the early fifteenth century, was also a lawyer.[2] Other London

graphy of the Social Sciences, 4 vols. (1931 and succeeding supplements); London County Council, *Members' Library Catalogue*, Vol. 1: *London History and Topography* (1939); Conyers Read, *Bibliography of British History: Tudor Period, 1485-1603*, 2nd ed. (Oxford, 1959); *Classification of London Literature Based upon the Collection in the Guildhall Library*, 3rd ed. (1966).

1 The two most prominent of these are George Norton, *Commentaries on the History, Constitution, and Chartered Franchises of the City of London*, 3rd ed. (1869), and Alexander Pulling, *A Practical Treatise on the Laws, Customs, Usages, and Regulations of the City and Port of London*, 2nd ed. (1854).

2 *Liber Albus: The White Book of the City of London*, trans. and ed. H. T. Riley (1861). The *Liber Albus* was relied on heavily by most of the seventeenth-century writers.

lawyers have performed similar services. That around 1274 a collection was compiled entitled *Liber de Antiquis Legibus* suggests that even in the thirteenth century the façade of the law was weaving its spell. Perhaps that spell was deliberately created on orders from the civic rulers, who wanted their regime to appear (regardless of reality) just, reasonable, honourable, attentive to the common interest, but above all conventional. At any rate, historians have been too impressed by the monuments erected by lawyers. Since the sixteenth century the essence of civic government has been understood mostly by referring only to the outward form of political institutions.

It was not until the early twentieth century that a fundamental change in historical outlook occurred, due largely to the work of the Revd. Alfred B. Beaven.[1] By means of extensive and systematic archival exploration, Beaven unearthed the raw material for a fresh look at London's constitution, to mention but one of the many subjects he opened for critical study. His insight was that social and economic history played a crucial part in political history, and he therefore set out to compile as much biographical information as seemed feasible for all the aldermen since the time of written records. His remarkable achievement continues to serve London scholars, for much that he anticipated has yet to find detailed treatment. Beaven opened the way for other studies of importance on London, though it was thirty-five years before the first of these was published. The work of Sylvia L. Thrupp provided the first, and still the only, comprehensive social history of the London ruling class, based on her studies of the fourteenth and fifteenth centuries.[2] Her treatment of politics itself, though restricted to a chapter, is solidly founded on civic records and summarizes the leading developments of the two centuries. It makes clear the oligarchic, self-interested nature of the governing class, as well as the great wealth and prominence of the rulers in London and in the realm. Being concerned almost exclusively with social setting, however, her work did not search out as many of the implications of a powerful merchant oligarchy for political practice as will be attempted here. The work of Gwyn A. Williams,[3] like this volume, is mostly concerned with London politics, but his book concerns the thirteenth and early fourteenth centuries, while I emphasize the sixteenth century, especially the reign of Elizabeth. At the same time the sixteenth century is placed in the longer span of the late fourteenth to the early seventeenth centuries, since I believe this period had an integrity of its own.

1 *The Aldermen of the City of London,* 2 vols. (1908-13).

2 *The Merchant Class of Medieval London, 1300-1500* (Ann Arbor, Mich., Ann Arbor Paperback, 1962).

3 *Medieval London: From Commune to Capital* (1963).

It is the major theme of this book that during what might be called the Renaissance London's government entered on a long period of stability, culminating in the age of Elizabeth. Despite the changes, indeed upheavals and disasters, which shook the realm during these years, even affecting the rulers of London itself, stability was the keynote in internal City politics. This study will show how that stability developed, it will illustrate stability at work in full flower at the time of Elizabeth, and it will suggest reasons for this stability, which was the more remarkable in view of the profound changes normally thought of in connection with the Renaissance and Reformation. London's political stability is the more unique when one considers other great cities of Europe during the same period.[1]

If, at a time when scholars find change and revolution so fascinating, studies of stable periods need a justification, I can do no better than refer to the Introduction of J.H. Plumb's *The Growth of Political Stability in England, 1675-1725* (1967). It might be said, too, that if we are to put into perspective the changes that racked seventeenth-century London, we should know rather more about the status quo ante, before the City rulers and the early Stuarts fell out with each other, before the constitutional changes of the Civil War era, and before the City's bankruptcy and charter controversy at the time of the later Stuarts. Since London's political stability was mostly due to her rulers, I have felt it proper to discuss them and their activity in some detail, but not to touch on all those topics that belong, in a general way, to the government of London. In other words I have not elaborated on London as England's chief market place, say, or the growth of crime, because such subjects deserve their own books. I have explained as much of such topics as seemed necessary to bring civic politics and the rulers into focus. Nor do I apologize for the concentration on elections, offices and procedures, levels of authority, different ranks among the rulers, and the connections between political rank and social standing. There is no other study that brings these things together for Renaissance London, and few that have tackled them for any period of London's history.[2]

But to clarify, and at times to correct, historical understanding of these local traditions, while necessary in itself, is not the only purpose of this book. The importance of London transcended its

---

1 See below, chapter 9.

2 The most general, but still one of the most valuable is Sidney and Beatrice Webb, *English Local Government from the Revolution to the Municipal Corporations Act*, 9 vols. (1906-29). The Webbs' work gave historians a penetrating glance into the general structure of English local government, but it did not pretend to portray individual communities in depth. Thus, for example, they

regional setting, and any study of London will have implications of a broad nature. Mentioning some of them at the start may make the details which follow more worthwhile. The critical, inquiring spirit of the Renaissance had its impact on individual rulers, but civic humanism never became a part of the City's make-up. Thus Alderman Henry Billingsley translated Euclid's *Elements of Geometry,* Alderman Thomas Offley learned some Greek, Remembrancer Thomas Norton became a successful poet and dramatist, Councilman Richard Grafton is better remembered as the printer, Alderman Thomas Whyte founded St. John's College, Oxford, and he was not alone among the rulers in patronizing learning. Yet these rulers never generated the kind of idealism, whether scholarly or political, so important in contemporary Italy. Humanist and governor never merged extensively in London. To be sure, the rulers possessed a sense of civic republicanism, but it remained implicit and was not articulated. Theirs was a republicanism based on the older roots of family, guild, and love of community. Neither their politics nor their ideology represented a break with the past, but rather a reaffirmation of it. For the rulers it can be said the Renaissance was, as Johan Huizinga saw it for France and the Netherlands, a culmination of the medieval, not the beginning of the modern.[1]

A similar traditionalism characterized their response to the Protestant Reformation. By the death of Elizabeth in 1603 most rulers were Protestants, but in 1558, at the queen's accession, the leanings of all but a few were ambiguous and may now never be retrieved. It would seem that Protestantism, and especially Puritanism with its doctrine of the elect, would have appealed to men who already saw themselves as a distinct and chosen community, albeit a worldly one. In fact one wonders if Protestantism did not ultimately succeed among them because of this predisposition; perhaps it gained an initial foothold for the same reason. What is more certain is that not all the rulers were of the same mind regarding doctrine − a potentially explosive situation. But no religious controversies among them are known. Instead friendship, marriage, co-operation, and harmony crossed denominational lines. So great was their abiding loyalty to the City and to each other, so deep and reverent their commitment to City politics, that their profoundest religious impulses seem understandable only if viewed as a blending of the civic and the spiritual.

The more mundane implications of the rulers' lives are no less interesting. It appears, to a greater extent than has been known before,

described the development across England of the secular vestry, but not the particular use that was made of it in London, or the important connections in London between vestry, guild, ward, Common Council, and Court of Aldermen.

1 *The Waning of the Middle Ages,* trans. F. Hopman (1924).

that the economic expansion of England resulted from the interests of this quite identifiable and particular group, the merchants who ruled London. To explain their motivation by the love of gain, or adventure, or even by religious zeal is no longer adequate. Fortunes made in trade were a kind of incentive in advance, taken not only to offset later costs of political activity, but also to permit a greater commitment to the City. Common business ventures were but one of the strands in City life that drew the rulers closer together; in turn these cohesive networks assured that the right men were advanced to the right places. Trade was developed, that is, like marriage, friendship, and other connections, to serve the interests of the City's rulers.

From the perspective of the twentieth century, the deep localism of the greatest men in the City speaks eloquently of the vitality and endurance of the medieval spirit in Renaissance London. This phenomenon is more understandable in light of the crown's permissive relationship with the City. The notion of Tudor paternalism, once apparently so appropriate, has received lethal blows before, and this study will do no more than drive a few more nails into the coffin. Not only did the City exercise a sweeping autonomy that bordered on de facto sovereignty, but the dependence of crown on City was rather greater than the other way around. The Tudor revolution in government, so forceful in revitalizing the central machinery of the state during the early sixteenth century, appears to be parochial, without cumulative effect beyond the royal bureaucracy, least of all on the behemoth just downstream. Thus untroubled in their own estimate of themselves and their sacred traditions, the rulers felt no compulsion to respond to new problems of urban growth, or to change with the times.

Another implication of this study concerns the role of different social groups in bringing about the Civil War. Some historians have shown that merchants had cause to find frustration in dealing with the establishment, and that as a result it is not surprising to find them in the camp of the opposition. This inclination of merchants towards what has been called the side of 'progress' seems especially attractive to the degree that merchants are also found to be Puritans, or to have had, as many did, some connection with members of the parliamentary opposition. It is particularly important to explore the attitudes of Elizabethan merchants since Sir John Neale has discovered in the queen's parliaments a kernel of dissent that preceded and encouraged its more famous Stuart successor.[1] Was there also at this time in City government the seed of an opposition that would foreshadow changes to come in the 1640s? Professor Pearl's study on London of the 1630s and

---

1   *Elizabeth I and her Parliaments,* 2 vols. (1953-7).

1640s, showing how staunchly royalist the City government was at that time, strongly discourages such a possibility. My own conclusions on the Elizabethan period are in harmony with hers, but with a change in emphasis that is suggested by exploring the traditional setting of the rulers' lives.

It will be appropriate therefore to introduce the Elizabethan rulers by getting to know their ancestors first, and by sketching the political development of London before the sixteenth century. John Stow, chronicler and antiquary extraordinary, cited with great pride the references from ancient and medieval writers that agreed in calling London the greatest city of the realm, the wealthiest, the most celebrated. 'London est caput Regni et Legum' he quoted approvingly from the laws of Edward the Confessor. Stow himself, in analysing the causes of this undoubted magnificence, felt that London's location on the Thames was easily the most decisive consideration.[1] In referring to this favourable location Stow was repeating one of the traditional explanations for London's commercial pre-eminence in the kingdom. Political, cultural, and social superiority followed upon economic success. London's dominance in the realm was enhanced by its proximate location to the seat of national government and its sheer size.[2] By the sixteenth century London had been the largest city of England

1 John Stow, *A Survey of London*, 1603 edn., ed. Charles L. Kingsford (Oxford, 1908), ii. 199-202.

2 Considering only the Elizabethan period, the population soared from just under 90,000 in 1558 to 250,000 by 1605. For the population by the latter date see F. P. Wilson, *The Plague in Shakespeare's London* (Oxford Paperback, repr., 1963), Appendix 2, especially pp. 214-15; and Wilbur K. Jordan, *The Charities of London, 1480-1660: The Aspirations and the Achievements of the Urban Society* (1960), p. 16, quoting Charles Creighton, 'The Population of Old London', *Blackwood's Edinburgh Magazine* 149 (1891), 477-96. Wilson and Creighton differ slightly: Wilson says 250,000 for 1603 and Creighton's figure is 224,275. Creighton's estimate for 1558 is the one shown above. He also said the figure for around 1535 was 60,000. Norman G. Brett-James, *The Growth of Stuart London* (1935), p. 512 estimated London's population at 250,000 for 1603.

These estimates are for the entire metropolitan area; the traditional City was considerably smaller, not only because the suburbs and certain liberties were not considered part of the City, but also because the large, unstable portion of the City's own population was not recognized by the rulers. In 1631 the rulers reported to the Privy Council that there were 130,280 in the 26 wards (W. H. Overall and H. C. Overall, eds., *Analytical Index to the Series of Records Known as the Remembrancia, A.D. 1579-1664* (1878) hereafter cited as *Remembrancia*, p. 389). It is uncertain whether this figure includes prisoners, hospital residents, servants, apprentices, and other dependents of the citizens; it certainly does not include the masterless men, vagabonds, most of the poor, or those numerous representatives of the underworld scorned by the citizens. A modern scholarly estimate for the 110 parishes within the 26 wards at the end of the seventeenth century is 123,089. This figure does not include prisoners, or those in hospitals and inns, but does count servants and apprentices (P.E. Jones and A.V. Judges, 'London Population in the Late Seventeenth Century', *Economic History Review* 6 (Oct. 1935), 45-63, esp 54).

since time out of mind and the political capital for five centuries. It owed its primacy not only to material power, for by that standard alone other commercial centres might have made claims for the honour, but also to its ancient freedom of all overlords save the king himself. London burgesses held the City by free socage as tenants in chief of the crown.[1] It was a tribute to London's ancient customs and powers that the Conqueror should have recognized a continuation of the laws of his predecessors. The Conqueror also granted the citizens the Sheriffwick of London. Henry I granted them the farm of Middlesex and the right to choose its sheriff, as well as other privileges, the most important of which was to name their own justiciar for holding pleas of the crown.[2] Since the coming of the Normans, the crown had supplemented and reaffirmed London's pre-eminence by royal charters. If Stow was proud then, certainly he had every reason to be, for there is a pithy truth in the words of one English historian who said 'Tudor despotism consisted in fact largely in London's dominance over the rest of England'.[3]

The formative period for London's constitution, and the period during which the world view of the rulers began to take shape, seems to have been the century or so after the establishment of the commune in 1190, an era that has been the subject of a careful historical study.[4] In surveying this period the author quite properly directed most of his attention to the tumultuous relations between the City and the crown. By 1200 London could boast of considerable political independence, its own elected mayor, and could support most privileges and customs by showing written charters. Yet London discovered that the needs of the aggressive and powerful Angevin monarchy were not compatible with its own continued independence. In accepting particular rights and privileges by royal charter London burgesses simultaneously opted for specific as opposed to general rights, and they recognized, in a quite concrete fashion, a higher authority. In the view of the crown, chartered rights could become but pieces of parchment because the rights granted or renewed depended on the strength of the king at the time. As a result, Henry II ignored his grandfather's precedent for allowing local elections of London's sheriffs, a privilege not restored until the second charter of King John. London was also to discover that its sacred privileges could disappear overnight, should the king choose to 'take the City into his hand' and govern it through his own officers. Although Henry III's charter of 1227 confirmed the privileges of the City as

1 Reginald R. Sharpe, *London and the Kingdom* (1894-5), i. 2-3.
2 Ibid. 36 and 40-44.
3 A. F. Pollard, 'Local History', *The Times Literary Supplement,* 11 March 1920.
4 Williams, *Medieval London.*

granted by King John, only twelve years later Henry deprived the mayor of his office for several months because the City would not accept his nominee to the shrievalty, the appointment of which legally lay with the citizens. This usurpation was repeated at the king's pleasure, and it is scarcely surprising that London joined the dissident barons who forced Henry to accept the Provisions of Oxford in 1258. Reconciliations were made with the king but not lasting ones, for the City supported the rebellious efforts of Simon de Montfort. After de Montfort's death at the battle of Evesham (1265), London was again deprived of its liberties and ruled for the next five years by a royal warden. The City was again deprived during the reign of Edward I, this time for thirteen years (1285–98). In restoring London's privileges the Crown managed to extract some money in the process, as it usually did in these cases.

The reign of Edward II was a decisive period for the City's political development. The rulers of London had always been wealthy aldermen who inherited much of their landed property in London and surrounding counties and who gained admission to civic life through their fathers, that is, through patrimony. These men enriched themselves through the older wool-export and wine-import trades. From the late twelfth century, however, new lines of foreign trade had given rise to a new group of merchants. Their trade was in such products as fish from the North Sea, German iron and Spanish leather. These new men gained the franchise through redemption (purchase) or apprenticeship, and few inherited much landed property. Their drive for a political power commensurate with their economic strength had been immeasurably advanced during the tenure of Edward I's warden, when many representatives of the old patrician class were deprived of their civic offices. During Edward II's reign, under pressure from these new men, the commonalty of London made what proved to be a lasting accommodation for a sizable assembly of citizens which was to have the essential political powers and responsibilities in London. This was the Common Council. Of equal importance, control over the freedom — which was the prelude to voting and holding office and selling by retail in the City — was vested in the guilds, or crafts, and the crafts were the political centres for these new men. Relations with the crown were also formalized at this time. The City took advantage of the king's weakness and baronial opposition to him to extract privileges as well as recognition of its autonomous administration. Although the City was to be taken into the king's hand again briefly by Richard II, the time of blatant interference was over.

In his book Williams has provided a detailed narrative of the leading developments of the period as well as an investigation into political structure which surpasses any other work on London of a similar approach. He showed that the favour of the crown was crucial, not only in maintaining London's autonomy, but in advancing the careers and fortunes of the civic rulers. He traced the rise of the leading salaried officers, the legal staff, who in his view went far towards making the government more professional and bureaucratic. He gave a perceptive account of the aldermen as leaders in their wards, which recognized the supplementary but essential role common councilmen have played at the lower echelons of government since the fourteenth century. Yet the meaning of what he has related is open to different interpretations. Williams dramatized the rise of the new crafts into a sharp class conflict which was said to have destroyed the older patrician rulers. But, as he himself showed, the new men married the daughters of the old. And although their places of origin and sources of wealth differed, once established the new men sought landed property in the counties in emulation of the patricians they displaced. Moreover, the new men proved to like oligarchic rule quite as much as their predecessors. True, they initiated an era of reform, but with what results? The so-called reforms would have transferred power from the commonalty to the crafts, especially the victuallers, yet this was not universally desired. The movement for craft rule met with partial success in the years 1376-83, when councilmen were elected by the crafts instead of by the wards, and aldermen were subject to annual election for the first time. But in 1384 the first of these reforms was abolished, and in 1394 the provision for annual aldermanic elections was annulled. Beginning in 1397, and continuing until 1714, the Court of Aldermen took over the election of its own members and left to the wards only the right of formally nominating candidates.[1] Ruth Bird's study on the reform period concluded that London's government was even more oligarchic after 1384 than before.[2]

For London the fifteenth century lacked the dramatic confrontations with the crown and the exciting periods of reform and constitutional theorizing which had marked the fourteenth. The monarchy was engaged in the Hundred Years War, then threatened by baronial

[1] See the fuller treatment of this subject below, pp. 63-5. By the sixteenth century nominees were those the court wanted nominated.

[2] *The Turbulent London of Richard II* (1949). In fairness to Williams it should be said that he did not discuss these developments of the late fourteenth century, for he ended his history after outlining the formal constitutional settlement worked out in the first three decades of the century. Yet an implicit point of his study (made explicit on his pp. 271 and 312) was that the base of political power in London from the mid fourteenth century was fairly broad, broad enough for London to avoid 'the closed corporation'. Yet, in considering the actual control over finances and elections, as distinct from the theoretical authority, there are grounds for recognizing a quite narrow power base, as will be suggested at greater length in chapter 2.

revolt and open civil war. The Lancastrians, Yorkists and later the Tudors were at once too poor and too unsure of their own support to risk alienating the largest and wealthiest of their cities. Their main concern was to keep London loyal and meanwhile to extract financial support from her. Ultimate authority over London rested in the crown's hands, but the City's autonomy was no longer in dispute. Left on their own, the aldermen were the true sovereigns in London, and during the fifteenth and sixteenth centuries they quietly strengthened their ancient hold on civic government. What looked like an emerging democracy in the middle fourteenth century was modified and largely reassembled around what proved to be the stabilizing influence of an elitist, merchant oligarchy.

That their influence was ultimately so stabilizing can be explained, I believe, by two characteristic attitudes of the rulers. First, the rulers established their identity with reference to the traditional City of twenty-six wards, not the whole megalopolis of London which included the seat of royal government (largely in Westminster), the legal centre (mostly wedged between the City and Westminster in independent jurisdictions known as liberties), and the centre of fashion (not uniquely in any part of London, but usually in the suburbs of the City and the liberties). To contemporaries and especially the rulers, it was the separateness of the City and Westminster and the petty jurisdictions contiguous to them that was most obvious. The rulers complained about conditions in the liberties, but did little or nothing to effect changes there, and they resisted strenuously all royal attempts to create a uniform political authority for the whole metropolitan region. With a few exceptions that are treated in Appendix 4, the authority of the mayor, aldermen, and Common Council existed only within the wards of the City. The City was the most populous and most influential of the several agglomerations collectively known as London, and the only one to experience stability during the Renaissance. By living and working in the City the rulers evolved their other characteristic attitude — that the City was more than an autonomous jurisdictional entity, it was a community. This community existed primarily for the benefit of its political rulers, and for the rulers City politics was the keystone of their lives. City politics was the central consideration in deciding how wealthy they became, whom they married, even how they felt about such things as religion, the poor, the queen, and their own rulership. In brief City politics shaped the world view of the rulers and was inseparable from other aspects of their lives. It is City politics in the setting of the rulers' lives that I have attempted to portray in the chapters that follow.

2

THE METHODS OF RULERSHIP

Almost anyone who lived in sixteenth-century London would have been able to point out the rulers as the twenty-six aldermen, the 212 common councilmen, and the handful of bureaucrats, who by virtue of certain qualities and deliberately assumed behaviour had long ago established themselves as the natural ruling class. Their unique characteristics as rulers will be discussed in later chapters. In a traditional and hierarchical society it was necessary that rulers be distinctive, but it may surprise the twentieth-century observer that the rulers believed themselves closely bound up with the ruled. Both shared a destiny as Londoners; all of them gloried in the City's wealth, its prominence, its ancient and peculiar rights. Even more than most citizens, the rulers rejoiced in being Londoners, and they articulated their identity in large part by referring to the 'commonalty' which was London. John Stow spoke for all of them when he said,

> And whereas commonwealthes and kingdomes cannot haue, next after God, any surer foundation, then the loue and good will of one man towardes another, that also is closely bred and maintayned in Citties, where men by mutual societie and companying together, doe grow to alliances, comminalties and corporations.[1]

To be sure, individuals did not share equally in the perquisites of citizenship. No one was unaware of varying social degrees, but the greater power exercised by the rulers was understood as a necessary concomitant of higher rank and greater wealth. Thus the rulers recognized the source of civic power to be the commonalty, not just their own loftier personal positions in London, but they also believed in their own rather special responsibility to monopolize the practical uses of that power.

To outline the ways in which the rulers governed is necessarily to discuss accepted practices, especially legislation, taxing power, and elections. In doing so we must resist the temptation to find too sharp a distinction between rulers and ruled, for such a view violates the reality of Elizabethan London. I have just mentioned the vague but pervasive sense of community that blurred the differences between all citizens. But even among the tiny minority who ruled, various levels of responsibility and power existed. The ruling class was not monolithic but stratified. Three obvious ranks developed among the rulers, and before discussing institutional operations it will be well to define these

1 *Survey of London,* ed. Charles L. Kingsford (Oxford, 1908), ii. 198.

ranks and to make the general observation that virtually all civic procedures were influenced to some extent by the existence of these three ranks.

Members of the ruling class have been distinguished according to their political service and are identified by the terms leader, notable, and élite. In justifying these categories I must digress briefly by discussing the source materials for this study and my use of them. Most of the high civic officers were elected; these included common councilmen, hospital officers, auditors of the Bridgehouse and Chamber, bridgemasters, chamberlains, aldermen, sheriffs, and mayors. Some officers were elected in the wards, some in an assembly called Congregation, to be discussed below, some in other gatherings that will be mentioned at the appropriate time, but summaries of all elections appear in civic records — except those for councilmen.[1] During the sixteenth century the gift of offices not filled by election, and the appointment of all committees, lay either with the Court of Common Council or the Court of Aldermen, most often the latter.[2] The records of both courts are complete for the period in minute books known as the Journals and the Repertories, which also contain the election summaries. These same minute books contain the names of all civic committee members, and many sureties who were liable for the City's debts. To the extent that the names of officeholders and commiteemen are preserved, therefore, they are recorded in the Journals or Repertories, and from the meticulous form of these it seems safe to conclude that virtually every office and committee of the period is mentioned sooner or later. By patient and systematic use of these records it has been possible to retrieve the names of all elected officers, again excepting the councilmen, of virtually all committeemen on the major permanent committees, and a large majority of those serving on ad hoc committees and in such lesser activities as tax collectors and supervisors of various civic accounts and properties.[3]

1 Partial election records for councilmen survive in only four wards; moreover the clerks of Common Council did not record in the minutes the names of councilmen attending meetings of Common Council, as they did for aldermen attending both Common Council and the Court of Aldermen. The names of councilmen can be discovered only in those entries that show committee assignments, or name officeholders, or identify sureties. Note 2 on p. 182 gives my reasons for treating officeholders as councilmen.
2 See Appendix 2 for a list of appointive offices.
3 I began by taking note of every office and committee in the records for the years 1558-63. In reviewing the detailed results it was obvious that a small number of men held most of these ad hoc assignments. I then jumped ahead to do the same exhaustive survey for the two years 1569-70. The same few men still performed most of this work, so it seemed that by selecting other consecutive years at regular intervals I would know most of the men who performed most of this supportive business. The other two-year periods selected were 1572-3, 1579-80, 1582-3, 1589-90, 1592-3, 1599-1600, and the single year 1603.

These men I took to be the rulers of London. Distinctions between them seemed necessary, first to account for the obvious differences of status between aldermen and councilmen. Also most aldermen had far more political activity than most councilmen. Further distinction became necessary because the experiences of councilmen varied enormously, from the many who served only as hospital governors, say, to those few whose activity outstripped some aldermen. Perhaps I should make it clear that the terms used for ranks among the rulers are my own and do not derive from contemporary usage. 'Leaders' held up to three offices, *or* had up to five ad hoc committees in a select number of years.[1] There were 118 leaders in the Elizabethan years, all of them councilmen.[2] 'Notables' held at least four civic offices *and* had at least five ad hoc committee assignments in the select years. Forty-one common councilmen can be identified as notables. The 'élite' were at first defined as those with over four offices, but this had to be changed for several reasons. Nearly all aldermen with over four offices also became mayors at some time; most of the remaining aldermen would only have qualified as leaders, if that, yet the dignity of a position on the Court of Aldermen seemed to warrant a more prestigious label. I deemed that the sixty-four mayors would constitute the élite; the fifty aldermen who served on the court for at least a year would be notables, along with the forty-one councilmen just mentioned.[3] Therefore the rulers consisted of 273 Londoners, and when speaking of the rulers I will usually be thinking of

---

1   See p. 13, note 3.

2   See Appendix 1 for the names of leaders, notables, élite, and other common councilmen..

3   See A.B. Beaven, *The Aldermen of the City of London,* 2 vols. (1908-13), ii. 29-48 for a chronological listing of aldermen. I counted as Elizabethans those aldermen on the court at the queen's accession and those sworn during her reign — a total of 138. To the 47 who served as mayors under Elizabeth, I added those who had been mayors before 1558 and continued as senior aldermen, and those who established themselves on the court during Elizabeth's reign but attained the mayoralty after her death — another 17 for a total of 64 mayors. Part of the distinction between the élite and the notable aldermen was seniority: only 4 of 64 élite served less than the average tenure for all Elizabethan aldermen, 11 years, and only 3 of 50 notable aldermen had a tenure exceeding 11 years. But another part of the distinction was desire to serve, for 18 notable aldermen resigned (36%) as compared with only 6 of the élite (9%). The average tenure of the notable and élite aldermen was 13 years.

Thus the 138 Elizabethan aldermen can be categorized as follows: the 64 mayors are the élite; the 50 who served at least a year are the notable aldermen; the 9 who resigned from the court almost at once but whose previous service qualified them as leading or notable councilmen are considered as councilmen, not aldermen; the 15 who served less than a year and lacked sufficient previous experience to qualify even as leading councilmen are excluded from the list of rulers.

these men. In chapter 6 and in a few places in chapter 4 I will refer to a select group of 141.[1]

The rulers organized their governance through three formal assemblies: the Court of Aldermen, the Court of Common Council, and the Court of Common Hall — known until the 1640s simply as the Congregation. The Court of Aldermen was the oldest of the three but was itself a descendant of the Court of Husting, which dates from Saxon times and consisted of aldermen and sometimes large numbers of citizens. This Court of Husting had always been mostly a judicial body, though in the fashion of early courts there was no clear separation of powers. As a result, at the conclusion of their sittings in the Husting the aldermen could make proclamations concerning whatever cases had come before them, while at the same time the court carried out general administrative duties, including the enforcement of the proclamations it handed down. Distinction between particular powers took place in London during the thirteenth century when the Court of Aldermen became, with the mayor as its director, the supervisor of all general administration. Sitting in another place, and under the name of the Mayor's Court, the mayor and aldermen continued to act judicially. Meanwhile the Court of Husting concerned itself mostly with real actions and those commenced by writ; it declined with the decrease in real actions and by the sixteenth century specialized in enrolling deeds and wills.[2] In the early fourteenth century it became desirable to assemble aldermen and representatives of the citizens on a more regular basis. The permanent institutionalization of this deliberative body, described in contemporary records as consisting of the mayor, aldermen and an 'immense commonalty', meant that subsequently power was to be shared by the aldermen with whatever citizens sat with them from time to time. At least that was the interpretation of nineteenth-century constitutionalists. Medieval and Elizabethan aldermen — and common councilmen, too, for that matter — had another view, for in practice the commonalty neither threatened nor questioned aldermanic dominance of London's government; quite the reverse, for ultimately the creation of 'the immense commonalty' and its descendant, the Common Council, did not diminish the aldermen's authority but enhanced it. This conclusion will be illustrated by tracing the development of legislative, financial and electoral authority.

Concerning the making of ordinances, an agreement of 1322 stated that 'two should be elected out of each ward by the men of the ward

1 See p. 92, note 2.

2 [Philip E. Jones], *The Corporation of London: Its Origin, Constitution, Powers and Duties* (1950), pp. 37, 50, 81-85 on the Court of Husting. (Hereafter cited as *Corporation of London*.)

who should make ordinances for the whole commonalty, and whatever they did on behalf of the commonalty should be held established by the commonalty'.[1] By a charter of Richard II in 1377 the mayor, aldermen and commonalty might alter any of their own ordinances and laws as they saw fit, a right that has been renewed frequently.[2] But while commoners were thus assured some responsibility in the legislative process, no charter or civic ordinance has ever specified that all legislation had to be initiated or approved by the whole commonalty. The aldermen's own orders and the mayor's precepts carried the same force as acts of the commonalty, and both were a great deal more numerous.

Formal acts or ordinances of the commonalty were promulgated whenever the support of representatives of the whole community seemed appropriate. It is well to remember here that elected citizens (later common councilmen) meeting alone did not constitute the commonalty or a Common Council, and there is no evidence at any time before the Civil War that councilmen tried to hold any formal assemblies without the aldermen. No Common Council was formed without the presence of the mayor, or his substitute (the *locum tenens*), and at least two aldermen.[3] Actually most of the council's work was done by aldermen, legal officers, or councilmen working outside the assembly. The Court of Aldermen would order the recorder, or several of his assistants, or all of them, to draw up a bill on a certain subject for presentation to the Common Council.[4] Or a committee of aldermen (sometimes a joint committee of aldermen and councilmen) was assigned to discuss the general framework of a bill, or sometimes to draw up the bill itself.[5] In either case bills came back to the aldermen for approval before being presented to the council for enactment. If approved, the court appointed a day and time for the council to meet and officially dispatch the business. Rarely a bill might originate in a petition of the citizens directed to the Common Council, as in 1593 when some inhabitants of Fleet Street petitioned for 'reformation of the annoyances and abuses in Water Lane'. In that case a committee of one alderman and several councilmen was appointed to study the situation and the relevant previous legislation; another act of Common Council finally resolved it.[6] Strictly speaking, the council itself could initiate bills, too, though

1 *Cal. Let.-Book E*, p.174.
2 Walter de Gray Birch, *The Historical Charters and Constitutional Documents of the City of London* (1887 ed.), p. 70.
3 *The Corporation of London*, p. 56.
4 CLRO, Rep [ertory] 15, fo. 369b.
5 Rep. 17, fos. 193b, 198.
6 CLRO, Jour [nal] 23, fos. 188b, 286b, 402b-04.

in practice it was nearly always done by the aldermen in their own court, or through one of the committees formed by that body.

By and large acts of the Common Council concerned economic regulation, but fifteenths or requisitions of men and arms to the queen's service were by act or formal approval of the council. The Common Council was employed to bring about formal constitutional changes in the City, such as the reviving in 1568 of the Court of Conscience.[1] Also letters from the queen or Privy Council were read before this body, if they contained more than routine announcements, so that all councilmen would be informed. And, of course, Common Council appointed its own committees. The council also had the gift of a few offices at this time, including the common crier, the common serjeant, the undersheriffs, the town clerk, the coroner, the bailiff of Southwark and the garbler of spices, though the aldermen often granted these places through an anticipatory device known as a reversion. The council was supposed to approve of every discharge of an alderman or sheriff, but it did not always do so.

The exigencies of war had played a part in the birth and early development of the Common Council in the fourteenth century; in the sixteenth century the same forces again influenced civic development. Despite its subservience to the aldermen, over the long course of Queen Elizabeth's reign the council was becoming a far more active body, largely because of the crown's greater demands in the 1580s and 1590s for money, arms and men. At the same time the council undertook an increasing responsibility for dispatching the routine work of the City. Many more committees than previously were formed by the Common Council itself. Individual councilmen were called upon more frequently to sit on committees of the Court of Aldermen. Furthermore, by 1592 common councilmen sat on the three permanent committees of the City — the Bridgehouse Estates Committee, the City Lands Committee, and the Committee for Martial (and/or Naval) Causes.[2] In the latter part of the reign the council became more diligent in approving of discharges for aldermen and sheriffs, in approving of City leases, in raising corn supplies for the City, and in appointing the few offices in its gift, rather than allowing the aldermen to grant them all away through reversions. The council even tried to limit the number of freedoms granted by redemption, and, more boldly, to prevent the aldermen

1 Jour. 19, fo. 121. The court was to deal in recovery of small debts and was also known as the Court of Requests.
2 On the Bridgehouse Estates Committee and the City Lands Committee, see below, pp. 21-2. The Committee for Martial Causes from its origin in the 1570s was composed of aldermen and councilmen; it supervised the mustering and paying of the City's trained bands.

18

from granting reversions for the seven years beginning in 1590.[1] It succeeded in the former endeavour, because the aldermen complied, but concerning reversions it failed completely.

But the legislative power did not lie exclusively in the hands of Common Council. Even after dividing their work into separate assemblies for general administration and judicial business, the aldermen retained a wide and diversified competence through their proclamations and orders. There were two kinds of civic proclamation: those made on behalf, and at the command, of the sovereign, and those made on the initiative of the City alone.[2] Both overwhelmingly concerned economic regulations and especially their enforcement: prices, quantity and quality of goods sold, condition of sale and manufacture, and so on. Civic proclamations were made 'in the Guildhall (in the place where the Court of Hustings [sic] is usually held) in the presence of the Lord Mayor and six aldermen ... (at the least) or in the absence of the said Lord Mayor, then in the presence of eight aldermen . . . (at the least)'.[3] The mayor and aldermen had exclusive authority over proclamations. That the proclamations are recorded in the same book with the council's minutes does not mean that the Common Council played any part in making them, for the queen's proclamations, over which even the aldermen had no authority, as well as a number of notes on orphanage matters that were actually determined in the Court of Aldermen, are also recorded there. The Journals in the sixteenth century were more miscellaneous record books than the exclusive book of any court; the council's minutes are only a small portion of the Journal's contents.[4]

1 Jour. 22, fo. 408.
2 The crown's own proclamations were distinct from these civic proclamations.
3 Jour. 23, fo. 108. This procedure suggests a parallel with the royal prerogative courts, for the Court of Aldermen (and previously the Court of Husting) acted exactly like the Privy Council sitting as a court in Star Chamber (formerly the whole *Curia Regis)* in making proclamations at the conclusion of a particular case. See Edward P. Cheyney, *A History of England from the Defeat of the Armada to the Death of Elizabeth* (1914-26), i. 107, and John B. Black, *The Reign of Elizabeth, 1558-1603,* 2nd ed. (Oxford, 1959), pp. 209-11.
4 The other materials in the Journals of the sixteenth century are: the records of prices and wages set by the aldermen acting in the capacity of justices of the peace; copies of various letters received by the City or sent on its authority (most of them ordered by authority of the aldermen alone); the mayor's precepts; miscellaneous statistics, for example, the number of men raised from each company for a muster, the amount each company contributed towards loans to the queen, or the debts owed to merchant strangers; the election results of Congregation; a collection of the various precedents or other relevant materials found in charters, letters patent, statutes, acts of Common Council, etc., by the town clerk when ordered to research a particular point — usually concerning a dispute over a civic privilege; depositions of individuals sworn before the mayor and aldermen, concerning cases before one of the City courts of law; and recognizances binding individuals to carry out the orders of these courts.

While not drawn up in the same detail and not proclaimed with such formality, the administrative orders of either the Court of Aldermen, or the mayor himself through his precept, were valid bylaws which carried severe penalties for the violator. The aldermen's orders were much more common, occurring at nearly every session of the court. For the most part they concerned the enforcement of existing laws, the discipline of civic officials, and orphanage business. More versatile was the precept, which symbolized the mayor's executive leadership over London. Precepts were ordered by the mayor alone, either while in court, in the council, or at any other time; they were then drawn up by the town clerk and delivered to the appropriate recipient by a member of the mayor's household.[1] Precepts were sent either to individual aldermen, or all of them, or to masters of the various livery companies. Through these orders the watch was set, inspections and searches were galvanized, lists of strangers or men fit for military service were drawn up, tax collectors were set in motion, scavengers were warned about the filthy condition of the streets, and grain was brought from the counties. The security and welfare of the City were the direct responsibility of the mayor, and for that reason his jurisdiction and his precept ran everywhere in the City and excluded nothing.

In regard to the right of the commons to consent to taxation, the earliest codification of this right was in the 1319 Orders for Government, agreed upon between the mayor, aldermen and commonalty, then sanctioned by the king.[2] This privilege and others were renewed

1 George Unwin, *The Gilds and Companies of London*, 4th ed. (1963), p. 237, said that precepts were sometimes issued on the initiative of Common Council. It may be that Unwin, with his far greater experience in earlier City records, encountered the Common Council initiating precepts. He cites no reference, however, and it is possible that he made this interpretation because precepts are recorded in the same book as minutes of the council. (See previous note on the contents of the Journals of the sixteenth century.) But during the sixteenth century the council had nothing to do with precepts, even in cases where the mayor ordered them at a session of Common Council.

Unwin also said that precepts were of two kinds, those issued on the City's authority and those done on orders from the crown. Here he is confusing precepts with proclamations, for proclamations were of two kinds. Precepts, however, were not ordered up by the crown in the same direct way as proclamations, though, of course, to enforce the wishes of the crown on any point the mayor commonly resorted to a precept. The important distinction is the intention of the crown. In giving particular orders to the City on, say, setting poultry prices, the Privy Council knew that the appropriate thing to do was to issue a mayoral proclamation; its orders therefore were often detailed and precise, making it easy for the aldermen to translate them into a proclamation. But when giving general instructions, like enforcing poultry prices, or making a request for a loan, or asking for a search to be made, crown officers did not presume to dictate how the mayor should go about enforcing the queen's will. The mayor might use a precept, but he might appoint a committee or assign a specific alderman to take the appropriate action.

2 W. Maitland prints an English version of these in *History of London* (1756), i. 115-16. For the point referred to see clause 6.

in a 1341 charter, and from these instruments stems the financial jurisdiction of Common Council.[1] By the sixteenth century the most common civic tax, and the one to which the commoners were entitled to consent, was the fifteenth. This was levied for a considerable number of recurring needs like timber and coal, or the men and arms recruited to the royal service, as well as for more occasional needs, like the expenses in connection with a coronation celebration in the City. Consent in these assessments was always granted for a specific amount. Only freemen of the City had a clear obligation to pay, and collections were made in the wards by men elected for that purpose, not by the aldermen themselves. But in practice the aldermen were very much involved, and the amounts raised were not limited to what Common Council had authorized.[2]

Outlining the various sources of money and saying something about accounting practices will best illustrate the far-reaching power of the aldermen over civic finances. Perhaps the most vital source of revenue was the orphans' money. For all children whose citizen-fathers died before they were married, or before they reached the age of twenty-one, the City was the official guardian of personal property and of all revenue derived from real property. Relatives, friends or associates of the deceased (or the executors and administrators of the estate — usually the same people) were sworn and bound by recognizance for a certain percentage of the estate to deliver the orphan's portion to him or her at the appropriate time, and in the meantime to maintain the child by periodic supplies called finding money. In times of civic need, the City could call the sureties in and take over the money, and the orphanage responsibility, itself. Alternatively, the executors might pay the orphan's money into the Chamber in the first instance; the Chamber then kept it until such time as payment fell due.[3] Of course the City invested or lent the orphanage money at its disposal, and sometimes the City used orphans' money to cover current expenses. Money moved around in this way was accounted for by other sureties, who were responsible for replacing the original sum if it were lost. In 1560 the City was engaged in buying wheat from the Low Countries to shore up its own inadequate supplies. Rewards in the form of loans

1 Birch, *Charters of London*, pp. xxvi-xxvii.

2 An example is the repair of St. Paul's Cathedral in 1561. The aldermen summoned special assemblies in their wards to urge contributions in excess of what Common Council authorized through three fifteenths. They even tried to collect from strangers and aliens. See Jour. 17, fos. 319b, 320-20b and Rep. 14, fo. 491b.

3 Money on deposit with the Chamber bore interest to the orphan's account. For the rates of interest during the sixteenth century see P. E. Jones, 'The Court of Orphans', *The Law Journal* 93 (6 November 1943), 357-8; and Research Paper 7.33 at the CLRO by the same author.

were granted to those merchants, like Thomas Bates, who were especially successful in getting the job done. In January 1561 the Court of Aldermen decided Bates should 'have £100 more of the next orphanage that this court may conveniently help him unto in occupying during the minority of the orphan to whom the same shall belong, over and above the other £100 of orphanage to him already granted, finding good sureties. . . .'[1] Aldermen and other City officers could also benefit from this arrangement. But aldermen were often bound as sureties themselves, sometimes when other sureties had failed. In June 1583 Alderman Martin was ordered 'from henceforth during the pleasure of this court [to] satisfy and pay unto Mr. Chamberlain of the City the sum of xxiii pounds to the use and behoof of the children and orphans of Richard Wycklyfe, goldsmith, deceased'.[2] The Common Council had no control over the management of this important source of revenue, which amounted in 1584-5 to at least £1,743-15s and in the next year to £2,635-8s-4d.[3]

A third principal source of income was the revenue realized by leasing out certain houses, stalls, shops, gardens and other properties. Most civic property fell under the supervision of the chamberlain. Originally leases were allocated and rents set by the chamberlain himself, with the advice and consent of the aldermen — or by the bridgemasters and the aldermen for the Bridgehouse leases — but in 1559 the aldermen took over responsibility for leases themselves and shortly thereafter created a committee of aldermen for this business, a committee that was the forerunner of the City Lands Committee created by Common Council in 1592.[4] This committee was composed of the chamberlain and between four and six aldermen, at least two of whom had to be senior aldermen (i.e., had served the mayoralty), and they were called 'the surveyors of the City's lands belonging to the Chamber'. Until 1592 the Common Council had no control whatsoever over this committee, or the City leases. In that year the composition of the committee was revised to consist of four aldermen, the

1 Rep. 14, fos. 442-3, 448 and Jour. 17, fos. 247-47[b].

2 Rep. 20, fo. 441[b]; and see fo. 449[b] on the same.

3 CLRO, Chamber accounts: sixteenth century, vol. 2, fos. 75[b], 109.

4 Rep. 14, fos. 158-9. This entry says nothing about setting up the permanent committee of aldermen; rather it says that from now on the mayor and aldermen, not the chamberlain (and not the bridgemasters for the Bridgehouse leases), would take charge. Thereafter from time to time, several aldermen and the chamberlain made reports to the court on the leases. By noticing that the members remained the same for long periods — as long in the case of most aldermen as they stayed on the court — it was established that this was a permanent committee. Their reports to the court are in the Repertories, at various times during the year, until 1589 (23 April) when a separate book, called the Grant Book, was begun for these records.

22

chamberlain, and six councilmen.[1] Other income accrued through the lease of property belonging to the Bridgehouse, property which had been bequeathed or assigned to the City with the provision that its rent should defray the cost of maintaining the bridge. From early times the Bridgehouse estates demanded a sizable administrative staff, and these officials might have become a practically separate department of civic government. But from 1311 the two wardens of the bridge were elected by the commonalty and were responsible to it; the City preserved even closer control because the wardens were usually aldermen or councilmen.[2] In the later sixteenth century there was a committee of aldermen that handled all leases of Bridgehouse property, virtually the same committee in fact which supervised the City's leases, since the membership of the two groups was identical in most years, except that the bridgemasters sat with the aldermen on what came to be known as the Bridgehouse Estates Committee.[3]

The policy of allowing separate administrative staffs to develop for particular purposes — each closely supervised and led by the councilmen or aldermen — was followed again and again as the government of London became more complex.[4] Markets especially called into being a vast and specialized number of weighers and meters, all regularly policed by the ubiquitous ad hoc committees of aldermen or councilmen. In the sixteenth century perhaps the largest group of administrative assistants was that created to manage the four hospitals, granted to the City from confiscated monastic property between 1544 and 1553.[5] The government of the hospitals was vested in the mayor,

1 Jour. 23, fo. 103. The act was on 24 April 1592. The purpose of the changes in 1592, I believe, was to bring councilmen into the work of the committee, as assistants to the aldermen, and to strengthen the City's control over the common lands. Since the Common Council formally held and exercised most of the City's legal privileges and powers, it was appropriate to vest this body with nominal control, though informally the aldermen continued to take the leadership on the committee. From time to time the aldermen alone continued to intervene in the business of civic leases, which was typical of their ceaseless, supervisory activity.
2 Williams, *Medieval London*, pp. 86-7.
3 Like the City Lands Committee, therefore, this committee had its origin in a committee of the Court of Aldermen; in 1592 both committees came under the authority of Common Council and councilmen began to sit with the aldermen on the two committees. It happened that while the Bridgehouse Estates and the City Lands Committees were separate bodies, their membership continued into the seventeenth century to be nearly identical. A separate Grant Book for Bridgehouse leases was begun in 1570; previously reports on Bridgehouse leases had been delivered to the Court of Aldermen and recorded, at irregular intervals, in the Repertories.
4 Other more or less permanent committees not mentioned in this chapter·are discussed in my doctoral dissertation, 'The Government of London in the Reign of Elizabeth I' (Columbia University, 1968), pp. 144-8, 258-9.
5 Corporation of London, *Memoranda, References and Documents Relating to the Royal Hospitals of the City of London* (1863) and *Supplement to the*

aldermen and commonalty, which meant aldermen and common councilmen. While the governors met independently of the court or council, collected and distributed their own income, still they were controlled and supervised at every stage by the Court of Aldermen itself, not the whole Common Council. As a result it happened that the aldermen — sitting in their own court, not in a general assembly of governors — issued orders for the management and direction of the hospitals. They ordered deposits into or payments from the treasuries, ordered hospital records to be kept at the Guildhall, and determined the number to be allowed admission to any hospital.[1] Individual councilmen, acting on orders of the court or on committees with aldermen, perused records and accounts, assisted in making collections and in determining who should have leases of the hospitals' properties, and assisted in devising new methods of raising revenue.[2]

Forced loans ordered by the aldermen to meet the cost of purchasing corn for the City's use were another important source of money, usually raised without consent of the commonalty. Only about half these assessments were agreed to by an act of Common Council. The rest were ordered by the aldermen alone. Even the ones consented to by the council were first discussed in the Court of Aldermen, where the proportional contributions of the livery companies who paid these sums were first allotted.

There are a few other sources of income to mention.[3] Fines brought into the Chamber a regular and often handsome sum, especially those levied on men who declined to serve as either sheriff or alderman. Other fines were paid by leasees of City property; it was common to pay both rent and a fine for a lease. Tradesmen or consumers who violated economic regulations also paid fines. Then there were fees, most of which fell to individual officeholders for performing specific services, but the Chamber collected a number: fees for licensing brokers, fees for admitting a man to the freedom by redemption, fees for enrolling apprentices with the chamberlain, or for translating a man from one livery company to another. Fees were also taken for enrolling documents, especially the wills and deeds at the Court of Husting, and for taking and enrolling inventories of estates. Other moneys came from tolls taken at the City markets. Selling offices and farming others brought in additional money. At the same time the Chamber could not

Memoranda Relating to the Royal Hospitals (1867) print the pertinent original documents relating to the hospitals.

1 Rep. 14, fos. 307, 512[b], 465 respectively.
2 Rep. 14, fos. 467[b], 474[b], 524, and Rep. 23, fo. 44[b].
3 For other traditional sources of revenue, see Thrupp, *Merchant Class,* pp. 87 ff.

have operated without the personal support of aldermen and the wealthier councilmen. They helped to raise loans, and contributed to them. They paid outstanding bills for the City and were reimbursed when convenient. They stood as sureties for the City and for moneys held on account by the City.[1]

To summarize, although joint committees of common councilmen and aldermen supervised the leasing of City and Bridgehouse properties after 1592, the whole Common Council was not consulted in these matters. It was consulted about, and obligingly approved, the fifteenths and sometimes the forced loans on the companies. And representatives of the council were summoned into the Court of Aldermen when the City's seal was used, usually to gain wider financial backing for civic agreements underwriting the queen's debts.[2] But over the orphanage money, the fines, fees, tolls, and most of the places for sale neither the council nor individual councilmen had much control, if any. All this was income. Over expenditure the council also yielded to the Court of Aldermen. The chamberlain handled most disbursements, but whether it was paying for a house the City had recently purchased, paying an annuity to a former parish clerk who sought relief, or granting a loan to the alnegor[3] of woollen cloths, or a loan of £1,000 to the city of Yarmouth for repairing the port, the chamberlain acted only on instructions from the aldermen.[4] There was a precedent from 1373 for two aldermen and two councilmen jointly 'to supervise the expenditure of all money thenceforth coming to the Chamber of the Guildhall for the business and necessities of the commonalty',[5] yet this precedent, if it ever became one, had no bearing on affairs of the late sixteenth century. True there was an annual audit of the Chamber accounts — by a senior alderman and four prominent councilmen — but there is no evidence that this group acted more than annually. More significantly, these auditors made their reports to the Court of Aldermen alone, as did the committees supervising the City's and Bridgehouse's leases.

---

1 Rep. 14, fos. 367, 385[b], 547[b] for examples.

2 An ordinance of 1312 prohibited use of the seal on letters binding the citizens 'before the commonalty be assembled for the purpose and have given unanimous consent thereto' (*Cal. Let.-Book D*, p. 283). By Elizabeth's reign the seal was used mostly at the discretion of the aldermen alone, or in the presence of a few councilmen summoned into court long enough to seal what was necessary then sent on their way; see Rep. 17, fos. 149-49[b] for a typical example. The Common Council even authorized this method of use (Jour. 23, fo. 75).

3 He examined woollens to check their quality.

4 Rep. 16, fos. 31, 29; Rep. 15, fo. 38[b] and Rep. 19, fo. 204[b] respectively. As another source of incidental income, the City sometimes took interest on these loans.

5 *Cal. Let.-Book G*, p. 316.

Elective power over certain offices had rested since the fourteenth century with the 'immense commonalty'. Included were one of the two sheriffs, the chamberlain, two bridgemasters, five auditors, and (beginning in the sixteenth century) four aleconners. Gradually the 'immense commonalty' actually became two bodies, the Congregation, which assembled for elections, and the Common Council, which passed legislation. By the sixteenth century both acted largely in accordance with the aldermen's wishes.

In the early fourteenth century one cannot distinguish between assemblies summoned for elective and legislative purposes; an assembly called to make elections might also approve certain ordinances. Beginning in the late fourteenth century the words 'Common Council' are used in the records to describe the legislative, or non-elective assembly. Meetings of the council thereafter are often identified as a 'Common Council', but other phrases such as 'mayor, aldermen and commons' or 'the good men of the wards' continued to be used. Elective assemblies were larger and included men not ordinarily summoned for legislative work. This is how the Congregation of 1384 was described.

> Wednesday the Feast of St. Matthew, 8 Richard II, ordinance made by Nicholas Brembre, the mayor, William Cheyne, the recorder,. . . . [15 names], aldermen, Simon Wynchecombe, one of the sheriffs, and all the good folk of the wards elected as a Common Council, together with other good and sufficient men summoned to the Chamber of the Guildhall, both for the City's business as well as for the election of sheriffs[1] . . .

From this time on, the Congregation was summoned only for elections and though other business might be discussed on election days, it was the Common Council that was regularly summoned for this other business.

After Common Council began developing as a separate and self-conscious body, who made up the larger elective assembly? Who, in other words, were the 'other good and sufficient men' summoned to supplement those elected in the wards? From an early time these other citizens were liverymen from the various leading trading companies[2]. The first time liverymen were specifically mentioned as part of Congregation was in 1467[3]. It gradually became the rule thereafter to limit membership of Congregation exclusively to liverymen of the companies, a privilege finally confirmed by statute of 11 George I, c.18 (1725).

---

1   *Cal. Let.-Book H,* p. 249.
2   For a discussion of what liveryman meant in the context of company offices, see below, p. 33.
3   *Cal. Let.-Book L,* p. 73.

How early the Common Council attended as a body at the electoral assembly is simply not known, but individual councilmen always made up part of Congregation. In the mayoral elections of 1384, 1442 and 1443 the council did attend as a body, supplemented by 'certain other citizens, powerful and discreet, from the several wards'.[1] Dr. R. R. Sharpe believed that these were exceptional instances, necessitated by threats of disorder. In 1467 and 1475 formal acts of the council demanded the council's presence for mayoral and shrieval elections.[2] That liverymen are first identified in the membership at precisely the time when the council began attending regularly as a body suggests that the aldermen were finally squeezing out the last citizens with whom they shared no civic or guild connections. During the Elizabethan period Common Council met on about half the various days when Congregation assembled, suggesting that the council was called as a matter of convenience, since its members would have been at Guildhall for the Congregation.

By the later sixteenth century it was openly recognized that the aldermen should have a large influence over the various candidates chosen. The records of Congregation state that the aldermen nominated two candidates for chamberlain and four for bridgemaster, of whom Congregation elected one chamberlain and two bridgemasters. Of the five auditors one was always a senior alderman, the other four were always common councilmen. Beginning in 1551, when four special aleconners were created, and for thirteen years thereafter, Congregation also chose these four officers, probably from nominees of the Court of Aldermen. But in 1564 the aldermen took over direct election of aleconners.[3] As to sheriffs, the mayor traditionally chose one by himself, who was then ratified by Congregation. The other, though officially elected by Congregation, was the most junior alderman who had not yet been sheriff — unless all aldermen had so served, in which case a commoner was chosen. A large majority of the Elizabethan aldermen served their shrieval year only after becoming aldermen. Concerning the mayor himself, since at least 1406, and perhaps since 1384, Congregation nominated two aldermen who had served as sheriff, and from them the court chose the mayor.[4] By the early sixteenth century, however, succession to the mayoral chair was according to seniority on the court, making nominations into formalities.[5]

---

1 *Cal. Let.-Book K*, pp. 275, 288.
2 *Cal. Let.-Book L*, pp. 73, 132.
3 Jour. 18, fos. 273-4.
4 *Cal. Let.-Book I*, p. 53, note 1 and *Cal. Let.-Book H*, pp. 241-2.
5 Beaven *Aldermen of London*, ii. xxv. Some mayors served ahead of other aldermen more senior than they, mostly in order to give certain men additional

Even over the election of MPs Congregation was not allowed a free choice. Half of the City's four representatives had to be, by tradition, the recorder and a senior alderman, who were the knights. These two had always been chosen by the aldermen alone.[1] Though Congregation chose the two burgesses, it invariably chose men of the ruling circle. Consider the Elizabethans: except for Thomas Norton, the remembrancer,[2] all the other burgesses were or had been leading or notable councilmen, and boasted considerable experience as committeemen or officeholders. Though there is no conclusive proof that aldermen regularly influenced Congregation's choice of MPs, it had been customary to do so since the earlier sixteenth century,[3] and aldermen did intervene during by-elections.[4] Given Congregation's lack of elective authority over other officers, we may suspect that the aldermanic interference was greater than formally acknowledged.

A few vestiges of Congregation's formerly broader consultative powers survived into the Elizabethan period. On 18 August 1586 it convened to hear the reading of a letter from the queen, confirming the arrest of certain conspirators (involved in the Babington plot) and acknowledging the expressions of joy the City had sent her on the occasion of their arrest. On 23 March 1597 Congregation assembled again to elect the first lecturers of divinity, astronomy, geometry, and music provided for by the will of Sir Thomas Gresham. A letter of James I, dated 28 March 1603, thanking the City for its warm approval of his accession and granting it a continuation of its rights, was also read to this assembly.[5] But since the late fourteenth century the

time to prepare for the mayoral year; such deferments were approved by the court itself and had nothing to do with Congregation.

1 *Cal. Let.-Book H*, pp. 98, 117-18 provide two early examples (1378 and 1379).

2 MP in 1571 and 1572, Norton was not exactly an unknown man. He had been remembrancer from the creation of that office in 1571 (*Remembrancia*, pp. x and 27 note 1). The remembrancer was charged to keep and engross copies of letters sent to the mayor and aldermen by the Privy Council. Later he wrote and kept copies of letters sent by authority of the mayor and aldermen. He had an annual salary from the Chamber (ibid. pp. v-vii). Like the recorders, common serjeants and town clerks of the period he was trained in the law, and like them he supplemented his salary with fees. He was very much more than a secretary, for he spent a great deal of time as an intermediary between the City and the crown. His particular role, even from the early years, had been to represent the City's interests in Parliament, whether or not he was actually an MP (Rep. 19, fo. 203[b] and Rep. 20, fo. 44).

3 Sharpe, *London and the Kingdom*, iii. 468-9 and Helen Miller, 'London and Parliament in the Reign of Henry VIII', *Bulletin of the Institute of Historical Research* 35 (1962), 128-9. Both authors pointed out that until after 1529 the Common Council, not the Congregation, elected the two burgesses and sometimes confirmed the aldermanic representatives.

4 Rep. 21, fo. 210. For a list of Elizabethan MPs from London, see Sharpe, *London and the Kingdom*, iii. 473-91.

5 Jour. 22, fos. 52-3; Jour. 24, fo. 206; Jour. 26, fo. 75[b].

Congregation had been steadily yielding influence to Common Council or the aldermen. There was an assembly in 1444, which approved an assessment on the wards, and two other non-elective meetings, in 1536 and 1551, summoned to show popular backing for particular policies.[1] By the sixteenth century the elective power of Congregation was limited to choosing from among the aldermen's nominees or ratifying the aldermen's preferences..

In conclusion, the increasing demands of the crown and the greater activity of the council were bringing about subtle changes in the Elizabethan period, changes not adequately measured by the council's more regular meetings or its greater responsibilities. Clearly, as in the attempt to limit reversions, there was a sense of political self-consciousness, a realization that government lay in the hands of the whole commonalty in Common Council assembled, not just with the more prestigious aldermanic leaders. The rhetoric was traditional, but the reality came to mean more too. But there were limits to this growing self-consciousness. It was a feeling that the whole council should rule, but it was not democratic or even anti-oligarchic, for the men who led the council were themselves closely bound to the aldermen and constituted what can only be called an oligarchy. In view of its supportive behaviour the greater self-consciousness of Common Council seems to have been the result of the aldermen's own need for more assistance in governing London. Neither the council nor individual councilmen were willing to take over from the aldermen their wide control over finances and elections or their leadership in legislation and general administration. The 1590s were still a long way from the hostile and divisive 1640s. In the Elizabethan period civic problems were tackled by men who worked, by and large, for a common purpose.

Jour. 4, fo. 64[b]; *Cal. Letter-Book* P, fo. 101[b]; and Jour. 16, fo. 118.

3

LOCAL OFFICERS AND LOCAL INSTITUTIONS

Despite a long tradition of citizen participation, the principal local institutions were subservient in one way or another to the aldermen, each in a way appropriate to its own history. So, too, were the local officers. In the localities, as elsewhere in the City, the aldermen ruled. Before plunging into the operation of local government, it will be well to introduce briefly some of the major officers, to indicate their approximate jurisdiction, and to identify the membership of the institutions to be discussed. Common councilmen acted as chief assistants to the aldermen in each of the local institutions operating in the ward, the parish, and the livery company. Though only assistants to the aldermen when acting for the whole City, their authority so far exceeded any other local officer's that, at least in this local context, it is more accurate to speak of councilmen as the aldermen's associates. This was especially true of the deputy alderman, chosen by the alderman from among the councilmen of his ward. The specific ways in which aldermen, deputies and councilmen involved themselves in the local institutions will be mentioned in the last section of this chapter.

To identify any of the local officers as belonging uniquely to ward or parish or livery company institutions would in some cases be to impose an unjustified simplification onto a complex reality. The overlapping network of men and positions will be untangled presently. To begin in the ward, the important officers were the constables, scavengers and inquestmen. The twenty-six wards of Elizabethan London were divided into approximately 242 precincts, and more than any other officer the constable had a close and unique association with the precinct.[1] This is suggested first by his duties. In the sixteenth century he still summoned juries from lists of precinct residents and assigned householders to their turn in serving the watch, which was organized along precinct lines.[2] One set of constable's accounts illustrates the variety of his work: he collected any number of assessments, assisted in military musters and pressed men for service; he made a number of surveys of the inhabitants and kept certain people under observation; he did so much that it was necessary to hire assistants.[3]

1   The most historically useful map of London at this time is one drawn by H.W. Cribb, who based his reconstruction on contemporary materials. A copy is provided with the Kingsford edition of Stow's *Survey*. On the number of precincts see below, p. 30, note 2.

2   Rep. 15, fo. 14 and Rep. 17, fo. 345.

3   MS 9680 at the GLMR. It begins in 1598. This precinct was so large as to have

The close similarity in the number of constables and precincts also points to their association. At the twenty-five City wardmotes north of the Thames 215 constables were elected for the year 1566-7;[1] the number of precincts in 1585 for the same wards was 226.[2] By 1598 when John Stow published the first edition of his *Survey* he counted 239 constables,[3] which closely approached the number of precincts. In the late sixteenth century neither the number of councilmen (212) nor scavengers (192 in Stow's *Survey*) bore close resemblance to the number of precincts; neither did the number of inquestmen. In later periods there is the same closer proximity in the number of precincts and constables.[4] Some precincts were too small to have their own constable (these fell under a neighbouring precinct), while others, particularly the larger ones coterminous with whole parishes, might require more than one.

Traditionally the beadle and the constables were the two ward officers most concerned with night watches. The beadle set the watch for the entire ward; the constable supervised and often participated at the precinct level. Possibly precinct and constable were first associated because of the watch. The beadle was an officer of the whole ward, and normally there was only one to a ward. But unlike other ward officers he had no apparent connection with either precincts or parishes, unless a precinct was large enough to deserve its own ward inquest. It was with the court of wardmote and the ward inquest that he belonged: he helped assemble both, then attended upon each. He was elected and paid by order of the court of wardmote. Although the constable was most closely identified with the precinct, by the Elizabethan period it was traditional to associate scavengers, inquestmen, even common councilmen with particular precincts as well.[5] Not all precincts were

two constables. In smaller precincts constables probably did not have paid assistants.

1 Jour. 19, fo. 59 and Letter-Book V, fo. 118b.

2 A book written by John Mountgomery in 1585, entitled 'A Book Containing the Manner and Order of a Watch to be Used in the City of London', gives the number of precincts for all 26 wards as 242 (on fos. 3b-4). The book is preserved on shelf 36C at the CLRO. Stow's *Survey*, ii. 69 shows that there were 16 constables south of the Thames in Southwark, or Bridge Without Ward.

3 At the end of each chapter Stow listed the number of officers that represented each ward.

4 For the number of constables and precincts by the early nineteenth century see the *Second Report of the Commissioners of Inquiry into the Municipal Corporations of England and Wales,* Parliamentary Papers (1837), pp. 138 ff. For the mid eighteenth century see John Smart, *A Short Account of the Several Wards, Precincts, Parishes in London* (1741), pp. 4-31. (This is Pamphlet 6894 at the GLMR).

5 This is clear from ward assessments, which often list those who paid by precinct. See, for example, the Cornhill W[ardmote] I[nquest] M[inute] book, fos. 57b-58b.

equally represented by these officers, and representation of a precinct did not depend on residence within it. In the vestry minutes of St. Dunstan in the West a general order of the vestry on 19 December 1587 put it this way: City officers 'should be chosen no more only by the precincts, but where they may be best had within the parish'.[1]

Scavengers began as street cleaners in the precincts. Often the word raker is used synonymously with scavenger, though strictly speaking the raker was a ward officer who supervised all the several scavengers.[2] On the basis of these duties scavengers could scarcely be important local officers. But like constables, scavengers were considered parish as well as ward and precinct officers. Like constables they served on parish committees and sometimes sat on the vestry. In other words, the office of scavenger entailed some specific duties (many possibly carried out by deputies), but also it signified attainment of a certain rank in the parish.

Inquestmen belonged to the ward inquest, which itself was a contingent of the larger court of wardmote. The foreman took first place on the ward inquest, and he was assisted by a horde of others, most importantly by three senior citizens responsible, respectively, for the financial transactions, the various records and papers, and a general auditing of the accounts. These three officers had different names in some wards, but they can be called treasurer, secretary, and comptroller. Some foremen had additional assistants peculiar to their own wards. Cornhill Ward had four speakers (high-ranking aids) and a pricker, who took attendance at meetings. Bridge Ward had four benchers, apparently similar to Cornhill's speakers. The remaining inquestmen — butlers, stewards, porters, fuelers, etc., — as their names imply, provided food, drink, essential supplies and performed minor services for the inquest while meeting indoors, for which they sometimes received a stipend.[3]

In the parish the churchwardens were the chief administrative officers. Generally two in every parish, rarely three, churchwardens were chosen for two years, usually by order of seniority among other vestrymen. They kept accounts of all money received and spent, safeguarded property and kept the keys to the parish chest, which contained miscellaneous records and valuables. They made sure that all preachers were licensed by proper authority before speaking in the

1 See the V[estry] M[inute] book, fo. 2. There were then three precincts sub-ordinate to the parish (VM, fo. 25[b]).
2 Cornhill WIM, fo. 148[b].
3 Aldersgate WIM, fo. 55[b].

parish.[1] They collected various church dues and commenced suit for any money not collected. The others on the vestry were usually the ancients — usually because occasionally a prominent parishioner appeared on the vestry who did not qualify as an ancient. Being an ancient did not necessarily imply advanced age, rather it designated those who had served in certain parochial or ward offices of sufficient importance to deserve a seat on the vestry.[2] Vestrymen normally served for life.

Several officers did double-duty, in the ward and the parish. Consider again the constable. In his oath of office in the sixteenth century[3] he was required to report monthly to one of the clerks of the Mayor's Court on the number of deceased freemen within his parish. Also, in reading the Tudor statutes on local government the constable is certainly seen as a parish officer. It was understood, I believe, that such duties and powers, though assigned through the parish, were executed in the appropriate precinct. In practice, therefore, the constable was simultaneously a ward, a precinct, and a parish officer. In keeping the peace, investigating nuisances, or enforcing ordinances he acted within the whole ward; in making most of his collections, in influencing elections, or setting the watch he was operating within a precinct. But he usually sat on a local parish vestry, where he had broad executive authority for a whole parish in addition to particular responsibilities in his own precinct. The jurisdictional relationship between precinct and parish makes sense when we realize that all precincts were considered to be part of some particular parish. When the precinct lay wholly within a parish, or was coterminous with it, there was no question which parish administered it. When a precinct lay in more than one parish, it was governed by that parish where most of its houses were located.[4] Thus the generating power in precinct and ward government was the vestry council. As a result, a variety of relationships ensued. It could happen that single parishes nominated most of a ward's officers, as St. Michael's did for the ward of Cornhill. But in the ward of Bishopsgate the ward's officers were chosen by

1 VM of St. Michael Cornhill, fo. 7.

2 In most parishes whose records survive the constable qualified as an ancient and sat on the vestry; the office of constable usually marked the transition to the rank of ancient. However, until 1601, when the vestry was 'closed' or officially limited, scavengers in St. Dunstan in the West also sat on the vestry and might well have been considered ancients (VM fo. 2).

3 This oath and many others are recorded in a book of oaths at the CLRO. From internal evidence it was written between 1584 and 1602. See fos. 27b-28 for the constable. An early fifteenth-century collection of oaths is in *Cal. Let.-Book* D. pp. 192-3.

4 This has been worked out from vestry minute books, court of wardmote and ward inquest records.

five different vestries. Also it was possible for a particular vestry to nominate officers for more than one ward. The church of St. Peter Cornhill lay in the ward of Cornhill, but the parish's boundaries enclosed the greatest part of three precincts, each belonging in different wards: Cornhill, Lime Street and Bishopsgate.

From the guilds or livery companies come the third group of local officers. Having gained the freedom of the City through his livery company, a Londoner became a citizen, with all the attendant privileges and responsibilities.[1] The initial advance in the companies was to the position of liveryman, originally meaning all those who wore the clothing, or livery, of the fraternity, but by the fifteenth century identifying those who had attained a certain rank in the company.[2] Liverymen performed a number of duties, largely on committees, and came together periodically in a court of livery, a large but not very powerful deliberative body. Those not yet liverymen were called bachelors or yeomen. Wardens audited accounts, kept records and looked after a variety of details. There were usually four, from renter warden (or sometimes fourth warden) up to first warden (also upper or senior warden).[3] Becoming a warden also meant initiation into the court of assistants, where members served for life and held the various wardenships by rotation. Like vestrymen in the parish, assistants in the companies held all the executive positions. The chief member of the court of assistants was the master of the company, who was chosen, generally by seniority, from among those who had served in, or paid a fine to avoid serving, the highest wardenship.

Between livery companies and the parishes and wards there existed less often the kind of overlapping institutional control we found between the parish vestry and the precinct. Occasionally members of one livery gained a plurality or even a majority of the vestry seats in particular parishes, as the grocers did in St. Stephen Walbrook. But there is no evidence that the Grocers Company, as distinct from individual grocers, governed St. Stephen's. Of course, liverymen were simultaneously in other ward and parish offices. Usually shortly after reaching the livery a man would be elected an inquestman for the first time; before his initial wardenship he would also have served as scavenger or constable, or both, and probably taken a place on a vestry.

1 Usually gained through apprenticeship, the freedom could also be inherited (patrimony) or bought (redemption). For a summary on the freedom see *Corporation of London*, pp. 220-1; for details and historical development consult Sharpe's Introduction to *Cal. Let.-Book D*, pp. i-xi.

2 George Unwin, *The Gilds and Companies of London*, 4th ed. (1963), p. 166.

3 In the Mercers Company the lowest ranking was the renter warden; then came second warden, and third warden, then master.

Assistants (members of the court of assistants) were normally vestrymen, as well as the higher officers of the court of wardmote and the ward inquest. The senior wardens and masters had often been churchwardens and foremen; even more were simultaneously common councilmen or aldermen.

In addition to such official ties the local officers built up numerous personal associations through the local institutions. Many of their wills speak of charitable donations to one or more parishes, and almost always to their livery company. Ward and parish inventories reveal that most of the property belonging to them came from inquestmen and vestrymen. Personal friendships grew up between them, frequently business connections and marriage ties too. Men of the same livery often lived in the same neighbourhoods.[1] Following the pattern of great merchant princes, and even the artisan elements in London, the local officers intermarried and built up dynasties with other families of similar occupation, wealth, and civic experience.[2]

How did these officers govern in the localities? The question raises further questions of origin, duties and procedures, and more generally of the co-optive nature of local elections. The institutions to be examined — the court of wardmote, the ward inquest, the vestry, and the several courts in the livery company — all show a similarity of development and operation.

Origin

The origin of the wards is difficult to separate from the earliest aldermen, who, from at least the early twelfth century, ruled their London wards as sokes.[3] By at least the late thirteenth century most of the wards were identified by the names they have had ever since, implying that the aldermen's proprietary controls had ceased by then.[4] The court of wardmote, and perhaps the ward inquest which sprang from it, probably existed from around the same time, for in 1311 the custom of holding four wardmotes a year was said to be by 'ancient

1   T. F. Reddaway. 'Elizabethan London — Goldsmith's Row in Cheapside, 1558-1645', *The Guildhall Miscellany* 2 (October 1963), 181-206.

2   This conclusion is based largely on a study of wills and local assessment records. For the details, see below. chapter 6. For the artisans, see David R. Ransome, 'Artisan Dynasties in London and Westminster in the Sixteenth Century', *The Guildhall Miscellany* 2 (October 1964), 236-47.

3   A.B. Beaven, *The Aldermen of the City of London*, 2 vols. (1908-13), ii. xiv-xvi; Frederick Pollock and Frederic William Maitland, *The History of English Law before the Time of Edward I*, 2nd. ed. (Cambridge, 1968), ii. 645-6; A.H. Thomas, ed., *Calendar of Plea and Memoranda Rolls, 1413-37* (Cambridge, 1943), pp. xxx ff.

4   *Cal. Let.-Book A*, **pp.** xi, 209-10.

ordinance'.[1] The livery company as a corporation only dates from the late fourteenth century, but the fraternal association, or mystery, whose members came together for religious and social purposes, is much older. The earliest craft guilds were themselves mysteries so that the several elements that later merged in the chartered livery company all existed separately, or in some senses together, from the second half of the twelfth century.[2] Government by a co-opting oligarchy of eminent men was traditional and became formalized during the fourteenth century for the greater mysteries, and during the fifteenth for most of the lesser ones, through the leadership of a master and a court of assistants. In the parish individual parishioners had probably always assisted on an informal basis in meeting the needs of their church. The first permanent officer, the churchwarden, came into existence by the late thirteenth century to administer funds or properties entrusted to the parish, and to collect church rates. By the middle of the fourteenth century the vestry had become a regular and indispensable supplement to the churchwardens: helping to assess and collect taxes, keep revenues and property safely, and supervise the churchwardens' accounts.[3] By the end of the fourteenth century the local institutions had assumed the form they would have even beyond the Elizabethan era.

The arrival of the vestry signalled secular control over parish finances; I believe it also made possible a reordering of local ward government along the lines already outlined, whereby the vestry took over essential business in the wards. Vestrymen were the ideal local authorities because they concentrated their administration at a truly local level, whereas the ward itself was too large and its officers too few to govern effectively. The interference of the vestry in ward elections, the coincidence in membership between the vestry and the ward inquest, the involvement of common councilmen and aldermen in ward business

1 Thomas, *Plea and Memoranda Rolls*, p. xxv.

2 On the evolution of the companies from fraternities, chartered trading groups, and craft guilds the best general history remains Unwin's *Gilds and Companies*. For a general bibliography of the companies see William F. Kahl, 'The Development of the London Livery Companies', *Kress Library of Business and Economics* 15 (Boston: Harvard Graduate School of Business Administration, 1960), and its supplement in *The Guildhall Miscellany* 2 (April 1962).

3 Pollock and Maitland, *English Law*, i. 532-71; F. W. Maitland, 'The Survival of Archaic Communities', *Law Quarterly Review* 9 (July 1893), 211-28; Sidney and Beatrice Webb, *Local Government*, vol. 1, *The Parish and the County* (1906); Charles Drew, 'Early Parochial Organization in England: The Origins of the Office of Churchwarden', Borthwick Institute of Historical Research, *St. Anthony's Hall Publication, no. 7* (1954). Joshua T. Smith [Toulmin Smith], *The Parish*, 2nd ed. (1857) collected some useful statutes, case decisions, and other legal precedents, but he incorrectly viewed the parish and the vill as the same institution, and therefore drew the conclusion that parish government was secular in origin. His views were corrected by Maitland.

through their parishes, and the consequent shifting of greater civic responsibilities to the parish probably began almost as soon as vestries became permanent features of parish life. By the sixteenth century this was traditional. The early development of Common Council also supports this view of the vestry. During the first half of the fourteenth century the council met irregularly, its membership fluctuated considerably, and the number elected varied sharply from time to time.[1] Moreover the power of the larger guilds, becoming greater due to incorporation during the century, was recognized in the years 1351-2 and 1376-83 by allowing guilds instead of wards to elect councilmen. Until late in the fourteenth century the council was a rather experimental body, experiencing growing pains similar to those of Parliament. From the end of the century, however, the council took on an increasing stability. The restoration of elective powers to the wards in 1384 seems to have been the turning point.[2] Though the number of councilmen continued to fluctuate, the council's size began to approximate the early modern form.[3] In 1384 the aldermen gave formal approval for the council to meet at least once a quarter, and regular meetings date from this time. The same act returned conciliar elections to the wards; the guilds never again intervened in the election of ward officers.[4] One reason for the growing stability of the council after 1384 may have been the vestry. Guild-dominated elections made even sharper the already keen political and economic rivalries of the leading mysteries; these rivalries left the City divided in the difficult times of Richard II and may have encouraged the king to suspend the City's privileges in 1392. It was feared at the time that continued guild control of elections would intensify the hostility of the craft fraternities and the wealthier commercial interests, as well as that between foodstuff importers and manufacturing exporters.[5] Thus to a commercial, political rivalry would have been added a deepening social one. Nor was this all. The men who wished to shift control of conciliar elections from the wards to the guilds also desired annual election for

1 *Cal. Let.-Books F, G, and H*, especially *F*, pp. 162, 237-9; *G*, p. 3; *H*, pp. 42-4, 59.

2 Ibid. *H*, pp. 227-8. From this time elections to the council became annual. By 1410 the date of elections coincided with the December meeting of the court of wardmote, 21 December (ibid. *I*, pp. 89-90).

3 In July 1384, 267; in 1385, 140; in 1386, 174; in 1388, 210 (ibid. *H*, pp. 237-40, 269-71, 279-81, 332-4). In the middle of the fifteenth century the number was around 189 (see Appendix 3 note 4). In the Elizabethan period the number was 212 (Appendix 3).

4 *Cal. Let.-Book H*, p. 241. The reformers who favoured mystery control of council elections had passed an abortive act in 1376, specifying at least two meetings per quarter (ibid. p. 40).

5 On the economic rivalries of the period see Unwin, *Gilds and Companies* and Ruth Bird, *The Turbulent London of Richard II* (1949).

aldermen.[1]   Obviously these two measures threatened the greater traditional authority of aldermen. It was far safer to disperse the power to elect councilmen among the wards, where the aldermen could muster their own considerable influence through the emerging vestries to secure election of the right men.[2]

Duties and procedures

The court of wardmote was the court held by each alderman in his own ward, but in the late sixteenth century it was not uncommon for the deputy to hold it for him. This court was the urban equivalent to the hundred court in the counties, whose main assembly was on St. Thomas's Day (21 December). This was the one time in the year when, theoretically, every householder could take part in civic government. The annual ward assembly brought together those serving the ward in some capacity, as well as those who had previously served, and those yet to take their first office in the ward or a parish. Potentially the wardmote was so large as to be chaotic, but not even all the adult males appeared on this annual occasion. That the beadle was empowered to levy a fine on absent householders indicates that there may sometimes have been difficulty in bringing a quorum together. Still, the annual wardmote best symbolizes the popular participation in local affairs that had developed in London centuries ago.[3]

A number of things were done on St. Thomas's Day — juries were named; brewers, bakers and innkeepers were licensed by the alderman; weights and measures were approved, and the several nuisances encountered in the ward by the inquest were presented before the alderman. The most necessary business was the election of ward officers for the coming year; scavengers, constables, inquestmen, the beadle and the common councilmen were officially chosen by this large wardmote. However, the wardmote preferred to play a passive role in elections, being content to ratify the nominations of parish leaders.[4]

1   This had actually been granted in 1319 by Edward II, then affirmed in 1376, though it never appears to have been effective (*Cal. Let.-Book D*, p. vi and n. 2, also ibid. *H*, p. 58, n. 2). In 1384 the ruling was amended, then finally annulled in 1394 (ibid. pp. 228, 409-10).

2   It is ironic that if the emerging vestry assembly offered a convenient way of offsetting guild influence in elections, it also eventually gave the frustrated reformers of the 1380s their chance to go beyond the guilds and build a base for councilmen in the vestries nearly as secure as the aldermen's claim to life tenure.

3   See Thomas's Introduction to the *Plea and Memoranda Rolls* and *Liber Albus*, pp. 32-5 for further details.

4   Nomination records for ward officers appear in over half the vestry books which survive. In other records there is evidence that vestries supervised

It could happen that parishes nominated more candidates for individual precincts than were needed, leaving it to the wardmote to choose from among their nominees. But this practice was exceptional, and there is no indication that the wardmote took it upon itself to nominate and elect candidates. Nor is there evidence of the wardmote challenging parish nominees.

The ward inquest met periodically throughout the year for a perambulation of the ward to search out nuisances or violations of civic ordinances. At the time of *Liber Albus* (1419) the inquest met at least twice in the year but in the Elizabethan period the prescribed frequency, by order of the Court of Aldermen, was monthly.[1] Presentment of nuisances to the alderman was supposed to be four times a year in the same period.[2] How did the ward inquest operate? First, it exercised a large autonomy in drawing up bylaws.[3] These encompassed time and place of meeting and general orders for discipline — forbidding, for example, swearing, fighting, speaking out of turn, or showing excessive reverence by tipping one's hat more than three times. Being late or absent also drew a fine. With the exception of a traditional grant every year from the alderman, and often the leading inquestmen, the inquest supported itself by fines, various fees, and a 'benevolence' raised from the householders.

The inquest also chose its own officers for the year, the ranking being according to seniority for the most part, and the wishes of the foreman. If, as sometimes happened, there was rivalry among the several precincts of the ward for the right to choose the foreman, the Court of Aldermen would intervene to settle all claims. In May 1617 the court made a general ruling through an act of Common Council that the alderman of the ward, or in his absence the mayor himself, should approve of every inquest foreman; further that if the inquest was evenly divided in its choice, the alderman, or the mayor in his absence, would cast the decisive vote.[4] Though the number of men

---

ward elections: for example, churchwardens collected fines from men unwilling to serve as constable or scavenger. At the same time there is no indication of precinct meetings held independently of the vestry. There are two precinct books, the earliest from 1594, but they contain no minutes of meetings, no discussion of precinct affairs, nothing to suggest a distinct assembly in the precinct. They were probably compiled by parish clerks as a list of nominees for ward officers. See MSS 1125 and 1162/2 at the GLMR.

1 *Liber Albus*, p. 32 and Rep. 45, fo. 84. This order was made on 11 January 1631 and seems to reaffirm older tradition.

2 Rep. 22, fo. 341b (10 January 1592).

3 For Cornhill, the WIM, fos. 1-2, 192b-93; for Aldersgate, the WIM, fos. 54-58b, 61b-62.

4 Letter-Book FF, fos. 265b and 305.

elected to the inquest varied from ward to ward,[1] as did their titles, their work was much the same in all wards.[2] The foreman conducted the proceedings, interrogated the witnesses and suspects, and had the major voice in making final presentments and in recommending punishments. He approved the selection of the lesser inquestmen. He enforced the bylaws and might supplement them with new orders if the leading inquestmen approved.

Though its work might influence more than one ward, the vestry operated within one parish. It made its own bylaws for meetings, and, except for the periodic visitations of the bishop or archdeacon, was left largely to itself. But while doing things in its own way, the vestry increasingly combined parochial with civic business. It was the vestry that took responsibility for raising the fifteenth, levied either by Parliament or Common Council. Minutes for the period are replete with lists of men named by the vestries as assessors or gatherers of fifteenths. The City utilized the parish for other special purposes. During one of the periodic Catholic scares in the early 1590s the rulers ordered the vestries to search out lurking Jesuits.[3] Powder, arms, and ammunition of the ward were often stored in the local church, where they were itemized and safeguarded by parish officers. One mayoral precept in August 1563, during an outbreak of plague, ordered that divine service should be held every day of the week at 8.00 a.m. until further notice; it went on to instruct churchwardens to warn every householder that at least two members of each household 'should come to their said churches to the said daily divine service and that they do then there remain and abide continually serving God devoutly by the space of one hour at the least'. Further the churchwardens were to warn all tavern keepers and victuallers to keep their places of business closed on Wednesdays and Fridays during the hours of worship. During the same two days they were to order 'minstrals, bowlers, archers, and other gamesters residing and dwelling within their said several parishes [to] desist, forbear and leave off the exercise and use of every of the said arts and sciences.'[4]

During plagues vestries also elected plague inspectors, whose job was to keep track of which houses and how many people were currently infected; different inspectors were named each week. They also reported

---

1 Sixteen in Cornhill; fourteen in Aldersgate; sixteen in Bridge Ward until 1632, thereafter only fourteen; the parish of St. Dunstan in the West held its own inquests; it had seven inquestmen.

2 For details on the presentments see my doctoral dissertation, 'The Government of London in the Reign of Elizabeth I', (Columbia University, 1968), pp. 175-8.

3 VM of St. Mary Aldermanbury, fos. 32 ff.

4 Jour. 18, fo. 140[b].

violations of plague ordinances.[1] Upon delegates of the vestry, or upon the constable in the precinct, fell such jobs as the killing of stray dogs that might be disease carriers, marking infected houses with a small blue cross, compelling vagrants to leave the City (done regardless of plagues), and preventing landlords from leasing out vacant rooms until the plague subsided.[2] Simultaneously, the vestries in 1563 were trying to collect a fifteenth that had been granted by Parliament in January of that year. For that reason the parishes had to keep track of everyone in the wards, as well as those who had fled during the sickness.[3]

The vestry accumulated a number of miscellaneous powers as well. One of the more important was redrawing precinct lines from time to time.[4] During the Tudor period parishes became responsible for birth, marriage and burial records. Later, parishes were given power to elect surveyors of the highways and overseers of the poor. Responsibility for these and other parish duties fell to churchwardens, constables, and vestrymen, or other parishioners active as ward or parish officers who would one day become vestrymen.[5] Armed with such powers the parish became the main organ of local government until the nineteenth century.

The vestry also acted in support of the ward inquest. In some of the larger wards the inquest could not deal effectively with the whole ward by itself, thus individual parishes made preliminary surveys of their precincts.[6] In the vestry book of St. Andrew Holborn (in the large ward of Farringdon Without) there is the following order concerning the inquests.

> There shall be a vestry held in every parish by the parson or the curate and churchwardens with the constable and the collectors for the poor and six other of the chief of the inhabitants at the least to inquire and understand of all idle persons, vagabonds, disordered persons, masters of dishonest houses, disordered children of the poor, disordered alehouses, and such like abuses as also of such as be or have been absenters of themselves from the Church on the sabbath and holy days, or other such like misdemeanors in their

---

1 For example, the VM of St. Andrew Holborn, fos. 6-10.

2 Jour. 18, fos. 136-36[b], 123[b], 139[b], and 151[b]-52.

3 Ibid. fo. 145[b].

4 VM of St. Dunstan in the West, fo. 25[b].

5 The best guide to the growing statutory authority of the vestry remains Webb and Webb, *Local Government,* which mentions most of the relevant acts under the appropriate topic headings.

6 When acting for the ward inquest it is clear that the vestry had the power to impose fines (VM of St. Andrew Holborn, fo. 13).

parish. And that such as they find faulty in those respects be duly
presented at the next wardmote or inquest.[1]

Other parishes in Farringdon Without following the same practice
included St. Sepulchre Without Newgate and St. Dunstan in the West.

Though the parish was developing from around the mid fourteenth
century as a centre of political influence and local government, it
obviously continued to be an ecclesiastical institution. As parish leaders
the vestrymen were concerned first of all with the repair and
maintenance of the parish church, and with all the property owned by
the parish.[2] Being in possession of considerably more houses and other
sites than they could use themselves, vestries leased some properties,
quite often to parish leaders. A condition of the lease was keeping the
property in good repair, also a typical practice in leasing City properties.
Despite greater involvement in secular affairs, the vestry never lost
sight of its narrower, strictly parochial existence. Indeed, the vestry
can be understood only by seeing it in both roles, and by keeping in
mind the essentially mixed character of its whole existence — that
is, men of a secular background concerned with their neighbours'
morals; men who administered the affairs of their parish yet
simultaneously were civic representatives, some of whom sat on the
high governing bodies; men who evolved a formal routine for local
government, yet men whose understanding of, and involvement in, the
vestry was nothing if not highly personal. And while the vestrymen's
jurisdiction was increasing, reaching into what could be called police
power, public works, sanitation, tax collecting, and old age insurance,
they dispatched their business not like modern bureaucrats representing
a collective authority but as prominent parishioners acting individually
and frequently relying on their own judgment.

Vestries also handled considerable amounts of money. There was
money raised by rental of property, by fines on individuals who
preferred not to take a parish or ward office, by burial fees, fees for
hiring the church, pew rates out of which the parson, the clerk, the
sexton, several choir leaders, and the occasional special reader or
lecturer were paid a salary. 'Strangers' who took communion in the
parish paid special charges; a double fee was taken for burying

1 VM, fo. 6. This order was contained in a 'Book of Orders for Bridewell
Published by the Lord Mayor, A.D. 1580'. Bridewell was a precinct of the same
ward as St. Andrew Holborn, though it was not within the parish. The order was
undoubtedly meant to apply in St. Andrew Holborn, though, otherwise it would
not have been copied into the vestry book. St. Andrew Holborn had first
petitioned the aldermen for its own inquest in the 1560s (Rep. 15, fo. 32[b]).
2 A useful study of the parish in this period, which pulls together much
specialized research, is Christopher Hill, *Economic Problems of the Church:
from Archbishop Whitgift to the Long Parliament* (Oxford, 1956).

'strangers'. The sale of property realized additional money, particularly chalices at the beginning of Elizabeth's reign. Special levies generated further funds. Of particular concern to the parish were the levies for its own repairs or enlargements, or for the purchase of additional property. Of importance to the ward and City as a whole are other assessments, like the salary of the scavenger and the beadle.[1] All this money was accounted for in the churchwardens' accounts, audited annually by several other vestrymen who had previously served as churchwardens. The vestry also handled money that did not appear in total on the churchwardens' accounts, but was accounted for elsewhere. Fifteenths raised for the City have been mentioned; to this would be added the tithe and most of what was levied for the poor. Also, not all details of bequest and trust transactions appear on these accounts; in particular this is true of money loaned out by the parish to young tradesmen.[2] Finally, some parishes had particular rates. St. Dunstan in the West helped to finance the repairs of Whitefriars Bridge out of wharfage (a tax on goods landed) and a rate on 'buckewashing' at the bridge.[3]

Vestry meetings took place usually on Sundays because that was the most convenient time for men to gather at their local parish church; holidays were used for the same reason. As a matter of habit a few members of the vestry probably met every Sunday to discuss particular affairs that did not require either a full meeting or the keeping of any records. Most of the full meetings probably took place without the clerk who kept the minutes. It was only when officers were nominated or elected, or leases allocated, or special assignments made (like tax collector), or when general orders of the vestry were resolved, or some particular memorandum drawn up that a permanent written record was required.

The incumbent was the only clerical member of the vestry. Since, on the occasions when he attended, his name was written first in the notes out of respect to his office, the clerk's indication of his attendance can be considered reliable. These notes show that the incumbent appeared infrequently. Much of the vestry's work by the late sixteenth century simply did not concern the minister because it

1 It may seem odd that the beadle, a general ward officer serving all precincts, should have had the parish supervise the collection of his salary. St. Dunstan in the West, a large parish with at least three precincts, had its own beadle because the ward (Farringdon Without) was too large for just one. In cases like St. Dunstan's the parish nominated the beadle and the annual ward assembly ratified its choice.
2 If all such sums in all the parishes that loaned money were totalled, a very considerable sum would be discovered. For examples see the VM of St. Dunstan in the West, fos. 15, 33, 37, 43[b] and 81[b].
3 Ibid. fos. 19[b] and 25. 'Buckewashing' was a process of bleaching clothes in a tub or vat by allowing them to steep or boil in an alkaline lye.

did not concern the church; sometimes the minister was indifferent even to parish affairs. He did not often meddle in the wider political concerns of the vestry, from which the deputy or the councilmen probably deliberately excluded him. The minister was not named on committees of the vestry and was not appointed to assess property or taxes. The only notice taken of him was to record his name when present.

Domination by a secular oligarchy was often written into the vestry rules, establishing a quorum of about twelve to sixteen men.[1] This kind of ruling is usually written out after a vestry had sought and received an official order from the bishop of London granting it a limited vestry of from twenty-four to thirty men.[2] But the idea of having a quorum, or minimum number to conduct parish business, was older. The reasons given for seeking a limited vestry were the same from parish to parish.

> Through the general admittance of all sorts of parishioners unto their vestries there falleth out great disquietness and hindrance to good proceeding by the descent of the inferior and meaner sort of the multitude. . . .being greater in number and more ready to cross the good proceedings for the benefit of the church and parish than able to furnish by counsel or otherwise the good thereof.[3]

Officially limiting the size of the vestry was usually necessary only in the larger parishes, where there were many more inhabitants available to serve, but virtually every London parish by the late sixteenth century was in the hands of a small group. In all the surviving vestry records of the period there is a common pattern: the vestrymen are recruited from those who have served as scavenger, constable and inquestman; vestry business is carried out by a small number of men, a quorum consisting of the few among those experienced in lower offices; it is these same men who are on the vestry year after year until they are replaced by younger, similarly experienced men.[4]

1   Two examples: W.H. Overall, ed., *The Accounts of the Churchwardens of the Parish of St. Michael Cornhill, 1456-1608* (1871), p. 206 (1504); and the VM of St. Andrew Holborn, fo. 1 (1570).

2   There were at least six parishes (out of approximately fifty whose records survive in some detail) that had their vestries officially limited during the reign of Elizabeth alone. They are, with the appropriate folio reference to the VM: Allhallows the Great, fo. 10 (1578); St. Botolph Without Aldgate, fo. 9b (1584); St. Martin Ludgate, fo. 82 (1592); St. Martin Orgar, fo. 64 (1593); St. Dunstan in the West, fo. 43 (1601); St. Magnus in 1603 (Chartae Miscellaneae, Vol. 7, pp. 4 and 104 at Lambeth Palace Library). A seventh vestry, St. James Garlickhithe, was apparently limited sometime before 1615, when its VM begins (see the first four folios). Between 1606-27 at least eighteen more parishes were officially granted a select vestry. See Webb and Webb, *Parish and County*, pp. 190-3 and notes.

3   VM of St. Dunstan in the West, fo. 43.

4   The select vestry was also the typical feature outside London at this time. See J. Charles Cox, *Churchwardens' Accounts from the Fourteenth Century to*

In moving to the livery companies it is surprising to discover how few of them held most of the power and carried most of the burdens in City government. By the end of the fourteenth century over sixty craft guilds had organized, yet with rare exception only seven managed to place representatives on the Court of Aldermen: the Grocers, Mercers, Fishmongers, Drapers, Goldsmiths, Skinners, and Vintners.[1] During the fifteenth century four other new trading groups placed members on the court: the Ironmongers, Taylors (not the Merchant Taylors until 1503), Haberdashers, and Salters. These eleven companies were the only ones, with a single exception, to provide aldermen during the fifteenth century.[2] In the sixteenth century the discriminatory tradition was breaking down somewhat. Henry Goodyere served as alderman from 1546-9 without translating from the Leathersellers to a major company.[3] But until 1551 other men chose to translate in order to reach the Court of Aldermen.[4] In that year Thomas Curtes, pewterer, began a long struggle to avoid translation, a conflict he only renounced in 1556 by becoming a fishmonger. Apparently this dispute encouraged the court to have second thoughts about the tradition favouring the major twelve,[5] for after his election in 1588 John Catcher, pewterer, made no move to translate and never did. Thereafter in the years 1588-1640 twenty men, representing twelve different minor companies, reached the Court of Aldermen.

These twelve companies have traditionally been spoken of as the twelve great companies of London. They dominated the membership of the Common Council and provided virtually all the London mayors until 1742 and an overwhelming majority of the sheriffs.[6] Looking more closely at livery affiliation among mayors, sheriffs, aldermen, leading and notable councilmen, and a selection of all other councilmen (see Appendix 1 for names and livery affiliation) shows that grocers, haberdashers, merchant taylors, and mercers accounted for 44 per cent

the *Close of the Seventeenth Century* (1913), pp. 12-14; Webb and Webb, *Parish and County*, pp. 175-90. The Webbs found one select vestry as early as 1443 (ibid. p. 189, note 2). They also mention that while some parishes were definitely open at one time and became closed, or selected, only gradually (ibid. pp. 178-83), other parishes may never have had an open vestry (ibid. p. 189).

1   Beaven, *Aldermen of London*, i.329.

2   The exception was Henry Pountfreyt, sadler, alderman from 1403-11 (ibid. ii.2 and i.329).

3   Ibid. ii.32.

4   Ibid. i.330-1.

5   The twelfth were the Clothworkers, incorporated in 1528 by merger of the Shermen and Fullers.

6   Until 1742 mayors had to belong to one of the twelve principal companies (Beaven, *Aldermen of London*, ii.xlvi). Mayors, of course, were simultaneously aldermen, sheriffs either aldermen or prominent councilmen.

of all aldermen and councilmen and approximately 52 per cent of all aldermen and the notable councilmen. By adding clothworkers and drapers, these six claimed 61 per cent of all aldermen and councilmen, or 70 per cent of all aldermen and notable councilmen. These six were among the largest and wealthiest companies, but they exercised a political influence exceeding the proportion of their numbers.[1] Probably the six had originally become important because the rulers of London were concentrated in them. At the same time the rulers' habit of developing business and social connections with their brethren in the livery gradually reinforced the greatness of these few companies. In other words it is likely that wealth and size among the companies were mostly a result, not a cause, of the political dominance of six particular companies. Of course, the more wealth and prestige accrued to a few companies, the more they continued to attract a disproportionate share of the politically ambitious.

Within the companies, as in the vestries, government was structured for the benefit of a few. The men who regularly attended the court of assistants were also the few active in other affairs, especially committee work. The average number in regular attendance in the major companies rarely exceeded twenty. The court of assistants was the executive and legislative directory of the company. It was meant to lead, and no one objected seriously to its oligarchic character, though the assistants were expected to confer with the entire fellowship on certain formal occasions. They met annually with all the freemen in a general court for elections, then met again with the freemen on quarter days for appointments and general business. The assistants met occasionally with various liverymen, in a court of livery, especially for raising funds. Mostly they met alone, that is, just the master, wardens, and assistants. Even when freemen and liverymen attended these courts, business was planned in advance and carried out under the leadership of the assistants, much as the aldermen directed Common Council, or the councilmen

---

1 During Elizabeth's reign over a hundred guilds or companies existed which might have been represented by the 138 aldermen and approximately 1,025 common councilmen of the period. However, only 48 did gain representation, perhaps a very few more. Put another way, of the nearly 800 men listed in Appendix 1, 697 (87%) represent one of the twelve principal companies of London. Not surprisingly, most of those not in the major guilds had little rank in civic politics: only 19 of 102 were élite, notables or leaders – 11 of them leaders.

A fair indication of the proportional size of companies is the number of liverymen. A list from 1501-2 (Jour. 10, fo. 373b) of 50 companies shows a total of 1,465 liverymen, only 440 (30%) of whom belonged to one of the six dominant liveries. Another list of 1538 indicates that the six leading companies accounted for 322 of 616 listed liverymen (52%). The list shows figures only for the twelve principal companies, and is defective in that not all aldermen and masters are listed; see it in *Middlesex and Hertfordshire Notes and Queries*, vols. 3-4, beginning at vol. 3, p. 39.

controlled vestry meetings. The court of assistants in one form or another met about once a month at least, but other gatherings of wardens and leading assistants probably took place more frequently. In the Clothworkers Company, one of the largest at this time, the assistants usually met over forty times a year.

Like the parish, the livery company performed a great deal of necessary City business. Among their membership the guilds counted the wealthiest group of men in London, and the City raised money for loans to the crown through assessments on companies. The City also met its troop obligations through the companies. It was nothing new in the sixteenth century for the City to divide its obligations among the leading trade associations; as early as 1363 they had shared the cost of a £450 gift to the king.[1] The City also made use of company organization to borrow money for civic purposes, especially the supply of corn.[2] Owing to the rapid growth of London's population during the sixteenth century the civic authorities had to reform the whole process of corn supply, which meant building new storage granaries and arranging for supplies to be furnished regularly and in specific quantities. Previously the City had bought most of its corn sporadically and more at the convenience of the individual merchants who supplied it. The companies were asked to help in the supply of corn as early as 1520, but it was not until 1578 that instead of loaning money to the City for corn purchase the companies themselves took over the responsibilities for supply.[3] This agreement had been foreshadowed in 1574, when a committee of twenty-four common councilmen (two from each of the twelve principal livery companies) was created to work with the mayor and aldermen 'concerning the making of any provision of corn for this City, either beyond the seas or within this realm'.[4] On 4 November 1578 Common Council resolved that responsibility for provisions should pass from the committee of twenty-four to the masters, wardens, and assistants of each of the great twelve. It was also arranged that either the mayor or an alderman would inspect the provisions weekly.[5]

Through the periodic searches carried out by each company an extensive examination was made into the production, sale, and distribution of most goods produced or brought into the City. There-

---

1   *Cal. Let.-Book G,* pp. 171-3.

2   Such civic loans, however forced, are to be distinguished from the straight assessment, or fifteenth, which was raised through the wards.

3   On the supply of corn for London during the sixteenth century see Norman S.B. Gras, *The Evolution of the English Corn Market* (Cambridge, Mass., 1915), ch. 3, especially pp. 82-9 for the part played by the livery companies.

4   Jour. 20, pt. 1, fo. 177b.

5   Jour. 20, pt. 2, fos. 442 f.

fore these searches acted to enforce the elaborate and extensive economic legislation that applied in the City. In enforcing economic regulations the mayor and aldermen did not hesitate to enlist the assistance of the companies, at any time of the year. Following the queen's proclamation of October 1560 on the revaluation of copper coins,[1] the mayor issued three precepts concerning the work of restamping. In the first he named the halls of eleven companies where inspectors would be available to view and stamp coins. In the second and third he directed the masters to have some of their company members attend and assist the inspectors in their work.[2]

The companies did their part, too, in keeping the peace in London and in enforcing measures to preserve general order. Keeping the peace fell mostly to the alderman and his assistants in the ward, but the City wanted the most effective kind of enforcement, which did not preclude the companies' help. Members of the companies still stood the watch at the City's gates on certain traditional days.[3] And in 1572 masters of the companies were instructed by the mayor to have apprentices withdrawn from fencing and dancing schools – those breeding grounds of disorder.[4] Companies also assisted in maintaining general security. Fire was a continual danger in a city of so many timber frame closely-packed houses, therefore the keeping of gunpowder had to be carefully regulated. It is not surprising that the act regulating its storage should conclude with admonitions to the ward inquests to search out violators, or that two months later the mayor empowered company masters to seek out violators as well, either members of their company or others.[5]

A number of other matters were arranged by the City through the companies, especially all the entrées, festivals, and civic ceremonies. We have examined the role of the companies in the elections at Congregation, an assembly open to all City liverymen, who came to the Guildhall annually (on 1 August until 1585, thereafter on 24 June) to elect various officers. But it was in the course of their own business that the companies did the greatest services for local government, services that otherwise some public body would have had to tackle. They gave considerable attention to the poor and the sick through their

1 See it in Jour. 17, fos. 272-3.
2 See the three precepts (all in the autumn of 1560) in Jour. 17, fos. 277, 280 and 273[b] respectively.
3 *Remembrancia,* pp. 549-50.
4 Jour. 20, pt. 1, fo. 32. Though it is not certain to whom the precept was directed, it is clear from the act (ibid. fos. 13-14[b]) that company masters were to help enforce it.
5 See the act in Jour. 17, fos. 256[b]-58 and the mayoral precept in ibid. fo. 261[b].

charities or by outright grants. Through their loan funds they encouraged young tradesmen. They supported schools and lectures, and sent scholars to Oxford and Cambridge. Because of their extensive real estate holdings in the City they had a direct interest in maintaining the security of thousands of buildings, tenements, and other properties. The courts of assistants, as well as individual masters and wardens, handled scores of disputes every year, some involving questions of trade, others concerning apprentices or property rights or individual debts. The courts acted promptly and apparently with great fairness because members continually brought difficulties before their masters and assistants; the alternative resort to the common law was expensive and slow.[1]

In supervising the operation of local government the ruling aldermen and councilmen sometimes intervened directly through the Common Council, or usually the Court of Aldermen. Constables in particular found numerous temptations to stray from the straight and narrow, by taking a bribe, procuring a contract for a friend, or keeping him off juries or out of burdensome offices. By 1583 the Court of Aldermen had appointed a special officer to supervise constables.[2] Where that expedient proved ineffective, constables were summoned before the court for reprimanding or a fine.[3] The court also reinforced the authority of local ward inquests, by summoning the habitual offenders before the aldermen and handing down special punishments. The traditional inquest was a quaint anachronism by Elizabeth's time. That the aldermen did not interfere more often attests to the effectiveness of vestries in the wards.

Mostly when the court interfered in the localities, it was with the livery companies. Despite the independence many companies preserved

---

1 Professor. T.F. Reddaway pointed out in this connection that resort to the common law courts was usually forbidden in the companies' ordinances without the permission of the wardens ('The Livery Companies of Tudor London', *History* 51 (1966), 292).

2 Rep. 20, fo. 434.

3 Rep. 17, fo. 461; Rep. 24, fos. 430 and 453 for examples. But this is not to imply that constables were normally corrupt or ineffective. Considering the difficulties involved in enforcing police powers through untrained citizens, constables are more to be commended than condemned as a group. In an otherwise useful article on how police powers operated in a particular crisis one author goes too far in saying, of the offices of constable and watchman, that 'neither attracted the best type of men'. (B.L. Beer, 'London and the Rebellions of 1548-49', *Journal of British Studies* 12 (1972), 23). Watchmen were appointed to the watch from precinct lists, thus were no better and no worse than other citizens, who were watchmen by rotation. Recalling that constables usually held places on their parish vestry, and later often became rulers, it is more accurate to say that they were chosen from 'the better sort', to use the contemporary phrase. For more on the place of constables in the hierarchy of local offices see chapter 4.

through charters of incorporation, during the sixteenth century many of them continued to bring disputes before the mayor and aldermen for arbitration, disputes between different companies and between individuals of the same company. Perhaps the best known of these was the periodic struggle, lasting off and on for most of the sixteenth century, between the Clothworkers and Merchant Taylors for jurisdiction over men in the clothworking industry.[1] So great did this arbitrating authority become that one mayor during the reign of James I claimed the mastership of all companies; furthermore, from the early seventeenth century companies needed the City's permission to seek new charters or the status of incorporation.[2]

Most of the explicit interference by the court in company affairs had to do with some aspect of economic regulation. In matters of price control the City had traditionally exercised authority over the food and drink trades particularly. During the sixteenth century butchers, bakers, poultry-sellers, soap and candle makers, woodmongers, and brewers especially were admonished, chastised, and regulated with unremitting vigour. Quality of beer and method of distribution were constant problems. Brewers were limited to the making of two kinds of beer — 'single beare' and 'doble beare' — but enterprising brewers had concocted a rather more potent mixture known as 'doble doble' which they had the additional shrewdness to sell only in barrels rather than in smaller vessels. So serious was this departure from accepted practice that a special act of Common Council was created to destroy it.[3] Enforcing poultry prices was just as difficult. As with other kinds of price violations, the first hint of trouble was the issue of a mayoral precept or a proclamation. In December 1559 the mayor issued a proclamation showing the specific prices to be allowed on particular fowl, quite a number being common songbirds. The proclamation warned that violators could face loss of civic liberties. This warning was insufficient to effect reform, however, and four months later another proclamation again set down the accepted prices, then established a series of punishments for violators. Nothing was said about loss of civic liberties; instead specific fines were set and provisions made for the public humiliation of violators. Finally, in July 1560 the City went even further; it encouraged price competition

1   George Unwin, *Industrial Organization in the Sixteenth and Seventeenth Centuries,* 2nd ed. (Oxford, 1957), pp. 114-15.

2   On these last two points see Unwin, *Gilds and Companies,* pp. 232 and 236 respectively. Unwin discusses the general grounds of the City's interference on pp. 231-7.

3   Jour. 17, fos. 261-61[b].

by an act of Common Council which permitted non-freemen to sell their poultry goods at market places every day but Sunday.[1]

A more direct supervision was maintained in approving the articles of government of many crafts, especially the unincorporated ones. Approval was by no means a formality, for the Court of Aldermen might throw out particular articles altogether, as in the case of the Brownbakers in 1560.[2]   In 1571 the court rejected the petition of the white and brown bakers to form one corporation.[3]   Of equal importance is the power the court exercised over individual members of the companies. In order to force the Leathersellers Company to pay its share of a loan, demanded by the City to buy wheat, the aldermen threatened Thomas Kyghtley, a common councilman and master of the company in that year, with imprisonment.[4]   In another instance George Cely, dyer, was jailed for three days for rudeness to his warden, for rebuking the searchers of his company, and for violating certain regulations on the colours of dyes.[5]

But most of the councilmen's and aldermen's involvement in local affairs depended upon their personal presence as powerful individuals. In their companies they normally appeared on the courts of assistants; in the ward their presence was less felt, except for formal appearances at the court of wardmote, but their authority was undeniable because through the vestries they watched over parish officials who performed ward business. Councilmen were especially active in the parish. They could summon meetings and preside over them; when nonparochial business was discussed they probably presided even if the minister were present. Councilmen determined the distribution of taxes throughout a ward.[6]   They imposed fines on those failing to appear before the ward inquest.[7]   They handled disputes between men unwilling to serve local offices, or cases concerning discipline of local officers.[8]   In any difficult business it was normal for the councilmen to resolve matters, even if they concerned a dispute over rental of parish property.[9] Perhaps the most forceful reminder of the councilmen's authority in the parish was the fact that they sat in the front pews of the church.[10]

1   Jour. 17, fos. 182b-83, 230b-31b, and 258-58b.
2   Rep. 14, fos. 327b-29.
3   Rep. 17, fos. 183b-90b.
4   Rep. 14, fo. 369.
5   Rep. 18, fo. 435b.
6   St. Dunstan's VM, fos. 21, 45b, and 75.
7   Rep. 22, fo. 345*.
8   Cornhill WIM, fos. 37, 81 and 108.
9   VM of St. Michael Cornhill, fo. 15.
10   Ibid. fo. 102b.

Though personally most active in his livery company, the alderman's authority was the cornerstone of local government in London. His very appearance — clad in his fur-trimmed robe (dark velvet or scarlet depending on the occasion), wearing the gold chain or velvet tippet, and accompanied by one or two servants — was a reminder, if any needed reminding, that this was a man of quality and power. By the late sixteenth century he was not in as much evidence in local administration as his several subordinates. He might still preside at the annual meeting of the court of wardmote which held elections, and whenever he attended vestry meetings he presided there too. But the aldermen attended vestry meetings usually only to emphasize and elaborate upon some order made by the Court of Aldermen, or when important rentals of parish property were under discussion, or when serious dissension existed among the other vestry leaders. Though responsible for all police powers, the daily keeping of order fell largely upon the constables. It was certainly as a magistrate then that he made his greatest impact. Within his own ward he had the same power as any two justices of the peace meeting in petty sessions.[1] Even before the statute of 1601 which gave him this authority, the powers of the alderman in his ward, especially because of his authority over civic defence, were certainly as great as any county justice's.[2] Those who ran foul of his jurisdiction could have a distraint levied upon their goods, just as a man who failed to show him proper respect might earn himself a few days' rest in Newgate Gaol.

In addition to his numerous committee assignments from Common Council or the Court of Aldermen, pertaining to his own and other wards, each alderman carried out a number of duties as the result of instructions in mayoral precepts. A typical precept directed each alderman to call together his deputy and constables and see to it that no 'stranger or alien born hereafter repairing to the City . . . be by any ways or means permitted or suffered to inhabit . . . within your said ward longer than one day and one night, not forbidding any such stranger as shall come hither for religion'.[3] Sometimes assemblies of virtually the whole ward were called to hear a lecture by the alderman, especially when the court had cause to complain of violations of the queen's peace. Through the alderman and his subordinates lay the

---

1   This was by statute of 43 Elizabeth, cap. 2, sec. 8 (1601). This considerable jurisdiction was given to all aldermen, despite the fact that then only the mayor and the senior aldermen were officially justices. Gradually, by charters of 1638, 1692 and 1741, all the aldermen were made justices *ex officio*.

2   Comparing a modern account of the sixteenth-century justices (Cheyney, *History of England* ii. 314-42) with the picture sketched here of the London aldermen shows the aldermen's jurisdiction and activity were even more extensive.

3   Jour. 19, fo. 132[b].

enforcement of every statute, proclamation, act of Common Council, mayoral precept, or order of the court. Thus, in early 1580, to give thanks for deliverance from an earthquake the mayor ordered that every householder should attend a special thanksgiving service at his local parish church at a specific time.[1] Or, again with his constables, the alderman was ordered to see that no common carrier delivered or picked up goods from inns on the sabbath.[2] Sometimes enforcement required special machinery. To execute properly the often-repeated sumptuary statutes, it was finally necessary to appoint four special assistants in the ward to bring offenders before the alderman; the alderman appointed his own assistants.[3]

In much of this work the alderman could safely delegate authority to his deputy or to the councilmen, who would oversee the constable, who in turn executed most general orders. The amount of actual participation by any alderman depended a great deal on the relationship he had with his deputy, the nature of his own personal and business affairs, on the size and unruliness of the ward itself, and finally on the nature of the order. Regarding his traditional powers of guarding the gates and walking the watch, he rarely did this in person, though he or the deputy often went out to set the watch or to participate in the earliest stages of special watches, like that on Midsummer Day. In special circumstances the alderman himself could still be ordered to keep the watch, or have the deputy do so.[4] By the same token the alderman was occasionally required to make a weekly patrol of his ward in order to identify and deal with anything out of the ordinary.[5]

For many of the things the alderman had to do, however, it was not possible to employ his deputy, or any other subordinate. He could not delegate the task of making a secret inspection in the ward to determine how many men were fit to bear arms, or the job of putting all resident aliens in the ward who were not church members under bond requiring them to leave the ward by a certain date.[6] Although the deputy might help in preparing the periodic lists of aliens, and though the whole ward could be exhorted to help root out recusants, still the alderman had to be well-informed in each of these matters, for invariably he was responsible for bringing back a report to the court. When his increasing statutory responsibilities as a justice of the peace are also

1   Jour. 21, fo. 5.
2   Jour. 19, fo. 138b.
3   Jour. 18, fo. 40.
4   Jour. 17, fo. 122b. The occasion was the watch of 1 May, the first important watch of the spring.
5   Rep. 14, fo. 402b.
6   Ibid. fo. 340, and Rep. 18, fo. 115.

considered, and when it is remembered that he did even more as a result of special committee assignments from the court in his own ward and others, it can be appreciated that the alderman was busy indeed. The greatest burdens on his time resulted from his own initiatives in keeping in touch with his subordinates, for he did not limit himself to serving on committees or executing precepts. Most of the decisions he made, most of the things he did, are not recorded because they were routine. No matter how mighty he was as an international merchant, therefore, when in London (and the court took care that he was there most of the time) the alderman could not escape the leadership of his ward.

4

RISING IN CITY POLITICS

The 273 rulers made policy for all 26 wards and supervised its enforcement in and through the 115 parishes and approximately 160 guilds of Elizabethan London. Assisting them were perhaps 500 men who served as an appointed staff of administrators. They will be introduced in chapter 5. Also subordinate to the rulers was an even larger and more amorphous group, numbering between 800 and 1,000, who deserve some recognition in the hierarchy of political London. A large number of them were at one time common councilmen, some of them held a City office, or worked with an ad hoc committee, but for the most part their official work was confined to the wards. They served as vestrymen and ancients in the parishes, officers of the ward-mote inquest, and as assistants, wardens, and lesser officers in the guilds. For convenience I shall refer to this group as the wardmen.

This discussion of rising in City politics begins with the wardmen, since an overwhelming majority of the Common Council at this time were wardmen. During the whole of Elizabeth's reign only a few councilmen qualified as leaders. Only a little over half the council's members during the first half of the reign ever undertook assignments outside their own wards. In later years more held civic office or served on civic committees, approaching 90 per cent of the council's membership at times, but most of them held only a single office, usually hospital governor, and sat on only a few ad hoc committees, if any; thus most were still wardmen. Despite the larger volume of business in later years, and the expansion of committees to dispatch it, membership of even the ad hoc committees belonged to a small minority, the rulers, who continued to dominate committee work year after year. For example, 60 per cent of the committeemen assigned by Common Council in 1559 reappeared in 1560; by 1599-1600 there was a 77 per cent continuity. Forty-one men engaged in committee work in 1559, yet twelve of them gained two-thirds of the assignments. In 1600 eleven out of sixty-six committeemen carried 40 per cent of the load. Perhaps half of all Elizabethan councilmen had some committee experience, but even during the busiest periods of the reign only about seventy men, or a third of the council, were active enough on committees to be identified as leaders.

Ward and parish records best illustrate the hierarchy in which wardmen operated and the extent to which they rose in it. The twenty-five men who constituted the select vestry of St. Dunstan in the West from May 1601 had considerable previous ward and parish experience, as shown in Table 1.[1] Their names are listed in order of seniority after allowing for the parson and churchwardens, who were always written before the others. A great majority began as scavengers and most then held a position on the inquest before becoming constable. Thereafter a second and third (rarely a fourth) inquest position followed before churchwarden. In the meantime membership on the vestry commenced sometime after constable and before churchwarden, but the timing of vestry membership is difficult to be precise about; it did vary. Some men were not permanent vestry members until after their churchwardenships, though that was unusual. Some joined a vestry before serving as constable, but that too was exceptional. Generally, if a constable had previously served as an officer on the inquest (foreman, foreman's assistant, treasurer, comptroller, or secretary) he then qualified for the vestry; if not his position there was less certain. Of the twenty-four secular members in St. Dunstan's, sixteen had become vestrymen before 1601, having served as churchwarden or an officer of the inquest. Perhaps another four also reached the vestry before 1601 if serving as scavenger, constable, and once as inquestmen had been sufficient qualification for the vestry before it was limited. The average time to go from scavenger to churchwarden was between fourteen and fifteen years.

The table offers a means of comparing the parish with others. In St. Michael Cornhill, similarly blessed with rich source materials, the picture is about the same. In St. Michael's, however, more frequent service on the inquest was expected, four and five positions there not being unusual, but men less often served as both scavenger and constable. In St. Michael's two positions on the inquest generally preceded constable. As in St. Dunstan's one usually became an officer of the inquest with the third position. The interval between first office and churchwarden in both parishes was nearly the same. Spotty survival of ward records makes it impossible to construct similarly detailed comparisons with other parishes. What lacks for the most part is information on wardmote inquest offices. However, fuller parish records frequently show the date at which men assumed higher positions on the inquest, as well as the offices of scavenger and constable; therefore, after becoming familiar with numerous careers in some fifty parishes I am satisfied that Table 1 portrays accurately the possibilities available to, and the moves made by, most wardmen. What varied most from parish to parish were the particular offices skipped

---

[1] The sources for this table are vestry minute books and ward inquest minute books. Offices and dates are found in the folios concerned with the annual elections in December.

TABLE 1: THE HIERARCHY OF PARISH OFFICES (ST. DUNSTAN IN THE WEST)

	1564	1570	1580	1583	1584	1590	1600	1603
Dr. Thomas White, vicar								
Henry Beverley						s s 1 1	2 2 2 2 3 3w w w4 4	w w
John Richmond (Richeman)						s s 1 1	c c c c2 3 3	w w
Henry Webbe	s s	1 1 c c c 2 2	c c c 4 4C C C	w w c	c c 4C C C	C C C C C C	C C C C C C	Cw Cw
William Crowche		s s 1 1	c c c	2 2c c	3 3	4C 4C C C	2C 2C C C	Cw Cw
Thomas Johnson		3 3 1 1	c c c 2 2	c c	3 3	c c c 1 1	C C C C	Cw Cw
Robert Jenkinson			c c c 1	c c 1 1		1 1	C FC C C	C Cw
Richard Grene		2 2	c c c 2 2		3 3	w w w4 4	2C 2C 3 3	23
Richard Hawes		s s s s 1 1	c c c	c1 1	2 2	w w w	w w3 3 3	c2 2
George Clark		s s	c c c 2 2	2 2		w w w		c c
John Howle			s s		1 1c c c	w w w3 3 3	w4 4	c2 2
Thomas Harris				c c	c1 1	2 2	w w w	1 1
Robert Johnson				s s	s s 1 1	c c c	3 3w w4 4	
Edward Tirrell					s s 1 1	2 2 2 2 3 3	w w4 4	
Mathew Payne						s s 1 1	3 3 3 3 w w	w
John Cockyn						c c	c2 c2 2 2	c c
John Huison						s s 1 1	2 2 3 3	
Robert Westwood						s s 1 1	F 2 23 3	
William Pascall						s s 1 1	c c c2 2	
Gilbert Fludd						s s 1 1	c c c	
John Waters (Walters)						s s	1 1 c c2 2	
Simon Penyale					?	? ?	1 1 ? ?	?
Andrew Field					?	? ?	1 1 ? ?	?
William Newton (Newby)						s s	1 1	
James Tackley						s s	1 1	c c c

s=scavenger; 1=first inquest position; 2=second inquest position; 3=third inquest position; 4=fourth inquest position; w=churchwarden; c=constable; C=common councilman; F=fined for the office of contable.

Continuations beyond 1603.
William Crowche C: 1594-1606;
Thomas Johnson C: 1598-1626; w: 1602-1605
Robert Jenkinson C: 1598-1615 w: 1603-1606

and the number of times men repeated in certain offices; generally the sequence of offices was similar everywhere. While working their way from the lowest inquest positions up to the vestry, wardmen would simultaneously have been moving from the rank of yeoman to liveryman in the guilds, and some to their first wardenship. Thereafter some served as assistants in the guilds, though less often as the higher wardens and rarely as masters. Later still wardmen became church-wardens and leading inquest officers in their parishes, and some common councilmen.

Before leaving the wardmen we must observe for the first time a phenomenon operating at all levels in the City and one that will be encountered again — office skipping. Typically the men gaining the highest offices in the ward, the parish, and the livery company did not hold as many of the lower offices as men who never reached the top positions. The purpose of skipping lower offices was to accelerate rising to the higher ones, where those so advanced were expected to devote more of their time. Rapid rising happened often enough among the eventually prominent men at all levels of City institutions that it seems to be the result of favouritism. In Cornhill Ward, for example, it was normal for future parish leaders to serve two or three times on the lower rungs of the inquest, in addition to serving as constable. But George Kevall skipped all the lower places on the inquest, though he served five times as an inquest officer. Another councilman, Thomas Piggott, began as a butler of the inquest, but thereafter he served three times as assistant to the foreman before becoming a councilman. A more striking example is John Slanye, probably the son of Alderman Stephen Slanye, who began in 1598 in a low position on the inquest, then was assistant to the foreman in 1601-2, constable in 1603-4 and a councilman in 1604. In his case the family relationship doubtless helped his rapid rise. The same can be said of Francis Gunter, son of Philip Gunter who was briefly an alderman then deputy alderman of Cornhill for over twenty years. The father was extremely active in parish and ward affairs, and the vestry of St. Michael's had no objection to bringing his son along in a hurry. His first office was speaker of the inquest in 1586-7; he was a member of the vestry from at least 1587. By contrast with these rapid-risers the typical pattern in Cornhill for men who became the local leaders, but never councilmen, was two places on the lower half of the inquest and up to five on the upper half, also including constable and sometimes scavenger. Two of the four councilmen in Table 1 from St. Dunstan's also skipped certain offices.

The same pattern is found in other parishes. In St. Benet Paul's Wharf Richard Ashbye was an auditor of the churchwardens' accounts before he became a councilman, was three times on the inquest but never constable or scavenger. John Pookye had one inquest office between 1578, when the parish records begin, and 1601, when he became a councilman. In St. Mary Aldermanbury John Comes was successively sideman in 1590, scavenger for 1591-2, then skipped all inquest positions and joined the Common Council in 1598. In the same parish Nicholas Warner had one place on the inquest in 1576 before joining the council in 1585, but no other parish or ward offices. Similarly, John Westwray in St. Olave Jewry had only two inquest positions (in 1591-3) before becoming a councilman in 1601.

Skipping offices was one sign of favouritism; it also happened that men marked out to be councilmen joined with the current councilmen to execute the more important parish business.

> It is agreed that Mr. Deputy Kevall, Mr. Harby [both councilmen] and Mr. Cowper [John Cowper, who became a councilman the next year] with the churchwardens shall have authority to confer and determine with the like number of persons in St. Peter's parish concerning the controversy risen about some parcels of the late 'Sonne' Tavern, now called the Mermaid.[1]

This strongly foreshadowed advancement to the council and was normal enough. Less often even more straightforward signs of favour appear.

> It was agreed that Mr. Thomas Wight should be discharged of all offices in this parish saving the place of common councilman, churchwarden and chancellor of the inquest, paying such fine as Mr. Webb and the now common councilmen of the parish should assess.[2]

On the same day he was admitted to the vestry; this was in December 1603. In 1606 a councilman's position became vacant, and Thomas Wight filled it.

In all these cases speed of rising depended very little on the size of the parish or ward in question. It might be thought that men in smaller parishes would rise faster because there were fewer men to hold the local offices, but the number of men on the vestry in large and small parishes was nearly the same. Opportunities being about the same everywhere, favouritism determined political advancement. In thinking about the elements in a man's life that made him a potentially effective ruler, the aldermen and greatest councilmen considered wealth, family, status, connections of various sorts, but also political service at all levels and of all kinds. Each of these often overlapping qualifications

---

1 VM of St. Michael Cornhill, fo. 80.
2 VM of St. Dunstan in the West, fo. 47. Wight had just moved to the parish; since at least 1599 he had been a councilman in another parish.

helped, and which was the most decisive varied from individual to individual. Because of important personal attributes or connections, some individuals rose despite only moderate political service. Individual ability mattered too. In organizing the records and funds of parishes, livery companies, and hospitals, or supervising supplies at the Bridge-house, councilmen needed basic administrative talents and some familiarity with accounting procedures. Common sense and alertness were probably more essential in view of the numerous investigations and inspections undertaken. By serving on the council for a few years councilmen developed wide experience. They kept in touch with local tradesmen and foreign merchants, occasionally statesmen and monarchs. They dealt with the royal government and other communities of the realm. In other words, to a certain extent previous political experience of the right kind indicated ability. The same can be said of seniority, with the same qualification. At each level of the City the most senior men usually possessed the greatest office and committee experience, but due to rapid rising of a few, the most senior and most experienced at all levels were the least likely to advance to the next level.

Before illustrating this further, we should ask by whom was favouritism controlled? An entry in the aldermen's minutes for 1527 answers candidly that every 'alderman in his ward, with his deputy . . . to appoint and name two of the most wisest, circumspect persons within his ward to be of the Common Council, and they four to name and appoint the residue of the most politic and wisest persons'.[1] From the first elections to the council in the early fourteenth century aldermen probably made their preferences known; by 1389 a specific order endorsing aldermanic interference had been codified.[2] Though the courts of wardmote traditionally nominated aldermen, occasionally the Court of Aldermen intervened pre-emptorily to the contrary. 'At this Court it is agreed that these persons by the assent of M. Mylborne, alderman of the ward of Cornhill, shall be of the Common Council for the year following, that is for to say [lists six names]'.[3] Usually the aldermen did not find it necessary to interfere so blatantly. Because of their close ties with councilmen, and because the vestries (under the leadership of councilmen) nominated all important ward and parish officers, the aldermen could rely on more subtle methods of promoting desirable candidates.

Men active enough to become leaders continued to move up in the local hierarchy, where they held a large share of the higher positions,

1 Letter-Book 0, fos. 52-3.
2 *Cal. Let.-Book H,* p. 347.
3 Rep. 9, fo. 42 (1534).

while simultaneously beginning on the lower rungs of another ladder, that of civic office. These offices will be discussed in ascending order, reflecting their importance in the City, and usually the order in which they were held. A few caveats should accompany this ordering of offices. Due to office skipping no one held all the offices to be mentioned, and different men skipped different ones. Duration of tenure in some positions varied. Even the order of assuming offices varied, but most men succeeded in the order indicated. Governor of one of the four hospitals was the first important civic office. In 1559 there were 48 governors, 12 aldermen and 36 common councilmen; in 1599 there were 176 governors, 24 aldermen and 152 councilmen. Other offices or duties might be assumed around the same time as hospital governor, though none had the same prestige. The Court of Aldermen appointed some men as tax collectors, or surveyors of various properties and accounts concerning miscellaneous transactions. Congregation, then later the aldermen themselves, annually elected four aleconners to inspect the quality of beer and ale. A substantial number gained re-election at least once, but serving more than four years was unusual. Most aleconners served only once for a year. Congregation also nominated councilmen for bridgemaster or chamberlain around the time of gaining their first office. Many were renominated frequently, and those most often renominated succeeded least well in gaining the City's top positions. For example, none became active aldermen, for Philip Gunter (alderman for eighteen days) was the only person ever nominated for either office who later gained election as an alderman. Twenty-four leaders were put forward for one of these positions, and seven notables, but significantly only one of them ever received a nomination to the Court of Aldermen.

The next two significant offices came closely together, the order of assuming them following no apparent rule. One was hospital auditor. The first auditors began their service in the 1570s, when there were twelve, three for each hospital. St. Bartholomew's was the first to have four auditors in the late 1580s; the others each gained a fourth auditor during the 1590s. The other office was auditor of the Bridgehouse and Chamber. There were five of these altogether, four councilmen and one senior alderman. Councilmen were elected annually, though they usually sat for two years unless excused upon becoming aldermen. Their terms were staggered so that two new men were elected each year; rarely a councilman might be elected for a second term of two years. Ordinarily the alderman's position changed every year, going in rotation according to seniority on the Court of Aldermen. The alderman usually began his year a full eleven months after the completion of his mayoral year. He might begin earlier only if the incumbent chief auditor died in office, in which case he completed that term then served his own. Unless another senior alderman was eleven months beyond his own mayoral year, the same man would serve another year.

Each hospital also had a treasurer, who was always a common councilman. Should a councilman gain election to the Court of Alderman while treasurer, he resigned the latter in favour of another councilman. Among the four auditors-general of the hospitals, after the mid-1560s two were aldermen and two councilmen. Their broad supervisory authority extended to all hospitals; there was no attempt to associate each auditor-general with one of the hospitals. Anytime after the first of the various offices mentioned, a councilman might be appointed to one of the City's standing committees.[1]

Two sheriffs were chosen annually by Congregation for one year only. Though one was elected for the county of Middlesex, the other for the City of London, their jurisdictions had overlapped for centuries. By the time they began serving their shrieval years, most Elizabethans were already aldermen, and their succession to the shrievalty followed by order of seniority on the Court of Aldermen. Only if all the aldermen had already served was a councilman elected and advanced to the court at the next opportunity. Not everyone elected sheriff was intended to serve in the office. The aldermen used shrieval elections to raise revenue from those who would pay fines to avoid serving, or purchase discharges after brief service. In 1591 thirteen successive electees declined to serve and paid fines. Only five belonged to the six livery companies that controlled 70 per cent of the higher civic positions, only one was later re-elected as sheriff. In short, these were not the sort of men the rulers wanted to serve as sheriff anyway. The years 1580, 1587, and 1593 proved nearly as fruitful in producing lucrative fines from reluctant candidates. In fact the same practice is found in some aldermanic elections. Twenty-four Elizabethan aldermen were discharged from the court shortly after their election. Only three did not pay to be discharged, most went unnoticed on committee assignments, only one held an important civic office while on the council, and less than half represented the six dominant livery companies — again, obviously not ruling calibre. Occasionally the financial motive manifested itself more flagrantly, in that some men were pressured to pay fines before ever being elected by, or even nominated to, the court. Robert Christopher, a secondary (assistant to the sheriff), would never have advanced to the Court of Aldermen with his previous experience, yet he paid £100 to avoid election as alderman

1 See above pp. 17, 21-2.

and sheriff.[1] William Blackwell, the town clerk since 1540, was discharged from ever serving as sheriff in 1561, though no town clerk had ever been sheriff.[2] Perhaps in this case, and one or two others, the discharge was honorary, for no sum of money is mentioned. Usually £400 or £500 was taken.

Mention of Robert Christopher, the secondary, affords an opportunity to notice some of the incidental places the rulers accumulated. While councilmen, some men might hold one or two of the offices usually reserved for the administrative assistants. For instance, Richard Young, grocer and notable common councilman, held the office of common packer for several years, yet he exercised no greater authority on the council as a result of his packership.[3] The office was a lucrative incidental to his career, not a stepping-stone to higher places. Such a combination of elective and appointive offices was not customary for the rulers. The rulers and the departmental chiefs used some appointive offices as rewards for political services, or as a favour to the friend or creature of some great man, or as an outright gift to a friend or relative. At the same time, to become a common councilman or alderman one did not begin as City attorney, or in any other legal office either, nor apparently was the study or practice of the law habitual among the rulers. Among all the rulers only two, both leaders, ever served as City solicitors, only one as a secondary. This absence of practicing lawyers from the large representative body of the City, doubtless deliberate, gives one indication of the differences between the Common Council and the Parliament, which had a sizable selection of lawyers.[4]

Two other important positions deserve mention before we go on to examine the offices open uniquely to aldermen. Chapter 2 suggested how important the position of MP was to the civic rulers. Two of the four City representatives were always councilmen, the third a senior alderman, the fourth the recorder. The rulers also filled officer positions in the London Trained Bands. The number of officers varied according to the number of troops raised. In 1588 there were forty captains and four colonels; four more colonels and three other captains served for the 'outliberties'. In 1599 there were fifteen captains for the City.[5]

---

1 Jour. 20, pt. 2, fo. 393b.

2 Jour. 17, fos. 300b-301.

3 Rep. 16, fos. 5b, 9-10, 12. For the value of the office of common packer see *CSPD* (1595-7), vol. 254/3.

4 J. E. Neale, *The Elizabethan House of Commons* (1949), pp. 302 ff. Neale says that of 460 men in the Commons in 1584, 53 were practising lawyers.

5 Lt. Colonel J. H. Leslie, 'A Survey, or Muster, of the Armed and Trayned

The normal expectancy of men raised to the Court of Aldermen was a year as mayor. Time of accession was predictable, since it followed the order of seniority on the court. Having served as mayor, senior aldermen filled the several offices open to them by rotation. Except for the chief auditor of the Bridgehouse and Chamber — normally held for one year — all were held indefinitely, often for life; therefore, it was possible to go several years without a new position. The normal order was as follows: chief auditor of Bridgehouse and Chamber, hospital president, surveyor-general of (all four) hospitals, and comptroller-general of hospitals. When a comptroller-general of hospitals died, his place was taken by the surveyor-general. The surveyor-general's position was filled by that senior alderman with the most executive experience in other hospitals. Usually this succession followed the order of seniority among aldermen, but not always, for in 1572 John Whyte became surveyor-general although Thomas Lodge, previously president for one year of St. Thomas's, was his senior. Similarly, Rowland Heyward was preferred to his senior, William Allen, for the same position in 1580 because his hospital experience was greater than Allen's. A very exceptional case is Christopher Draper, who in 1573 was made surveyor-general in spite of having had no previous executive experience in hospitals and despite there being other men his senior with the requisite experience.

Succession to presidencies of the four hospitals did not at first follow any discernible order. The court apparently felt that all senior aldermen, and some juniors, should have the leadership. There was frequent shuffling of men from one position to another in order to give as many aldermen as possible some responsibility. After about the middle of the 1570s, however, procedures began to crystallize. Thereafter succession to a presidency was usually to the most senior of those beyond the chair who had not yet held such a position. Each succeeding presidency then went to a man the junior of his predecessor.

How long did it require to become a member of the élite? A term of six years on the Common Council before the first nomination to the court was average. The duration between nomination and election could be days or years, but the average was between one and two years.[1] The number of years as alderman before the mayoralty

Companies in London, 1588 and 1599', *Journal of the Society of Army Historical Research* 4 (April-June 1925), 62-71.

1 This must be considered a minimum figure because it has not always been possible to discover when a man first became a councilman, or how long he served before holding an office or working on committees, at which points he would be noticed in the records. Generally, this interval was not great, however, and the minimum figure shown can be considered close to the whole number.

depended on the number of junior aldermen but was rarely fewer than eight or more than twelve. As a result, reaching the highest level of authority in City politics required about eighteen years as councilman and alderman. A number of considerations influenced whether councilmen and junior aldermen would move into the next rank, and, if so, how long it would take. Delays in rising to the Court of Aldermen were especially common. At the appropriate court of wardmote usually two commoners were put in nomination for each vacancy on the court, along with two aldermen, the senior of whom had first choice in translating from his present ward.[1] Since aldermen, unlike councilmen, did not have to reside in the ward they represented, translation was a device utilized to place every alderman, in so far as possible, where he wanted to serve. Preferences were largely personal matters, depending on residence or property held, but also on the ward in question; the richer ones offered greater perquisites, the larger ones more administrative headaches.[2] If either alderman chose to translate, his wish was granted and nominations were then made in his former ward. Since 1397 the aldermen themselves had been choosing between the nominees, and this could cause further delays.[3] The usual practice was to reject all the nominees if even one was deemed unsuitable, necessitating a new slate.[4] After 1397, moreover, should a ward make three successive nominations which were unacceptable, the court itself nominated and elected.[5] Reasons for rejecting nominees were, officially, lack of sufficient estate, and we cannot doubt that this was sometimes true. More than a few examples exist, however, where all the men put forward possessed adequate wealth, and the only apparent reason for delaying election was the lack of a candidate with sufficient political experience.

1 Between 1397-1401 there were only two nominees; normally four between 1401-1710, though occasionally three or even four commoners were put forward along with the two aldermen; after 1711 only two again, one alderman and one commoner (*Cal. Let.-Book I*, p. 18 and Jour. 55, fo. 261ᵇ).

2 Translation was known by the early fourteenth century and became an ordinary custom from the middle of the fifteenth century to the later seventeenth century, at which time it came to an end. For details, consult A.B. Beaven, *The Aldermen of the City of London*, 2 vols. (1908-13), i.240-1 and ii.xx-xxii. For the special case of Bridge Without see also J.J. Baddeley, *The Aldermen of Cripplegate Ward from 1276-1900* (1900), pp. 198-201, and David J. Johnson, *Southwark and the City* (1969).

3 *Cal. Let.-Book H*, p.436 for the 1397 act.

4 Before Elizabeth's reign the court took this liberty on 83 different occasions, but only 11 times during her reign (Beaven, *Aldermen of London*, i.244-9).

5 This happened twelve times within a forty year period at the end of the fifteenth century, but the court tightened its control thereafter and only had to exercise this power four times between 1503-36, and four more thereafter: in 1633, 1669, 1833, and 1877 (ibid.).

In analysing the reasons for electing the nominees they did, the aldermen obviously took a sharp look at previous experience.[1] More often delays ensued because the court could only choose one nominee at a time, and, to protect against death of incumbents, as well as unwillingness or inability to serve, the aldermen had to keep in mind a larger number of names than there were openings. The aldermen kept a fairly small number of names in mind, for once nominated a candidate was renominated periodically until elected. During the Elizabethan period nominations took place on 204 occasions, meaning at least 816 individual nominations, since at least four were nominated at a time. Yet there are only 179 names in the records over forty-four years, meaning that on the average a candidate rose only after the fourth or fifth nomination.

Occasionally personal hostilities delayed or prevented the election of individuals. But we should not exaggerate this possibility. It might appear the motivation for delaying Thomas Cambell (19 nominations before election) or Richard Saltonstall (6), or for blocking Geoffrey Walkedon (8) or Anthony Cage (5), neither of whom were elected. Explanations already recited, however, account for most of these cases. More to the point, none of the four belonged to any of the six dominant livery companies. Men representing the other guilds were less frequently nominated; also most aldermen with more than average previous nominations belonged to other guilds. In sharp contrast to these delays, any recently chosen sheriff was nominated at the next possible vacancy on the court and promptly elected. In all cases involving a sheriff or sheriff-elect the court used the same haste, and it is usual to to find few previous nominations for these men. [2]

For junior aldermen poised to become one of the élite further reasons for delay in rising existed. The burdens of the mayoral year discouraged more than one. William Masham was discharged from the court on 8 January 1594 for £600, because of being 'grievously tormented with gout, colic, and stone, unwieldiness and disability of body'.[3] Despite his plea of bad health, he did live another six years, and it also happened that in 1594 Masham was next in line to assume the mayoralty in October of that year. Part of his desire for the discharge can be attributed to his unwillingness to take the next step in City

1 Men like Richard Pype, with at least eight years experience on the Common Council by 1567 plus active committee work, were passed over for this reason. Normally the court preferred its candidates to have office experience too.

2 Both sheriffs were officially chosen by Congregation, but one was nominated previously by the mayor (tantamount to election) through his prerogative, traditional since the mid-fourteenth century at least (Cal. Let.-Book F, pp. 169, 306).

3 Rep. 23. fo. 146.

politics. The same is the case with Thomas Starkye, discharged on 20 September 1588. Since the end of October 1587, when George Barne completed his mayoral year, Starkye had been the next in line and should have taken the chair immediately after Barne. He did not, however, and George Bonde, the next in line after Starkye, took the chair instead. The pressure on Starkye to take his turn was not relieved, and his discharge came just nine days before the time for choosing George Bonde's successor. The standard excuse of 'age and infirmity' is less credible in view of the unwritten law against staying on the court without serving the mayoralty. [1]

In that connection two practices that have traditionally been interpreted to show the unwillingness of aldermen and councilmen to hold civic office need to be re-examined. Paying a fine instead of serving a particular office was acceptable in City politics, even among the rulers; it was not necessarily a sign of disengagement or reluctance. If one tallies the offices they actually held versus those fined for, it is found that they served much more often than they fined. It was not thought necessary for a man to serve in every position for which his ability or his seniority qualified him, and in order to accelerate rising it was necessary to fine for certain offices. Another supposed sign of reluctance was the fact that a number of aldermen had to be imprisoned in order to persuade them to serve. That interpretation is untenable because there was no way to compel a man to serve the aldermanry. Some were briefly imprisoned, it is true, but as a practical precaution, until they decided whether or not to assume the position. It was vital to have their decision promptly, one way or the other, if there was to be legal and political continuity in the twenty-six wards of London. In view of the costs, commitments, and other personal matters which the aldermanry entailed, it is not surprising that some men needed time to make their decision, or to complete their preparations for taking up the dignity. While they reposed in Newgate Gaol there was no dishonour to them, and the legal position of the City was protected.

This chapter on political rising concludes by illustrating the careers of the rulers. Table 2 shows the experience of each rank among the rulers with respect to the various offices mentioned. The table brings together most City offices of the rulers during Queen Elizabeth's reign. [2] Because I looked for the names of hospital governors in only a

---

[1] Rep. 21, fo. 590. Eighteen Elizabethan aldermen served several years but resigned in time to miss the mayoralty. It was possible to delay the mayoral year, and five others did this, but only William Hewet managed to postpone his obligation for as long as two years.

[2] In my research I tried to keep track of all the experience of all the rulers, regardless of date. I am satisfied of being aware of most of their positions, but

select number of years, some have certainly been missed.[1] The same will be true of hospital auditors and treasurers, and auditors-general of

TABLE 2 : POLITICAL EXPERIENCE OF THE RULERS

	Leaders (118)	Notable councilmen (41)	Notable aldermen (50)	Élite (64)
Common councilmen	118	41	45	51
Aleconner	9	6	–	–
Tax collector	12	6	3	4
Hospital governor	89	31	25	20
Surveyor of accounts	9	8	1	–
Auditor of Bridgehouse and Chamber	22	29	14	15
Hospital auditor	22	20	7	11
Bridgehouse Estates and City Lands Committees	16	12	13	43
Hospital treasurer	15	7	9	9
Captain of Trained Bands	2	1	1	3
Auditor-general of hospitals	4	4	6	11
MP (burgess)	2	9	–	2
Bridgemaster	2	1	–	–
Chamberlain	1	–	–	–
Alderman	7	2	50	64
Sheriff	–	1	42	51
Provost marshal	–	1	1	1
Mayor	–	–	–	47
Chief auditor of Bridgehouse and Chamber	–	–	–	40
Hospital president	–	–	1	45
Surveyor-general of hospitals	–	–	–	13
Comptroller-general of hospitals	–	–	–	6
MP (knight)	–	–	–	10
Total positions	330	179	218	446
Average per officer	2.8	4.4	4.4	7.0

some of what I learned was based on chance or random searches beyond Elizabeth's reign. In order to assure accurate comparisons between the ranks for this table it was necessary to restrict the dates of offices to 1558-1603, when all ranks received an equal amount of attention. It should be said that Table 2 is the result of more thorough investigations than those previously summarized in my article, 'Politics and Community in Elizabethan London', in *The Rich, the Well-Born, and the Powerful*, ed. Frederic C. Jaher (1973).

[1] See above, p. 13, note 3 on the select years.

hospitals, though additional efforts were made to search out more of them because of their obviously greater importance. Tax collectors and surveyors of accounts were also gathered only in the select years. All other offices are complete for the period 1558-1603, and the gaps due to selective searching do not result in a bias favouring any rank over another. General comparisons between ranks are therefore possible.[1]

The most apparent conclusion is that with higher rank came greater commitment to civic responsibilities, not less. Seniority increased the opportunities for positions, and with some exception the higher ranks also served longer: the aldermen averaged twenty years, the notable councilmen fourteen years, and a random sample of thirty-six out of 118 leaders fifteen years. It would also seem that on the average each ruler spent most of his effort at the highest rank he attained, illustrating again the results of rapid rising by favour. Thirteen of their twenty years were spent by the aldermen on the court; a large majority of all their City offices could only be held by aldermen. It is difficult to be precise about comparative periods of time councilmen spent as leaders or notables, but proportionally more notables were active in every office than leaders, and in general the proportions became greater with higher offices.

All ranks of the rulers participated actively as hospital governors, auditors, treasurers, and auditors-general, auditors of the Bridgehouse and Chamber, and members of the Bridgehouse Estates and City Lands Committees. A comparative proportional study

1 One or two other comments on the table are in order. Some of the special ad hoc committees created by the Court of Aldermen or Common Council endured longer than their creators had anticipated. This makes it difficult to decide which committees were genuinely ad hoc and which became standing or permanent in the minds of the rulers. Because of this difficulty, I have included only those two permanent committees of greatest importance to the City: the Bridgehouse Estates Committee and the City Lands Committee (shown in Table 2 as one committee because the membership was identical with respect to the rulers).

I have found no reference to provost marshals before the late 1580s, and evidence in City records suggests that this officer was appointed irregularly on an experimental basis in the late sixteenth and early seventeenth centuries, to assist the aldermen in supervising lesser officials charged with police powers. He seems distinct from the marshal and the provost, both of whom were known earlier, especially in connection with the civic militia. See Stow, *Survey*, ed. Kingsford, i.63 and Strype, *Survey of London and Westminster* (1720). ii.452-6.

It may seem odd that any councilman should be listed on the table as an alderman. The seven leaders and the two notables, however, were among those who resigned the office almost as soon as they were elected; their previous experience qualified them as leaders or notables. Two other notables were aldermen outside the period for this study: Lawrence Wythers (alderman, 1550-6) and Roger Jones (alderman, 1604-5), who actually served as councilmen during Elizabeth's reign, not aldermen. The single notable who became a sheriff was Geoffrey Walkedon, who seems to have served only a partial term.

of how many from each rank served in these offices shows that the notable councilmen were the most involved in the first four of those places.[1] The notable aldermen had the edge for hospital treasurers, and the élite for auditors-general. Measuring their activity in these six offices against their total office involvement shows the following concentrations: leaders 51 per cent, notable councilmen 58 per cent, notable aldermen 34 per cent, and élite 24 per cent. In other words, the rulers regarded six particular offices as important enough for all ranks to involve themselves there, sometimes perhaps as a requisite to further advancement, but the higher a ruler's rank the more likely he was to skip inferior places and concentrate on others. Positions like aleconner, bridgemaster, or chamberlain, even MP (the burgesses anyway) were left almost exclusively to those who would not become aldermen, as was the work of collectors, surveyors, and certain committee members. This does not mean that the lower ranks performed most of the humdrum detail — in fact, the next chapter will show the reverse — rather that each rank tackled details considered appropriate to its status.

We can now discuss the entire careers of a few rulers, from offices in the wards to those of the whole City. Table 3 brings together the ward, parish, guild, and higher civic experience of ten men who attained political prominence. The ten rulers were selected at random — four are élite, Barnes, Harbie and Towerson are notable councilmen, three are leaders. The table illustrates the kinds of positions held and shows various durations between positions. It is complete for civic positions up to aldermen, but not for local positions, where it is difficult to distinguish office-skipping from gaps in the records. The table cannot be used to make comparisons between the three ranks because the sample is far too small, and unfortunately the gaps in ward and parish records are so great that even a larger sample might not provide an accurate comparative basis.[2] We might compare the ten rulers as a group with the wardmen mentioned above in Table 1. The more rapid rising of some rulers seems evident, but on the average they required sixteen years to progress from the freedom to churchwarden, as compared with the fourteen to fifteen years it required the wardmen to go from scavenger to churchwarden — scavenger being somewhat later than

1 From the figures given the Bridgehouse Estates and City Lands Committees would seem to be an exception, but since councilmen only joined these committees during the 1590s there is a bias favouring the aldermen over all of Elizabeth's reign. During the period when councilmen and aldermen both belonged, councilmen outnumbered aldermen.

2 Further sources for this table were wardens' account books, minute books of courts of assistants, freedom registers, churchwardens' accounts, Repertories, and Journals.

TABLE 3: THE HIERARCHY IN LOCAL AND CITY OFFICES

	Freedom	Livery	Constable	Vestry	Church-warden	Fourth warden	Third warden	Common councilman	Auditor of Br.&Cham.	First warden	Sheriff	Alderman
R. Barnes (died 1598)	1543	1552			1553-5	1561-2	1570-1	1558	1567-9		E:1577	D:1585
H. Campion (died 1588)	1548	1555		before 1574	1585-7		1568-9	1571			Ex:1584	N:1571
T. Cambell (died 1614)	by 1563	by 1567	1584-6	by 1577	1579-81	1573-4	1577-8	1579	1584-5; 1588-90; 1596-8		1600-01	1599-1614
R. Chamberlain (died 1607)	?	by 1567	1578-80		1574-5	1573	1576-7				Ex:1597	1596
L. Duckett (died 1587)	1537	1549			1550-51	1558-9		1558	1559-61		1564-5	1564-87
B. Durham (died 1610?)	1561	1568		by 1574	1582-4	1580-1		1589	1584-6; 1600-02			
L. Holliday (died 1612)	1564	by 1579		1576	1582-4; 1593		1588-9	by 1592		1593-4	1595-6	1594-1612
J. Harbie (died 1609/10)	1564	1566		1567	1571-2; 1573-4	1574-5	1579-80	1578	1585-7	1587-8		
J. Hawes (died 1582)	1540?	by 1549		before 1563		1554-5		1560		1559-60	1565-6	1565-82
W. Towerson, Sr. ?	1559	1562		by 1567	1568-9; 1570-1	1567-8	1570-1	1561	1580-2	1580-1		

D:=discharged; E:=elected, did not serve; Ex:=exempt; N:=nominated.

the freedom. The table reminds us that there was no normal pattern for all careers, even among the rulers: John Harbie became a churchwarden within seven years of his freedom; Henry Campion required thirty-seven.

More of the variety and some of the typical moves can be found in eight individual careers. George Forman's early history is lost in obscurity. He first emerges in 1536 when he took the livery of the Skinners Company; by 1545 he was on the court of assistants and within seven years he had held all four wardenships. His earliest appearance on the Common Council was during the middle 1550s, and he remained a councilman until his death in 1575. He was a vestryman of St. Michael Cornhill from at least 1567, when appropriate documentation begins. He twice attained the mastership of his company, in 1571-2 and 1572-3, though he was never nominated to the Court of Aldermen. He seems to have been typical of those leaders who clearly had no chance of rising further, since he was nominated six times for chamberlain between 1564-73, and he was released from ever serving the shrievalty or aldermanry in 1572 after paying for a discharge.[1] He was of more than comfortable means, having been assessed at £275 in the subsidy three years before his death. He was able to provide the usual charitable bequests in his will, including a £100 loan fund for young skinners.[2] Another leader, William Hewet, possessed less wealth (only a £120 subsidy payment in 1572) but certainly had a more prominent family connection: his father had been an alderman and mayor. Having gained the freedom of the Clothworkers Company through patrimony around 1552, he advanced successively to the livery, two wardenships, and the court of assistants. In St. Olave Jewry he was constable in 1576-8, rather unusually after having been a councilman for two years. He was a governor of St. Bartholomew's Hospital in the 1570s, and on the Common Council for approximately sixteen years. Apparently he earned some favour, for he was nominated once to the court in 1578, and actually elected one of the sheriffs in 1580, though he never served. Despite his connections, his commitment to London was not as great as Forman's, all or most of whose property lay there and who took up much more ad hoc committee work. Hewet had close friends and relatives in the country, as well as most of his real estate, and seems to have retired to Kent in around 1593. He died in 1599. While little is known about the business interests of either leader, Hewet was a merchant adventurer and a director of the Spanish Company in 1577.

1 Jour. 19, fo. 430. Unless otherwise noted, biographical information is based on the same sources mentioned above pp. 55, note 1 and 69, note 2, plus A.B. Beaven's work, and Theodore K. Rabb, *Enterprise and Empire: Merchant and Gentry Investment in the Expansion of England, 1575-1630* (Cambridge, Mass., 1967), pp. 233-410.

2 P[rerogative] C[ourt] of C[anterbury], 39 Pyckering.

A very typical notable councilman of the lesser sort is Roger Warfeld, grocer. After gaining the freedom in 1544 and the livery by at least 1563, he was an assistant from 1575 and held two wardenships. In St. Stephen Walbrook he was churchwarden in 1562-3, sideman 1579-80, and numerous times an auditor of churchwardens' accounts. As a councilman between 1577-89 he made his contribution primarily on routine committee assignments, though he became both a hospital governor and treasurer. Never considered as a potential alderman, he was once nominated to be bridgemaster in 1588, four years before his death. He leased several messuages in London and was probably a moderately successful domestic trader, being assessed at £50 in 1572. There is no hint that he ever engaged extensively in overseas trade. Quite different was another notable councilman, Robert Offley, senior. After he took the freedom in around 1540, gaps in the records do not permit us to record his company activity, but he was an active assistant of the Haberdashers Company by at least 1583. In St. Mary Magdalen Milk Street he served as churchwarden in 1557-9. He was a councilman from 1558-97, serving on numerous committees, as auditor of the Bridgehouse and Chamber, 1562-4, a hospital governor, and later auditor-general of all hospitals. He probably became a captain of the London Trained Bands in 1588, though this may have been his son. He was a prosperous merchant of the staple at Bruges, paying subsidies of £160 in 1559, £200 in 1572, and £200 in 1589. Both from property acquisitions and civic committee work it is clear that he was deeply involved in London life, and, not surprisingly, he was nominated to the Court of Aldermen three times between 1567 and 1577. He was a member of the famous Offley family to be mentioned in a later chapter. By the time of his death in 1597 his son Robert had followed him to the council and had embarked on even more overseas trading ventures.

Among the aldermanic notables Ralph Woodcocke seems typical in most respects. He was a grocer who assumed moderate activity in his company. He reached the vestry of St. Lawrence Jewry by 1556, was churchwarden in 1560-2 and auditor of accounts several times over two decades. He began on the Common Council in 1571, serving as hospital governor and auditor before being elevated to the Court of Aldermen in 1580 on only the third nomination. His prompt election was doubtless due to his being the mayor's nominee for sheriff in 1580-1. He died in September 1586 before his chance for the mayoralty came. That he was of rather modest estate for an alderman (£67 assessment in 1559; £100 in 1572) may be due to his twenty-four children. A more active notable alderman is Thomas Smythe (died 1625). Despite his prominence as an overseas merchant, his extensive crown service, the fact that he was three times an MP, and his forceful zeal to spread the gospel overseas and among his merchant friends,[1] he did not ignore the traditional ruling class of London from which he sprang. He was a grandson of Alderman Andrew Judde. Not much survives concerning his early local experience, but he reached the vestry in St. Alphage London Wall by at least 1594, served as an assessor for the parish in 1597, and was on the Common Council in 1595-9 and the Court of Aldermen 1599-1601, then briefly again in 1604, serving as sheriff for a partial term in 1600-1. His alleged connections with the Essex rebellion of 1601 cost him further promotion in the City, but his previous experience is impressive: master of the Haberdashers Company three times between 1583 and 1600, captain of the London Trained Bands in 1588 and 1599, a surveyor of Bridgehouse lands, 1596-7, an auditor of the Bridgehouse and Chamber, 1597-8, and treasurer of St. Bartholomew's Hospital, 1597-1601. Through propery transactions and personal friends he remained to the end close to the traditional City setting.

Smythe's brother-in-law, Rowland Heyward, was probably the most impressive of the élite aldermen during the Elizabethan period. His political rise was rapid. Born around 1520,[2] he gained the freedom of the Clothworkers Company in 1541 or 1542, became a liveryman by 1549, renter warden 1550-1, quarter warden 1554-5, master 1559-60. He reached the vestry of St. Mary Magdalen Milk Street in the early 1550s, became a councilman at around the same time, and served as churchwarden in 1552-4. Elected to the Court of Aldermen in 1560, aged forty, he served thirty-three years, for the last seven and a half as Father of the City, or the most senior alderman. No other civic ruler matched his long list of offices, his assiduous attendance at court, his remorseless devotion to committee work. To mention only the places he held after the mayoralty: chief auditor of the Bridgehouse and Chamber 1572-3, MP 1572-83, president of St. Bartholomew's Hospital 1572-93, surveyor-general of hospitals 1580-2, comptroller-general of hospitals 1582-93, and surveyor of Bridgehouse lands 1579-93. He was one of only two Elizabethans who served more than one term as mayor, the first in 1570-1 succeeded a generation later in 1591 when he finished the term of a deceased colleague. He amassed a large fortune through extensive investment in overseas trade, real estate, and money lending. His subsidy assessments were £400 in 1559 and 1572, £200 in 1589. He was an honorary member of the

---

1 See the *Dictionary of National Biography* and Louis B. Wright, *Religion and Empire: The Alliance Between Piety and Commerce in English Expansion, 1558-1625* (Chapel Hill, 1943), chapter 3.

2 Thomas S. Willan, *The Muscovy Merchants of 1555* (Manchester, 1953), p. 103, n. 1.

Inner Temple from 1561, and, like all the élite, received knighthood after the first mayoral year. The final example is another élite alderman, Thomas Cambell, who shows that not all the élite enjoyed rapid rising due to favour. Free of the Ironmongers Company in 1562 or 1563, he rose to the livery by 1568, held three wardenships, and served as master three times between 1595-1613. In his ward he was both scavenger, inquestman, and collector for the poor before reaching the vestry of St. Olave Jewry by 1577. Thereafter he was churchwarden 1579-81, constable 1584-6, common councilman 1590-9, and deputy alderman for the ward of Coleman Street 1591-9. As a councilman he was twice an auditor of the Bridgehouse and Chamber, surveyor of the Bridgehouse lands, governor, auditor, and auditor-general of hospitals. He needed nineteen nominations before gaining election to the Court of Aldermen. Despite many family ties in City politics and numerous ventures in overseas trade, his did not seem to be an easy life: his subsidy assessments were £50 in 1572 and £80 in 1589. In the wardens' accounts of the Ironmongers Company is a note that in 1574 he was fined ten shillings 'for unkind words'.

Even after looking at these individuals, whose careers were more fully documented than most, one distorted impression remains regarding rising in City politics. Because City offices and committees are nearly all known, but only some of the local ones, most men seemed to spend more of their time in City offices. Sufficient examples have been found of rapid rising by office skipping at all levels of London politics, and we cannot doubt the importance of this phenomenon for those enjoying favour, yet we cannot say how typical this was. In conclusion, then, let us attempt to reassess the balance between local and City office. Due to incomplete local records very few of the rulers can be found holding parish offices, yet virtually all who appear in parish records also held some office.[1] Furthermore, where the rare records of ward offices survive, future rulers, like the wardmen, held a surprisingly large number of places. More complete records would probably confirm both rapid rising for a few and considerable tedium for the large majority of rulers. This is substantiated by the livery records, whose survival and completeness are both more satisfactory. Information on livery offices was available for twenty-six out of thirty-six leaders and nineteen of forty-one notables.[2] Twenty-two of

---

1 Thirty-six of 141 rulers were found in the surviving parish records.

2 This means that beginning with dates of apprenticeship and the freedom there were continuous enough records to find any higher offices for 26 leaders and 19 notables. I excluded numerous others because only partial records existed, which would have meant incomplete recording of their offices. The material at hand seemed adequate for illustrations, which is about all one can offer without complete records.

the twenty-six leaders and seventeen of nineteen notables held at least one of the four wardenships. For the leaders, two held only one wardenship, fourteen held two, five held three, and one held all four. Four of the twenty-two repeated in a wardenship once, five repeated twice. Fifteen of the twenty-six leaders achieved the highest eminence in the livery company by becoming master at least once. Among the notables, five held one wardenship, six held two, three held three, and three held all four. Two repeated once, one repeated twice, and one repeated five times. Ten of the nineteen notables served as masters. Fifty-two of sixty-four élite were masters, and though I have not taken the pains to search out all their wardenships it was normal to serve twice as warden before becoming master. With their first wardenship, it will be recalled, men joined the court of assistants, and usually served for life. Thus even as they rose higher in civic office, the rulers continued to serve in the localities where they began political activity.

5

PROCEDURES AND ATTITUDES

It is arguable that institutions have a life of their own, independent of the passing generations of men associated with them, and that therefore any government operates as a reflection of certain forms and limitations inherent in particular institutions. To an extent this was true of Elizabethan London, but the remaining chapters of this book also show that political institutions reflected the deeper, sometimes unconscious, assumptions of the men who created and reshaped them from time to time.

An inquiry into political attitudes prevailing among the rulers of sixteenth-century London is enlivened by the fascination of attempting to understand the minds of other men at other times, just as it is frustrated by a lack of explicit contemporary comment. A considerable part of the fascination, and virtually all the frustration, can be attributed to the nature of the source materials. The scarcity of 'private' papers in the early modern period can be blamed with some justice on the fates, which are said to have been unkind to such materials. Thus historians assume that a great deal of material once existed which no longer survives. On the other hand, is the comparative abundance of 'public' records due only to the fact that they have been better cared for over the years? It would seem not, because while neglect is no friend of paper, parchment, or canvas, it is conspicuously less harmful than the furies which threaten and occasionally ravage centrally collected materials: fire, water, deliberate acts of destruction to conceal a shameful deed, or to protect a guilty conscience. Even after allowing for the heaps of scrap lying hidden in dusty attics or dank cellars the world over, the preponderance of public records may well reflect their greater abundance in the first place. This seems especially true regarding the Elizabethan rulers. Not finding tracts on political theory by London merchants, or letters discussing political issues, we are liable to conclude, erroneously, that the rulers gave little self-conscious thought to the nature of rulership; or that what thoughts they did have on the subject were not invested with much meaning. Such conclusions would seem to be supported both by the scarcity of private papers and by the lack of explicit political comment in the corporate sources that do survive. And yet the City's records do speak forcefully and continually, even if indirectly, of political attitudes. The agenda of the court — what came before it, and what did not — tells us as much about the rulers' priorities as about their jurisdiction;

procedures reflect attitudes on efficiency and competence, not to mention duty and loyalty. Even the form of the records — how lengthy, how detailed, how formal, how regular in codification — is based on implicit notions about the purposes of ruling. Therefore while treating the regular governmental procedures of the City, I shall also try to look behind the specific acts to reconstruct the attitudes at work.[1]

The usual meeting place of the Court of Aldermen was the Guildhall. Though there is no full description of the Guildhall for the Elizabethan era, it is known that in addition to the great hall — the walls of which have been standing since 1425 — there were several other chambers built off the hall which served as offices for City officials and meeting rooms for the many legal and administrative courts. Writing at the end of the sixteenth century of the fifteenth-century construction, Stow said there was a Mayor's Chamber, a 'Counsell' Chamber, 'with other rooms above the stairs'.[2] Above the stairs meant above the ground floor where the great hall was. Among these upper chambers was one known as the Inner Chamber and another called the Outer Chamber. In the former the aldermen met in an administrative capacity, at which times they were officially styled the Court of the Lord Mayor and the Aldermen in the Inner Chamber. In the Outer Chamber met the Mayor's Court, a judicial court usually presided over by the recorder. The 'Counsell' Chamber was doubtless for the Common Council, not the counsellors or legal officers who met with one of the two main courts when their services were required. There are also references in the early seventeenth century to a new and larger room for the council, completed around 1614. Occasionally the full court met elsewhere — the mayor's house being the usual place. Once in 1599 it met on Good

1   What follows is based mostly on the Court of Aldermen's minute books (the Repertories), but it draws on the Letter-Books and Journals too. Concerning the Journals, see note 4 on p. 18. In the sixteenth century the Letter-Books were used almost exclusively for fair copies (parchment) of orphanage transactions and important acts of Common Council or orders of the aldermen, which were copied from the Repertories or Journals (paper). Concerning their form, it should be admitted at once that the various minute books are apparently fair-copy summaries of notes drawn up by clerks on the spot; unfortunately none of the clerks' notes survive. The Repertories are rich in details on innumerable subjects and persons and contain some petitions, committee reports, and other information drawn up by, or presented to, the Court of Aldermen. But essentially they are a record of proceedings. As such they are often annoyingly abbreviated or evasive, since they do not record the sort of things contemporaries took for granted, but which historians would dearly love to know. There are no debates, no indications of disagreement, and usually no hint of how business once before the aldermen, but resolved elsewhere, was settled. To the aldermen these records were a list of names, dates, circumstances, decisions, and legally-binding agreements that they needed, or might need, to remember.

2   *Survey,* ed. Charles L. Kingsford (Oxford, 1908), i. 272.

Friday at St. Paul's, where the aldermen always attended in state on that day. Committees of the court or informal groups of particular members might meet anywhere they chose, though the permanent and even some of the ad hoc committees met at the Guildhall at this time.

Anything important enough to be worth preserving must be subject to some routine, and by Elizabeth's time there was a highly developed sense of regularity to government: courts met in the same places and individual assemblies had their own chambers. Civic government was held in high respect, for not only was there a separate building assigned to it, but the building could grow according to need. At the same time the rulers were assisted by a host of lesser officials. Beyond the Guildhall they took part in periodic ceremonies that had nothing specific to do with their jurisdiction, but which attested to their power, dignity, and rank, as well as to the pride which the City felt in its rulers. As a reflection of the esteem in which it was held, the Court of Aldermen developed a formal quality in its proceedings, which enhanced the regularity and dignity of its work. A further example is the method of voting in court. A number of matters were probably settled by a show of hands, but in 1532 it was resolved that 'in every matter of gravity which shall pass or not pass by this Court, the box shall be brought into the same. And by putting in of the white piece or the black the matter to take effect, or not effect'.[1] The box had been used at least as early as 1525, perhaps on an experimental basis.[2] In another entry, concerning the handling of petitions from 'strangers', the aldermen resolved that speaking in court should be according to seniority, a practice probably pertaining to other business as well.[3]

A more extended example of deliberate regularity is the way in which aldermen categorized the business that came before them. They dispatched much of it at once, on first hearing as it were. What could not be settled immediately was put forward to another specific day, or assigned to a committee. Delays were permitted when a particular witness or advisor was to be summoned, or an individual against whom a decision of some kind was going to be made. Gathering of appropriate information, usually by committees, caused more delays. Much time, too, was taken up in listening to committee reports, after which a

1 Rep. 8, fo. 263.
2 Rep. 7, fo. 56[b].
3 Rep. 14, fo. 402[b]. With the exception of the mayor, who always had primacy, rank on the court was by seniority. This was measured in two different ways. Date of actually joining the court, not date of election, determined precedence for junior aldermen. For men beyond the mayoralty, rank followed the order of holding the chair. An alteration in precedence took place between 29 September, when the next mayor was chosen, and his assumption of the office on 28 October. During that time the mayor-elect took second place in the court.

discussion either settled the matter or hit upon another problem, in which case the committee worked on. In an effort to expedite committee work the composition was often enlarged if the business was obviously taking up too much of the original members' time. Assignments to committees were made in court, probably by the mayor, who might appoint even those not in attendance at that particular time. The senior alderman on the committee, regardless of its composition, was its leader or chairman. Committees undoubtedly had clerks before 1579 (probably assigned by the mayor) but in that year an act of Common Council permitted committees to choose their own clerks and counsellors. Committees also determined the fees of their clerks.[1] Moreover from the middle years of Elizabeth's reign an increasing number of committee reports are summarized in the Repertories.

Formalism was occasionally elevated into ceremony, whenever solemnity was required. Appropriately enough, each court meeting began and ended with a stately procession of aldermen, important civic officers, and clerks — all arranged in ranks and marching behind the mayoral sword, carried by the swordbearer. (This is still the practice today.) There is no specific mention of ecclesiastical men present in court during Elizabeth's time, but there may have been formal or informal prayers all the same; this was apparently the rule during the seventeenth century.[2] That such rituals were celebrated in the Court of Aldermen, however, speaks of more than solemnity. Such ceremonies underlined the legitimacy of the proceedings and the participants. Ceremony was the most formal acknowledgement and the most joyous celebration of legitimacy.

The amount of formal routine in their work points to the considerable practical, perhaps even experimental, experience the aldermen had accumulated over several centuries. Their acceptance of formalism broadcasts their satisfaction with the ways they had learned, an attitude that might have engendered a rather relaxed pace in government. As models of industry and involvement, however, the aldermen of the sixteenth century would win accolades even from modern activists. There is even a strenuous quality in their work. Before 1545 the court met at different times, depending on the season: in the autumn and winter quarters sessions began at 9.00 a.m., but from 25 March to

1 Jour. 20, pt. 2, fo. 498.

2 *Corporation of London,* p. 56. In other official minutes of civic bodies there is explicit evidence of informal prayers. The Wardmote Minutes of St. Dunstan in the West end in this fashion on one occasion: 'And thus we end our wardmote, desiring Almighty God to forgive us our offenses and grant us all grace to live in faith to him, and love one towards another in neighbourly charity, for Jesus Christ's sake unto whom be all glory' (fo. 58 of the WIM). The date was 21 December 1580, the date of annual ward elections.

29 September members had to be present and ready to begin work at 8.00 a.m.[1] On 3 November 1545 hours were set at 8.00-11.00 a.m. regardless of the season, and these were the effective hours through the Elizabethan period.[2] Special meetings, of course, could be called at any time, some even before 8.00 a.m., but afternoon meetings of the court were more common when the pressure of business was heavy.

The frequency of meetings was recorded in an early published account (1629) of the ceremonials of the mayor and aldermen. 'Courts of Aldermen in ordinary are held at the Guildhall every Tuesday and Thursday through the whole year, except holy days, the month of August until Bartholomew Day [24 August] be past, the week before Christmas, Shrove Tuesday and the week before Easter'.[3] The practice was the same during Elizabeth's reign, except that vacations were often encroached upon, even Sundays when events demanded it. It was often more convenient to take the Christmas holiday in the week, or sometimes two weeks, after Christmas, not the week before. The August holiday was less well observed, and it is the exceptional year without several meetings before 24 August. Two assemblies a week constituted the minimum, a third or fourth meeting was normal. In the first year of Elizabeth's reign, for example, the aldermen held court 115 times: forty times on Thursday, thirty-eight on Tuesday, fourteen on Saturday, nine on Friday, eight on Wednesday and six times on Monday. In the same year the lowest number of courts per month (six) was in December, because of the Christmas holiday. July had only seven, and February eight, but both preserved the traditional average of two courts a week; all other months, including August, had between nine and thirteen courts. The busiest season in any year was often September, October, and November, because of the many searches to be made and reported on, and because the sheriffs and mayor were finishing their one year of duty and had to make way for their successors. In other years it was the wintry January to March period that was the most active, but such seasonal variations were insignificant and made no impact on the routine of the court's sittings.

Frequent sessions were matched by assiduous attendance by the individual aldermen. The quorum of the court was thirteen, based on the ancient tradition of only twenty-four aldermen, instead of the

1 Rep. 10, fo. 228[b]. In both cases morning sessions were meant to end by 11.00 a.m.
2 Letter-Book Q, fo. 150.
3 *The Order of my Lord Mayor the Aldermen and the Sheriffes for their Meetings and Wearing of their Apparrell Throughout the Whole Yeare*, p. 32 (at the GLMR).

twenty-six there have been since 1550.[1] The aldermen disregarded the quorum when necessary, though in the first regnal year of the queen only eleven out of 115 courts were attended by less than the quorum; in 1577 eighteen out of one hundred courts, and in 1593 (one of the worst plague years) forty-two out of ninety-seven courts were held by a similar minority.[2] Aldermen did not always flee the City during sickness, and during 1569 — also a year of mild plague, or perhaps influenza — attendance fell to twelve or fewer only twice.[3] In normal times and during less serious visitations of sickness, around fifteen aldermen usually attended. It was not at all unusual for courts to be held by twenty-one or twenty-two, or by twelve or thirteen. But it was very rare for all twenty-six to appear together, and equally rare for five or six to hold the court. Gaps in a man's attendance usually stretched no longer than a few weeks or a month. Some individuals did not attend for months at a time, for reasons of health or business, but these were exceptional. Prolonged absence from the City, hence from civic duties, was discouraged by the act of Common Council of 1545 which disenfranchised freemen away from the City for over one year.[4]

Given the large number of critical or serious outbreaks of various epidemics over the Elizabethan years, one is struck by the courage and steadfastness of the aldermen. In the year November 1558 — November 1559 the aldermen who attended at all were present on average at 63 per cent of the courts; in 1569 it was 67 per cent; in 1577, 57 per cent; in 1593 (again, a serious plague year), 59 per cent. Omitting the several who were permitted an unusually long leave, and those who joined the court in mid-year, each alderman attended between two-thirds and three-quarters of the courts during most years. For some attendance was even higher. The mayor presided at every meeting. Pressing business abroad or away from London had to wait or be dealt with by deputies; only grave illness excused him. Sheriffs showed nearly the same faultless attendance. There were always a few men, usually

---

1   Farringdon Ward divided into two parts in 1394, and both wards were allowed to have their own alderman. The twenty-sixth has represented Southwark, or Bridge Without Ward, since the charter of Edward VI (23 April 1550). Thirteen as the quorum is confirmed by the wording of an act of Common Council in 1564 stating that aleconners could make certain regulations for brewers provided that they informed the mayor and twelve aldermen.

2   The minutes of every court meeting show the names of the aldermen attending.

3   That 1569 was a serious year for sickness, even if not one of the most serious, is clear from the City's plague ordinances for the year. On the plague at this time and the authorities' efforts to deal with it see F.P. Wilson, *The Plague in Shakespeare's London* (Oxford Paperback, repr., 1963).

4   Letter-Book Q, fos. 138b-39b. This was revised in August 1564 to allow aldermen to make exceptions, but they took no liberties for themselves.

senior aldermen, whose attendance was also much higher than average. In 1569 Rowland Heyward attended fifty-six out of eight-four courts, about average for the year; in 1577 he attended eighty-four out of one hundred, way ahead of the average, and in 1593 — the year of his death — he still managed to come to sixty-two out of ninety-seven courts, also over the average. Richard Martin in 1593 and again in 1599 was far ahead of the average attendance and was probably the most active senior alderman in the 1590s. Thomas Offley showed the same pattern: in 1559 he was well over average attendance, again in 1569, and just over average in 1577.

If age commanded rank and greater respect, it was not accompanied by retirement but by an even more onerous engagement in politics. The industry and dedication of the seniors is particularly well illustrated by their committee work. In 1573, not counting orphanage business, eight senior aldermen earned seventy-four committee posts between them (average 9.3); nineteen juniors had 179 (average 9.4). Two seniors and four juniors had over ten each. In 1577, counting orphanage business to show the impact it could have, eleven seniors had 158 committee posts (average 14.4), sixteen juniors only 122 (average 7.6). Seven of thirteen with ten or more were seniors. To keep the comparisons between juniors and seniors in their proper ratio, it should be remembered that there were always more juniors serving than seniors, usually around twice as many. More important was the work done by specific committees. Over and over again in every year juniors were busiest on committees handling most disputed estates, repair and construction of City property, provision of supplies, investigation of company disputes, and matters concerning the appointed officers. The seniors often took the lead on committees appointed to see some representative of the central government, whether it concerned some point of disputed privilege, foreign trade, or the enforcement of economic regulations. Seniors also handled discipline of other aldermen, and estate matters of other seniors. Seniors represented the City in its dispute with Lord Rich over rights to City water intended for the poorhouses. A survey of the 107 committees formed by the court in 1579 appears in Table 4; the only committees shown are those involving aldermen.

In 1579 the activity rating of seniors exceeded that of juniors: thirty-five per cent of the aldermen (nine seniors) carried forty-three per cent of the jobs. This was normal in all years. It was customary to mix juniors and seniors on most committees, but there were also times when seniors acted independently of juniors, doubtless more frequently than is suggested by a rare entry like the following. 'Item, it is ordered that Sir Rowland Heyward, Sir Thomas Ramsey, Sir George Barne, and

Sir George Bond, knights, shall have conference with the right honourable the Lord Mayor touching certain causes importing the estate of this City'.[1] Even if seniors did more often establish policy or make final decisions, that was part and parcel of rank and greater experience, but seniors never became a group apart by shirking tedious detail. Increased attention to both great and small matters was the characteristic of seniority. Individual examples stand out. In the early part of the reign Martin Bowes, William Garrarde, and Thomas Offley were the exceptional men, just as Lionel Duckett, John Ryvers, Wolstan Dixie, and George Barne were in the middle years, and Richard Martin and John Harte in the later years. The most remarkable alderman of this time, Rowland Heyward, was extremely active throughout the reign until his death in 1593.

TABLE 4: COMMITTEES OF THE COURT OF ALDERMEN IN 1579

No. of Committees	Dealing with	Junior members	Senior members
20	orphanage	29	11
17	royal government	26	24
11	City property	20	17
11	misc. disputes	15	8
9	civic officers	14	8
9	livery companies	13	11
8	markets, etc.	14	5
7	City's rights	12	14
6	miscellaneous	5	13
3	the poor	6	6
3	repairs, etc.	7	1
1	drafting bills	2	0
1	raising money	0	4
1	apprentices	0	2
107		163	124
	Average number of posts held	10.2	13.8

---

1   Rep. 22, fo. 105.

More than any other alderman the mayor epitomized the attitudes and the resulting behaviour of the ruling élite. Of all the aldermen the mayor was the most important and the busiest. During his year in office he led the court and the City. He presided not only in the Court of Aldermen but in Common Council, Congregation, the Court of Husting, and at any court of wardmote which nominated an alderman. In the Court of Aldermen he probably still directed business himself, made committee assignments, ordered reports, and approved the schedule of business. Because of the considerable demands on his time during the mayoralty, he avoided most committee work. In addition to his broad executive and administrative duties, every mayor faced a traditional and formal routine. The prices of bread, beer, poultry goods, wood, and candles were set in November; a general court was held in early January for hearing appeals from the several courts of wardmote; in June a report was made to Chancery on the wages established by the mayor and his fellow justices for servants and labourers, and so on month by month throughout the year.[1] Other duties and privileges emphasized his constitutional as well as ceremonial pre-eminence.[2] He attended in state with his brethren at scores of ceremonies, he greeted the sovereign at the City's gates should she be passing through, he received and entertained dignitaries. Pride and even exuberance were not inappropriate to the mayoralty, but there was a heavy cost: Alderman Richard Martin is said to have spent £7,000 as sheriff for one year and mayor for parts of two one-year terms; Alderman Pemberton spent between £4,000-5000 just on a house suitable for his mayoral year.[3] It is small wonder that the financial decline of Alderman Thomas Lodge began during his mayoralty.[4] That more mayors did did not follow Lodge to the debtors' prison is a testamony to the great wealth and acuity of the ruling élite.

Naturally, the aldermen did not do everything themselves. Much was done by common councilmen, household officers, and various other civic administrators. What the aldermen delegated, and to whom, also reveals something about their attitudes towards ruling. During the last quarter of the sixteenth century the pressures on civic government forced the aldermen to convene Common Council more often than

1 For a schedule of the mayor's activity by the month in these routine affairs see a book at the GLMR, *Generall Matters To Be Remembred of the Lord Maior, Throughout the Wholeyeare,* which was published sometime between 1574 and 1585.

2 For a sketch of these other traditional duties see the preceding note and *Corporation of London, passim,* but especially pp.20-1.

3 Robert G. Lang, 'The Greater Merchants of London in the Early Seventeenth Century', D. Phil. thesis (Oxford Univ., 1962), p. 344.

4 See below, pp. 145-6.

ever before.[1] For similar reasons individual councilmen became much more active than ever before. There were around forty councilmen on committees in 1560, only seven of whom had more than one assignment, and all seven had close personal and business connections with the aldermen. In 1593 around fifty councilmen had committee assignments, twenty-three of whom served more than once. In both years greater participation was directly in proportion to experience and rank. The contribution of these active councilmen approached but did not quite match the effort of the aldermen themselves. Five of the fifty councilmen with committee experience during 1593 did have more assignments than twelve of the aldermen, it is true, but for very good reasons: four of the twelve aldermen devoted part of the year to the shrievalty, when it was normal to be excused from nearly all committee work; five of the twelve were seriously ill with plague and died during the year or in early 1594; one alderman did not join the court until the last month of 1593; another, for uncertain reasons, did not attend all year, and the last — whose assignments numbered only three less than the most active councilman — was simultaneously holding crown office as a customer of the Port of London.

The work of household officers and civic administrators was more specialized; both acted in supportive capacities to the aldermen. In preparing for meetings of the court the mayor relied on all the aldermen, as well as the chief department heads, but especially on the members of his household. This household staff was larger than that of any other officer and better able to cope with petitions and agendas.[2] Some household officers were personally attendant upon the mayor at all times: in his home, on the streets, or in one of the several courts over which he presided.[3] Various members of the household were responsible for summoning individuals before the court, for notifying councilmen of forthcoming meetings of the Common Council, and for sending and receiving messages.[4] The household was the one body large

1 During the first half of the queen's reign the council met infrequently and apparently for only short periods of time. Until 1579 it was the exceptional year that saw as many as four sessions. Thereafter, monthly or even fortnightly sessions were not uncommon. In August 1599 the council met six times, by far its busiest period; the Court of Aldermen met seven times that month.

2 Stow, *Survey,* ii. 187-8 shows the names of the household officers and counts a total of thirty-two. MSS 90.12 at the CLRO, from the 1590s, has only thirty-one; it shows one less 'young man', or 'gentleman's man', but adds the foreign taker to the household. It does not show the coroner in the household.

3 MSS 90.12 at the CLRO.

4 This is clear from entries in the Repertories, for example, Rep. 19, fo. 244. The men ordered to do these jobs, in this case one of the water bailiff's men, were not specialized functionaries as their titles might suggest. They were all attendant on the mayor and might do any number of services for him. Their titles help in clarifying the circumstances of their creation, but are not an accurate guide to

enough and close enough to the mayor to keep him informed from day to day concerning the various business which might ultimately come before the Court of Aldermen.

The civic administrators fell into two groups, in accordance with two rather distinct attitudes about their whole nature and purpose: first, the bureaucrats, or department heads, and then all the others, including the sheriffs' subordinates, petty officials, collectors, inspectors, weighers, clerks, assistants, and artisans who performed much of the City's daily work. In Elizabeth's time there were approximately 479 men in this second grouping (see Appendix 2); there were only seven bureaucrats. Most of the officers and clerks served in specific capacities, usually involving little skill and even less training, and were rigorously supervised by the bureaucrats, or councilmen and aldermen, or both. Strictly assistants, they possessed little or no independent authority or right of initiative.

The bureaucrats differed both in function and degree. The two bridgemasters and the chamberlain belonged to the same merchant group of which the councilmen and aldermen were the chief representatives. The town clerk, common serjeant, and recorder were prominent lawyers. Less is known about the swordbearer, though, as the leader of the mayor's household, he deserves to be included among the bureaucrats.[1] The lawyers in particular were highly trained and occasionally gained sufficient position to marry into families of the ruling councilmen and aldermen. Simultaneously, they were assigned large responsibilities appropriate to their training, which in turn involved extensive supervision of the rest of the civic administration. The recorder was the chief legal officer of the Court of Aldermen;[2] the common serjeant had a similar capacity in Common Council. Both directed the lesser legal clerks of the City, helped in drawing up legislation, and represented London before the crown whenever legal assistance was necessary. The common serjeant also had a special responsibility for the orphans of the City. The chamberlain had certain responsibilities over apprentices in addition to his special concern for civic revenues.

duties. For the duties the Elizabethan Oath Book at the CLRO is a helpful beginning. Concerning the historical development of the household see Betty R. Masters, 'The Mayor's Household Before 1600', in *Studies in London History Presented to Philip Edmund Jones,* ed. A.E.J. Hollaender and William Kellaway (1969), pp. 95-114.

1   The remembrancer might also be considered a bureaucrat, especially in view of his connections with parliament (see above, p. 27, note 2). In his secretarial capacity, however, he was subordinate to the town clerk, and he did not attend the Court of Aldermen.

2 I have given details on the bureaucrats elsewhere: for the recorder *The Guildhall Miscellany* 4 (October 1972): for the other bureaucrats 'Government of London', diss. (Columbia University, 1968) pp. 110-22.

The town clerk kept the City's many records, but he also gave legal advice and probably conducted the proceedings of Common Council at this time, even though the mayor presided. The bridgemasters supervised the maintenance of London Bridge, as well as its estates, and kept corn supplies in the Bridgehouse.[1] Despite their specialized behaviour, and their undoubted abilities, the bureaucrats were not like modern boards of experts who devise plans and recommend them to the politicians for enactment. Initiative and final authority remained with the aldermen. The chamberlain did not submit proposals for the collection and expenditure of revenue; the aldermen discussed these matters then gave orders to the chamberlain. Similarly, the recorder and common serjeant did not initiate legislation; they only prepared the actual instruments after the aldermen had indicated what was required. A number of the bureaucrats served for life, though as officeholders (frequently as pluralists), not as rulers.[2] All the bureaucrats were appointed, paid, disciplined, and discharged by the rulers. None of them ever advanced to the dignity of an aldermanry.

It is a testament to the political sophistication of its rulers that London's government could grow so large and multifarious by virtue of employing experienced, often highly-trained men in the higher bureaucratic positions, but could also remain fixed in its traditional form, by subordinating all departments, committees, officials, and even the Common Council to the central, supreme authority of the Court of Aldermen. The persistence and devotion of the aldermen exhibit their essentially paternal interest in civic government, an attitude even more explicitly revealed in the traditional routine of business they established for themselves. Analysing the concerns taken up by the court shows that orphanage work demanded the most attention, accounting for a third to a half of the items in the records. In view of the City's traditional role as guardian of all freemen's orphans, it is easy to see why orphanage business so dominated the agenda, and its preponderance in the records may well suggest the proportion of time it demanded. Orphans needed the permission of the court to marry before the age of twenty-one. The court had to be notified by the appointed guardian in case of the death or mental incompetence of the

---

1   After 1550, when the City bought the various royal manors in Southwark from the crown, the administrative duties of the bridgemasters were increased in various ways: they collected the traditional rents of the manors, kept the streets clear, and for a period at the end of the sixteenth century actually rotated in the office of bailiff of Southwark. For details consult David J. Johnson, *Southwark and the City* (1969).

2   Some of those who retired before their deaths are known to have received a pension or a sinecure of some kind from the City. Rather different were the recorders, who at the conclusion of their service to the City found further promotion through the offices of the crown.

orphan, and upon his or her coming of age. Virtually every aspect of an orphan's life, including employment and leaving London, was subject to the approval of the court. Upon reaching twenty-one, when the orphan was paid his share of the father's estate, he appeared to officially acknowledge receipt of his lawful portion, and to discharge the court and the sureties from any further responsibility. Most of these affairs were routine and could be dispatched in a short time.

Other matters required more time. Immediately after the death of the freeman father, the local parish clerk became responsible for notifying the common crier of the death, and the common crier brought the executors and administrators of the estate before the court. They were responsible in turn for bringing in an inventory of the deceased's personal goods, which was registered with the common serjeant. The testator usually named his own administrators (commonly relatives or members of his livery company) who, unless they chose to pay over the estate to the City directly, were then bound to the Chamber to assure that the orphan's portion would be paid at the appropriate time. Delays could arise at any stage of this process, beginning with delivery of the inventory. Even after it was compiled, the court could challenge the inventory or make further inquiries of the sureties. In a number of other ways difficulties could arise. Disputes often developed between rival beneficiaries of the estate. Some administrators needed prodding to pay the orphan finding money. Others assigned revenues from properties they owned or leased to cover the cost of maintenance, but these properties then had to be appraised. Men who died intestate provided a particular problem because then considerably more time was required to draw up inventories and disputes were more likely. The aldermen assigned a great deal of the resulting orphanage work to the common serjeant, the common crier, and their assistants. But they handled just as much themselves. Estate disputes concerning former aldermen, for example, were always worked out by one or two other aldermen or a committee of them. Any disputed estate for that matter, if not taken care of within reasonable time, became the responsibility of individual aldermen. Finding sufficient sureties who would keep up with their responsibilities also consumed much time. In order to accelerate the binding of sureties the court often took a recognizance of an alderman for a high sum, obliging him to find the sureties and in the meantime to carry the burden himself.

At first glance this almost obsessive concern with orphanage strikes one as peculiar, if not downright irrelevant. Surely larger concerns were, or should have been, at the centre of the aldermen's attention. There were, of course, and these must be articulated so that the high priority of orphanage can make sense. In the relatively uncomplicated

scheme of things in the sixteenth century it was possible to insist upon
visions and controls which today our more elaborate governments
would blush to consider: not just fixed prices and set qualities, but the
precise supply of materials and provisions was often established,
especially for the essential goods of poulters, woodmongers, and coal
meters.[1] Not only material goods and conditions, but the whole
moral condition of human beings was subject to thorough examination.
Many people had to be disciplined by the court. A man who stole a boat
from a Thames waterman and rowed up and down the river, apparently
for his own pleasure, paid a fine of 13s. 4d.; another was jailed tempor-
arily for ringing the bells of St. Sepulchre's 'awkwardly in manner of an
alarm'. When one considers the great amount of such trivia which
reached the aldermen, and recalls that most of it probably came to the
court only after initial attention in some lower tribunal, the magnitude
of petty abuse is obvious. Even more interesting is the aldermen's
willingness to confront it. In the first regnal year of Queen Elizabeth
the court considered and decided no less than sixty-three such cases
involving social or moral infractions. It is not easy to distinguish
these from economic violations, and the court also ruled on forty-eight
cases of that nature. There is something rather humourous, if not a little
heroic, about great men spending so much time on such apparently
inconsequential affairs. From this point of view virtually all of what
remains in the records seems to be incredibly beside the point. In the
year in which they heard these sixty-three cases (5 per cent of the
records for the year), they made 482 entries concerning orphans
(37 per cent), 301 on economic regulation (23 per cent), 140 on local
officers and offices (11 per cent), 76 on City property (6 per cent),
fifty-two on the freedom (4 per cent), thirty-two on the hospitals
(2 per cent), but only ninety-one (7 per cent) on matters beyond the
City, including the affairs of greater London, the queen, and the
central government.[2] And in addressing themselves to such topics the
aldermen passed easily from considerations of theft or vagrancy to the
price of coal or quality of meat, then on to disturbing the peace or in-
subordination to a civic officer. It also mattered little whether they
were acting in an individual capacity, in their own wards, or in their
formal assembly in the Court of Aldermen. The force of law, after all
emanated not so much from certain courts, or even very conclusively
from particular laws, as from the authority of those entrusted with its
creation and protection.

1 As an apt illustration of a point made earlier, individual aldermen or councilmen were often requested to use their own money and connections to buy up
requisite supplies.
2 The other 5% of the items concerned miscellaneous topics, like apprentices,
the Common Council, or aliens. These proportions are representative of the
aldermen's focus in other years.

The orders they gave and the punishments they assigned seem to have been based on certain assumptions about a moral and material universe that was both static and harmonious. It followed that the general purpose of government and justice (parts of the same phenomenon) was to preserve the fundamental though rather ineffable form of things which the controls assumed. Translated into its broader implications, this meant that controls, like the forms and harmony they protected, were a part of what must be: that is, Providence. Fortune, that fickle manipulator of transient events, might be scorned or sometimes even ignored, but since all the eternal verities were part of Providence — order, authority, and tradition among them — man had always to hold before himself the goal of preserving these truths since that was God's will.[1] There is the further assumption, therefore, of an autonomous will, or a personal responsibility, upon which law and the social order were predicated. This can be illustrated in the manner of punishing infractions, perhaps most effectively in recounting the familiar treatment accorded those who sold goods of inferior quality or unwholesome produce. It was the custom to parade the person through the several markets with the offending goods carried before him or hung from his neck. The purpose was public humiliation. The parade was followed by the formal and ceremonial destruction of the goods, after which the transgressor might spend several hours in the pillory. Before beginning this public penance, it was common to spend a day or two in gaol, and before being released fines were sometimes exacted, or, especially for violators of economic regulations, recognizances were taken which became forfeit upon recurrence of the misdeed. At every stage there was the suggestion that correct behaviour is a simple matter of will, and every effort was made to show the will the propriety of reform.

Within the context of civic government, preserving the fundamental forms was based upon this final assumption: that government existed of and for the citizens of London only, that is the freemen.[2] The numerous regulations concerning materials, markets, craftsmen, and working conditions were drawn up with the responsible and productive

1 Acknowledgement is made to Durant W. Robertson Jr., *Chaucer's London* (New York, 1968), pp.8-10 for his suggestive distinction between Providence and Fortune. I hope I have shown how it is possible to arrive at similar ideas from different sources.

2 The percentage of freemen in the gross population of London cannot be stated with assurance. In 1631 the rulers reported to the Privy Council that 130, 280 lived in the traditional wards (*Remembrancia*, p. 389). This estimate has been criticized as much too low, but it may represent the rulers' conception of legitimate residents, that is citizens and their dependents. If so, they constituted around 40% of the entire population in the early 1630s, when greater London amounted to approximately 320,000. See above, p. 7, note 2 on population.

citizen in mind. Those punished, corrected, supervised, healed, patron-
ized, assisted, and advanced were also citizens. In other words the
freedom determined the limits of control and responsibility within
which tradition was to be preserved. Thus aliens and strangers were
subject to special regulations. Many, probably most, of the poor and
helpless were ignored, brutalized, or driven out. Prostitutes and
vagabonds, and other such degenerates, were regarded as hopeless
because their wills had been surrendered into the hands of evil forces.
Not being in possession of themselves, persuasion was of no avail.
Whippings might encourage the evil spirits to desert a tortured body,
but the number who relapsed into idleness or immorality was notorious;
it was far safer, and easier, to simply banish such people from the City
and be done with it. After all, they were not citizens. Unlike the freemen who might fall victim to bad fortune, they were not subject to the
controls of guild, parish, or wardmote, nor the relief offered by charity
and patronage. Paternalism, then, blended with a parochial concern to
protect and maintain a rather unique community within London, this
was the fundamental attitude of the rulers regarding government. Thus
the abundant concern for the City's orphans is understandable. Thus,
too, there was force and meaning to the common contemporary
phrase, so bland to modern ears, 'the custom of London.'

6

POLITICS AND COMMUNITY

Something of the rulers' spirit was captured by the contemporary dramatist, Thomas Middleton. In 1617 he wrote a panegyric of London, its wealth, its famous merchants, and especially its venerable traditions, epitomized by the annual Lord Mayor's Show. The main business of the day, which preceded all the pageants, was the mayor's journey to Westminster where he gained approval of the sovereign and thus formally entered into his mayoralty, an event Middleton symbolized as entering 'the Castle of Fame'. 'About this Castle of Fame are placed many honourable figures, such as Truth, Antiquity, Harmony, Fame, Desert, Good Works; on the top of the Castle, Honour, Religion, Piety, Commiseration, the works of those whose memories shine in this Castle'.[1] Appropriately enough, Middleton's description of the Lord Mayor's Show was entitled 'The Triumphs of Honour and Industry'. As we have seen, similar outlooks and abundant shared experience forged a mutual identity among all rulers, not just the mayors. This chapter will investigate elements of their shared experience beyond City politics — status, residence, business ties, wealth, family, and friendship connections. These bonds did not exist independently of each other, since often the most intense political participation was accompanied by greater achievement in business, more family ties, and so on. Indeed, there was a close relationship between political rank (élite, notable, leader) and levels of socio-economic prominence.[2]

To begin with status: all the rulers lived in London and all were businessmen, thus according to the canons of Tudor social thought, all were men of rather middling status. But distinct groups existed within this middle stratum of the hierarchy, set off from each other by birth, wealth, and connections. Some were moderately wealthy retailers, others great international merchants; some lived quite modestly and had few possessions, others bought lands in several counties, intermingled with

1 Arthur H. Bullen, ed., *The Works of Thomas Middleton* (1885-6), vii. 304.
2 In the comparisons that follow of élite, notables, and leaders I refer to 141 of the 273 rulers: all 64 élite, all 41 notable councilmen, but none of the notable aldermen, and a randomly selected sample of 36 leaders out of all 118. In comparing the three ranks I dropped the 50 notable aldermen since I already had sufficient aldermen, and because I was more interested in comparing aldermen with councilmen. I worked with only a sample of the leaders, since the research necessary to compare wealth, social status, community and family connections was very laborious. Originally the random sample included only 35 leaders, but I later discovered that one of the 42 notable councilmen should be classified a leader.

the squirearchy, or gained titles. Titles are an obvious reflection of the gradations of status. All the élite except Thomas Skinner became knights, and he only failed because he died a month after beginning his mayoralty, the completion or near completion of which was the usual requirement for knighthood.[1] However, only one leader (Baptist Hicks) and one notable (Roger Jones), and perhaps one other (Thomas Bramley, the haberdasher), achieved knighthood. Forty-nine per cent of the notables and 25 per cent of the leaders were declared armigerous at the London visitation of 1568.[2]

Membership in one of the Inns of Court also carried a certain status. Memberships were honorary, not based on studying or practising the common law, for most of these connections began well after rising in the hierarchy of London government. Thirty-nine per cent of the élite (twenty-five different men) were affiliated with an Inn, but only 17 per cent of the leaders and 17 per cent of the notables.[3] Those interested in formal education might spend some time at Oxford or Cambridge, but university experience had no perceptible impact on subsequent careers in London. Attending a university before settling down in London may have added to family prestige, but in view of the small number who did the ruling class of London took little stock in the universities. Only two of the élite (Henry Billingsley and perhaps William Chester) pretty certainly went to Cambridge, and only one leader, Baptist Hicks. Twenty-eight men with the same names as other rulers appear in the records of Oxford or Cambridge, or both, but even assuming that all are rulers the total is not impressive. Twelve are élite (19 per cent of the élite), eight are notables (20 per cent), eight are leaders (22 per cent).[4]

So far as the rulers themselves were concerned, residence in London generated enormous status. There they began an apprenticeship. There they entered into other associations which might result in a favourable marriage or open the door to City politics. And, of course, London was the centre of their foreign business ventures. In view of their extensive

1 At least that was the case until the 'inflation of honours' of 26 July 1603, when James I knighted all members but one of the Court of Aldermen who were not already knights (A.B. Beaven, *The Aldermen of the City of London*, 2 vols. (1908-13), i. 255-6).

2 The figures are based on those old enough to be so declared in 1568. William A. Shaw, *The Knights of England* (1906); The Harleian Society, *The Visitation of London, 1568*, vols. 1 (1869) and 109-10 (1963).

3 Joseph Foster, *The Register of Admissions to Gray's Inn, 1521-1889* (1889); William H. Cooke ed., *Students Admitted to the Inner Temple, 1547-1660* (1878); W. Paley Baildon, ed., *The Records of the Honourable Society of Lincoln's Inn*, vol. 1: *Admissions, 1420-1799* (1896); H.A.C. Sturgess, ed., *Register of Admissions to the Honourable Society of the Middle Temple*, vol. 1 (1949).

4 John and J.A. Venn, *Alumni Cantabrigienses* (Cambridge, 1922); Joseph Foster, *Alumni Oxoniensis, 1500-1714* (Oxford, 1891-2).

lands in the counties, it is revealing of London's importance to the rulers — and to their own status — that they preferred to live in town.[1] Probably no other group of merchants was in as much evidence there, particularly as shown by their attention to City government. A few found the routine unfruitful and retired to country estates, but not many. The further a man went politically, the less likely he was to retire from London, since business and social connections multiplied with the passing of time. Doubtless some retired from City life because they failed to establish any very profitable connections that would have made staying more interesting. Even the less prestigious rulers, however, mostly stayed in London.

A testimony to the great attraction of London is the fact that few of the men, from élite to leader, were born there. Only twelve of the élite (19 per cent) were certainly or probably born in London, whereas thirty-four (53 per cent) were not, or very likely not.[2] Among the notables and leaders there is less certainty about birthplace, making statistical surveys less useful, yet where the evidence exists the tendency was the same: most were not born in London. Those born in London had a decided edge in two respects essential to successful political advancement. At least at the beginning of their careers, they possessed more ties with families already, or soon to be, involved in civic politics, and they more often secured an apprenticeship with a prominent ruler as a result.[3] In both domestic business and foreign trade apprentices found entry into companies facilitated by their association with patrons. So commonly did patrons advance their protégés in the major trading companies that in 1591 Lord Burghley complained about apprentices becoming members of the Turkey Company even before they could

1 Whenever records of landowning were found, the élite were much more likely to mention county as well as City property. Eighty-eight per cent of the élite mentioned county lands in their wills (or it is recorded in *inquisitions post mortem*), but only 59 per cent of the notables and 67 per cent of the leaders held lands outside London. Ironically the men who might most easily have retired were the ones least likely to do so.

2 Birthplace for the other 28 per cent is uncertain, but probably few were born in London. Place of birth has usually been determined by the residence of a man's father at the time of some particular documentation: a herald's visitation, or the drawing up of a will, for example. Needless to say, this is not a completely reliable guide to the places where their children were born, for there may have been family mobility before or after any of the documents that have survived were compiled. Nonetheless, a number of men took the trouble in their wills to reveal their birthplace, and this confirms that most were not born in London.

3 The names of apprentices and masters are found in the records of the livery companies, usually in apprenticeship registers, or freedom registers, or in the wardens' accounts. To determine family relationships I have relied primarily on wills, heralds' visitations, *inquisitions post mortem,* and Beaven's work. Use has been made of the *DNB* as well, and the unexpected notes in a City minute book or a livery company record that clarifies relationships.

provide any stock or engage in the trade.[1] Undoubtedly ties like these account for the rapid rise of such men as Henry Billingsley, John Braunche, John Garrarde, Henry Rowe, or Nicholas Woodroffe. Twenty-one of the élite, a third of them born in London, served their apprenticeship with a man who was important politically, or soon became so.

But these initial advantages were not indispensable to upward mobility, and certainly not relied on exclusively. Twelve of the élite (36 per cent of those whose masters are known) had masters of no political prominence; at least half, and probably all but one, were not born in London. Still, such early London connections often presaged the ultimate rank attained by the rulers. With few exceptions the masters of the élite were men of greater political and social prominence than those of the notables and leaders. Most notables and leaders served an apprenticeship with political bigwigs, too, though a large minority had masters of no political consequence.

Among their various business and social endeavours overseas trade ranked as one of the most attractive and useful for advancement. Of the twenty-two men named by John Strype as the greatest merchants of the early Elizabethan years, twenty, most of them merchant adventurers, were rulers of London. Interest in foreign trade grew as opportunities increased during the course of the queen's reign; for the Jacobean period it has been estimated that between one-third and one-half of the aldermen had their principal source of income from foreign trade, while perhaps 70 per cent joined in a venture occasionally.[2] In the case of foreign trade, however, as in so many of the rulers' achievements, the associations formed can often be traced back to ties in the livery companies. Rulers commonly married into the families of their liveried brethren. Those whom they remembered most fondly in their wills were fellow liverymen. Liverymen usually served as overseers of each other's estates, and it was the rare ruler who neglected to remember his guild by way of a present, perhaps a silver cup or a memorial dinner. Largely through their livery companies the rulers dispersed charitable donations, to the poor, to schools, to other young merchants. The liveries also acted as trustees for most of the lands and capital endowments left by the rulers. In short, they created a kind of nucleus for other business

1   *CSPD* (1591-94), vol. 239/140.
2   Strype, *Survey*, vol. 2, bk. v. 291; Robert G. Lang, 'The Greater Merchants of London in the Early Seventeenth Century,' D. Phil. thesis (Oxford Univ. 1962), pp. 94-6. The particular trading activities of many rulers are already known; see especially Astrid Friis, *Alderman Cockayne's Project and the Cloth Trade* (Copenhagen and London, 1927); Thomas S. Willan, *The Muscovy Merchants of 1555* (Manchester, 1953); the Lang thesis just cited, and Theodore Rabb, *Enterprise and Empire* (Cambridge, Mass., 1967), especially the bibliography and the appendix.

enterprises. Particular connections were more valuable than others: of the forty-four élite known to have invested in overseas trade, thirty-five (or 80 per cent) belonged to only six livery companies.[1] Among the notables 51 per cent of the investors in foreign trade belonged to the same six liveries; among the leaders 83 per cent. In all the trading associations of the time a significant percentage of members would be from the six liveries, but nothing like the same concentrations, since many members would have had no London livery affiliation. In the Muscovy Company of 1555, for example, only ninety-one of the 201 members (45 per cent) belonged to one of the six.[2]. The significance of this small group is greater when it is recalled that approximately 70 per cent of the men who rose to the highest political standing in the City were affiliated with these six livery companies.[3] Just as suggestive of the concentrated, and doubtless deliberate, character of their connections is the preference of all rulers for three particular trading ventures, the Spanish Company, the Merchant Adventurers Company, and the Muscovy Company; 41 per cent of their investment flowed to these three companies alone, whereas the same three attracted only 29 per cent of all investment.[4] Even among the most active foreign traders who did not belong to the charmed circle of six liveries there are close family and livery connections. The numerous activities of Thomas Cambell, an ironmonger, or Richard Saltonstall, a skinner, testify to that.[5] Cambell was the son-in-law of a very wealthy and politically active councilman and ironmonger, Edward Bright, while Saltonstall was a close friend and associate of an even more prominent councilman, William Towerson, also a skinner, who had a part in several overseas ventures.[6] William Towerson, furthermore, was a close friend business associate, and relative by marriage of John Harbie, another skinner and notable councilman.

Among all ranks of the rulers, level of business achievement was closely proportional to political rank. Considering foreign trade, more

1   The Grocers, Haberdashers, Merchant Taylors, Mercers, Clothworkers and Drapers.   The figures on investment are primarily from Rabb, pp. 233-410, though especially for the period before 1575 it has been necessary to supplement Rabb by reference to the standard printed material on overseas trade.

2   Willan, *Muscovy Merchants,* pp. 75-132.

3   See above, pp. 44-5.

4   See the next chapter for further discussion of the rulers' trading activity, especially Table 5, p. 105 which is the basis for my figures.

5   Cambell was a member of the Spanish, Eastland, Levant, East India, Irish, and French Companies.   Saltonstall was a merchant adventurer, backed a privateering venture, and was a member of the Muscovy, Spanish, Levant, and East India Companies.

6   Towerson's activity was similar to that of Saltonstall: a merchant adventurer, backed a privateering venture, also one of the Frobisher-Fenton voyages, was a member of the Muscovy, Spanish, and Eastland Companies.

of the élite invested (69 per cent) than either notables (44 per cent) or leaders (50 per cent). It did not follow, however, that the greatest businessmen were exclusively the most active politicians, or vice versa. Of the ten most active politically, only four were also among the ten most active traders. Therefore, rather than overlapping extensively in the leadership roles, the élite exhibited some specialization of behaviour — some preferred politics, some trade, a few both — suggesting how little they desired to create a dominant faction capable of enjoying a monopoly of political power and trade connections.

A comparative measure of wealth reinforces the major conclusions regarding the relationship between politics and foreign trade.[1] Subsidy assessments (set according to the value of lands and moveable property) are a useful guide to the various levels of wealth in the City, where £50 and up was the top bracket. Most of the leaders and notables and all the élite fell in this bracket; aldermen and wealthier councilmen were often assessed at over £200. Aldermen in particular were reluctant to admit any man to their court who was not of financial independence, and the most common excuse for rejecting the nomination of a candidate for the aldermanry was insufficiency of estate. From the earliest records of aldermanic elections it had been ordered that the 'wealthier and wiser' men be chosen, and by 1469 a specific requirement existed that his goods, chattels, and expectant debts amount to £1000.[2] By 1525 this qualification was up to 2,000 marks[3] (£1,333) and by the 1640s it was £10,000.[4] No specific valuation was required for councilmen's estates, but substantial levels of wealth were expected. Councilmen were not paid either, and from their ranks came the aldermen.

Two examples can illustrate the variance in personal wealth between men of different political rank. Élite alderman James Harvye, an ironmonger, owned a house with a garden and nine tenements in Lime Street, as well as unspecified lands in the Old Jewry and in the parish

1 As a guide to wealth I have examined three subsidies: for the 1559 subsidy see MS 2859 at the GLMR; for 1572, MS 2942; for 1589 see *The Publications of the Harleian Society*, vols. 109-10 (1963), 148-64. Various local records from the wards, parishes, and livery companies have also been consulted. Two representative ones are an assessment on the assistants of the Ironmongers' Company in 1569 (fo. 76[b] of the Court Book), and a parish assessment for a fifteenth in 1582 collected in St. Olave Jewry (VM, fo. 9[b]). Councilmen, aldermen, and the local leaders always rated higher proportional assessments, as did those about to move into civic positions. All this emphasizes the fact that wealth was a qualification for political service.

2 *Cal. Let.-Book L*, p. 85. This was an order of the Court of Aldermen on 29 July 1469.

3 Rep. 7, fo. 45[b] and Letter-Book N, fo. 287[b].

4 Valerie Pearl, *London and the Outbreak of the Puritan Revolution* (1964), p. 60.

of St. Benet Gracechurch. Outside London he held a manor and other assorted lands in Wiltshire, another manor in Staffordshire, and various lands in Essex, some in Hornechurch near London. A considerable part of his business developed through the Antwerp market, and he purchased a house there. At his death he settled 2,000 marks on each of his five children still unadvanced.[1] In 1572 he had been assessed at £300 towards the subsidy voted in 1571. One of the leaders, Councilman William Chelsham, a mercer, was assessed at £80 for the same subsidy. He had a share in the tenure of five City tenements and shops, in addition to a leasehold in St. Mary-le-Bow. He held a manor in Clapham which he expected to sell for £1,366-13s-4d. He settled £600 on his wife outright, over and above the third portion of his personal estate to which she was entitled. His eldest son had already been given some financial help, that is, had been advanced, but he now received £550; two married daughters were given £200 each, and his only unadvanced child, Magdalen, had £300 set aside for the day of her marriage.[2]

But political rank alone did not determine distribution of wealth among the rulers. Generally the élite were richer than the notables, who in turn were richer than the leaders. But sometimes steep differences existed within the same group. More importantly, the relationship between political power and wealth was close, even fundamental, but it was not rigidly defined around a particular group of men. The men of greatest political power, for example, did not all share the same level of wealth; nor did the very richest exercise a proportionate influence in politics. Considering again the ten most active politically, six appear once, but only once, among the top ten in one of the three subsidies examined; thus only 20 per cent of the richest were simultaneously the most politically active. Conversely, while the richer merchants were more likely to be involved in civic politics,[3] level of wealth had only a loose relationship with political rank. Men of equivalent wealth worked at all levels of city government.

As with other connections, so with family, close relationships existed among all the rulers, while simultaneously there were differences among the particular ranks. More of the élite found wives, and later husbands for their daughters, among the wealthiest mercantile families of London, families that shared interests in the same overseas

1 PCC 39 Rowe.
2 PCC 25 Peter.
3 An exception was Sir Thomas Gresham, who founded the Royal Exchange and was probably the most famous Elizabethan merchant. He never entered City politics. His disinclination is the more surprising since his father and uncle had been aldermen. Extensive crown service doubtless explains his exceptional reluctance.

trading companies, and membership in the small circle of City livery companies. The notables and leaders also normally chose brides from among the families of fellow liverymen, though the tendency seems rather less and was certainly not as concentrated in the circle of six companies. Despite the spectacular success some aldermanic families had in marrying their kin into houses of the aristocracy or squir-earchy,[1] the élite mostly preferred their closest ties with those involved at some level in the politics of the City; the notables were somewhat less inclined, the leaders still less. Ninety-one per cent of the élite had at least one relation who was or became involved in City politics (notables 61 per cent, leaders 53 per cent). Sixty-nine per cent of the élite had more than one (notables 39 per cent, leaders 31 per cent). Eighty-nine per cent of the élite had at least one close friend in civic politics (notables 78 per cent, leaders 64 per cent); seventy-two per cent had more than one (notables 54 per cent, leaders 44 per cent).[2] Each of the three groups had extensive links within each of the other two, but the élite were most often associated with other aldermen, especially other élite. Even the leaders and notables had more of their connections with them than with other notables and leaders, especially where family ties were concerned. All this underlines the importance attached to family by those rulers seeking to make the most of their careers.

One's family became increasingly useful the higher up the political and social ladders one went, which can be illustrated by showing family ties on the Court of Aldermen at a particular time, say in the year 1580.[3] A number of close links developed between several of the twenty-eight men who sat together for part or all of that year. Four could say that they sat with a brother-in-law; three others could point to a son-in-law on the court, and one of them, Alderman Draper, had two sons-in-law with him. One of the three sons-in-law, Alderman Starkye, had been married twice: both his fathers-in-law sat with him during 1580. These close relations among the aldermen of 1580, as well

1 Beaven, *Aldermen of London,* ii. 168 ff. for examples.
2 It is not possible to identify all the family and friends of these men, but their wills mention a number of these ties. See above, p. 94, note 3 for other sources used. Individuals that were both relatives and close friends of other political bigwigs were counted for the statistics here as either a friend or a relative, not both. Percentages may not seem appropriate when based on incomplete data, but the sample sizes seem large enough to assure general accuracy: 84% of the élite left wills, 73% of the notables, 72% of the leaders. Virtually all the élite without a will were found in some visitation, as were 83% of the notables, and 92% of the leaders. It is difficult to see how even complete data would alter the conclusion that leaders and notables had far fewer connections than the élite, thus I have let the figures stand for comparative use.
3 The year was selected because it demonstrated rather more connections than 1560, but rather less than 1600; it was not an untypical year.

as their ties with other aldermen, past and future, can be summarized thus: one was a grandson of an alderman; one married the grand-daughter of an alderman; three were sons of aldermen; nine were sons-in-law of aldermen; two were brothers of aldermen; six were brothers-in-law of aldermen; one married the widow of an alderman; two were fathers of aldermen; seven were fathers-in-law of aldermen; one was a grandfather of an alderman; one's granddaughter married an alderman.

There were other indirect links between members of the court in 1580. The son of Alderman Avenon had married a daughter of Alderman Harvye. Thomas Offley and Nicholas Woodroffe were linked because Offley had been the brother-in-law of former Alderman Stephan Kyrton, who somewhat later became the father-in-law of Woodroffe. Relationships of this kind, based on ties through marriage, were considered as important as more traditional ties of blood, which is clear enough by the deliberate way in which the rulers built up and maintained such connections. It is the more remarkable that the English language has never produced a word which gives concrete recognition to those ties based uniquely on marriage but not blood. Cousin and kin were sometimes used to indicate such relations, and other rather vague connections as well, but those words primarily described blood ties. In order to draw attention to the important ties based on marriage but not blood I have used the word compernupt.[1] Another example is the pair of Alderman Avenon and Alderman Ramsey. Avenon's daughter, Alice, married John Farrington (the brother of Alderman Richard Farrington), and she was referred to in the will of Ramsey as a cousin. Avenon and Ramsey had no blood tie and no very direct links of affinity, yet they considered their tie to be close and important. They were compernupts. Searching out similar links discloses that no fewer than twenty different pairs of men had these compernuptial ties, though some of them may not have been established by 1580.

Such connections as these were especially important because family had so much to do with business success. In the 1590s Alderman Robert Lee took his two sons, Henry and Robert Jr., into the wine-importing business with him. James Cambell, a future alderman, followed his father, Alderman Thomas Cambell, into various enterprises which

---

1 Affinity is not satisfactory either because it usually refers to very close marriage ties, for example, between a husband and his wife's blood relations, or vice versa. Compernupt stretches affinity to encompass those whom the rulers actually recognized as closely linked. Whether they saw these ties as strictly family or not does not matter much; what matters is that they saw themselves closely bound to groups made up partly of blood relations and partly extended affinity connections.

included wine imports and exports of woollens and draperies.[1] The same occurred in domestic companies. George Barne, a future alderman, owed his rise in the Haberdashers Company to his father, also an alderman before him, but his rise in the Company of Mineral and Battery Works was through his father-in-law, Alderman William Garrarde.[2] Through their wills some rulers even assigned to relatives their memberships in overseas trading companies.[3] The older generation of a family was an important source of capitalization to the younger, too, not only because of the traditional dowry, but also the custom of London, whereby one-third of a citizen's estate had to be divided among his orphaned children.[4] One further example will emphasize the instrumental role of the livery companies in nourishing all sorts of connections. Three compernupts — Councilman Richard Springham, future-Councilman Mathew Field, and Geoffrey Duckett, probably a relative of Alderman Lionel Duckett — were each shareholders and directors of the Company of Mines Royal in 1568. They had each married a daughter of Alderman William Lok, mercer, and all three were themselves mercers.[5] Among the thirty directing shareholders of the same company were five other members of the Mercers Company: George Nedham, Francis Nedham, Sir Thomas Revett, Richard Barnes, and the governor of the company, Alderman Lionel Duckett.[6]

But even among the élite some possessed more family connections than others. In Elizabethan London fifteen families stood out because of the sheer number of their marriage ties, their large progeny., and their good fortune in surviving. For these reasons the fifteen were related to more rulers than any other similar group of families. Neither the Pakyntons nor the Whitmores produced Elizabethan aldermen, though the Pakyntons had been represented by an MP, and they married into eight aldermanic families. George Whitmore, son of a wealthy merchant adventurer of Elizabeth's reign, became an alderman in 1621; his family was closely linked to at least seven aldermen. The Gore, Chamberlain, and Quarles families produced Elizabethan councilmen and aldermen, though in three cases the aldermen paid fines instead of

---

1 Lang, 'Greater Merchants', pp. 174-6 and 189-94.
2 Maxwell B. Donald, *Elizabethan Monopolies: The History of the Company of Mineral and Battery Works from 1565 to 1604* (1961), p. 37.
3 For example, the wills of Richard Malorye (PCC 9 Stonarde) and Thomas Whyte (36 Stonarde).
4 Orphanage money was an important indirect contributor to overseas ventures; see Charles H. Carlton, 'The Court of Orphans: A Study in the History of Urban Institutions with Special Reference to London, Bristol and Exeter in the Sixteenth and Seventeenth Centuries', Ph. D. thesis (UCLA, 1970), ch. 6.
5 Maxwell B. Donald, *Elizabethan Copper: The History of the Company of Mines Royal, 1568-1605* (1955), pp. 91-2.
6 Ibid. ch. 3.

serving a normal tenure on the court. The other ten families showed more civic dedication because at least one representative of each rose to become mayor.[1] Each of these fifteen families can be considered the centre of a cluster of closely related families (blood relations), the indirect ties of which (compernupts) ultimately extended to 67 per cent of the élite aldermen, 39 per cent of the notables, and 42 per cent of the leaders.[2] The Offley cluster was certainly the most extensive. In addition to its patriarch, Sir Thomas Offley, the family included his two brothers, Alderman Hugh Offley and Councilman Robert Offley, and three other Offleys, probably his nephews or sons, who were lesser councilmen. Between them the Offleys could boast of relations among twelve aldermanic families and marriage ties with no fewer than nineteen others, including representatives of seven of the other fourteen cluster families.

The fifteen cluster families further illustrate the tendency among the élite for different groups to show specialized behaviour. But it would be wrong to see these fifteen as the most powerful or influential families. The cluster families developed more ties with other eminent families, but they were no more cohesive than many other groups of families. They had no particular unity through trade, wealth, or political activity. Only three of the fifteen ranked in the top fifteen in trade; only three had an equivalent ranking in wealth; five were among the fifteen most active politically. Many other families gained ties to individuals of the highest rank and maintained extended clusters only slightly less impressive than those among the fifteen. At least twenty additional families had direct blood ties with three or more aldermanic families, and their compernupts included still other aldermen and councilmen. Any number of families existed which, when collected together, could show links with two-thirds of the élite or a high percentage of all aldermen and councilmen. Though some important marriages were useful for families of political consequence, nothing as impressive as what the fifteen cluster families arranged was mandatory. Indeed, so far as I can tell from incomplete records, five of the élite lacked connections with other political families, and numerous others had only one or two such ties, not infrequently to the more humble governing families. Even the cluster families absorbed a number of obscure connections, and within most families of consequence there

---

1   The other ten families (with given names of élite aldermen in parentheses) are as follows: Heyward (Rowland), Lee (Robert), Offley (Thomas), Draper (Christopher), Hewet (William), Rowe (Thomas, father of Henry and cousin of William), Lowe (Thomas), Garrarde (William and his son, John), Weld (Humphrey) and Barne (George and his father, George).

2   In working out these figures I counted as compernupts those families that were joined by only one intervening family.

were links with notables and leaders, not just other members of the élite. Similarly the personal friends and business associates of the élite cut across a broad section of London mercantile society, embracing different levels of wealth, trading activity, and political rank.

In conclusion, the rulers shared much beyond their commitment to civic politics: great wealth, high status, similar trading activities, common links of family and friendship, and connections through the same livery companies. Their similar experiences encouraged a sense of community among them, which reinforced their political dominance in the City. This community was distinct from the larger merchant class of London by virtue of certain close ties, but especially because of their commitment to City politics, which in turn drew men and families into the various connections that forged the ruling community. Among the rulers ties varied, but they varied in similar ways for men in the same political rank. Rank was an accurate measure of the quality and extent of other ties. Over the two generations of the queen's reign the community of rulers consisted of 273 men, in a number of different but interlinking families. Within the group a few individuals and a few families stood out as more influential, but they shared both more connections and more intense dedication to the government of London. These greater men never saw themselves as a group apart; they were simply the most prominent among the community of rulers.

7

THE RULERS' ETHIC

Given the close community that they developed in London, the rulers could scarcely prevent signs of their mutual association from appearing beyond City government, in virtually all their other activities. Because so many of them were great merchants, a central question is how much impact did they have on the dramatic growth of trade that began during Elizabeth's reign?[1] Table 5 shows their investments.[2] Naturally, many of the rulers had investments before 1558 and especially after 1603, since the greatest boom in trade followed the queen's death. But to have assessed the investments of all rulers would have meant retrieving the names of rulers before 1558 and after 1603, a task which has been accomplished for the aldermen but did not seem worth the great labour involved for the councilmen. Also, extending the range of the study did not seem advisable in view of the concentration on the 1558-1603 period that has been the main focus elsewhere in this book. Similar considerations suggested how best to represent the companies shown in column 1 of the table. Obviously in showing only the charter members of the Eastland Company a sizable percentage of the company has been neglected, but since so many joined at an unknown date the

---

1 This section on overseas trade draws heavily on the 'List of Names' provided by T.K. Rabb as the Appendix to his *Enterprise and Empire*, in which he has listed all known investors in overseas trading ventures during the period 1575-1630. I have corrected the errors in the 'List' regarding the rulers and gained a few pieces of information not in his book by an exchange of letters with Professor Rabb.

2 Because of the well-known difficulties in distinguishing people of the same name, I cannot claim always to have made the correct choices when trying to identify the rulers among Rabb's list of investors. Fortunately there were not many cases where two people had the same name, either one of whom could have been the man I was trying to identify. The two John Marshes (see p. 107, note 2 below), two Thomas Wilfords, two John Stones, three Richard Reynoldses and Richard Youngs, and the four Richard Wrights (two of them councilmen) were problematical. Most namesakes were not difficult, however, for City records made it quite easy to distinguish between Alderman Thomas Lowe, a late Elizabethan haberdasher, and Councilman Thomas Lowe, a rather earlier vintner. A greater problem arose with a man like Thomas Heaton, a prominent mercer and leader in London during the 1560s, 70s and 80s. In all likelihood he was the merchant adventurer, privateer, and Russia Merchant who flourished at the same time, but was he also the MP of 1593 (not of London), the Spanish Company member in 1604, or the investor in the Irish Company of 1611? Lacking a will or other evidence of death or retirement, I have had to guess in such cases, and my general rule has been to avoid classifications – like the three questionable ones for Heaton – that were subject to some strong doubt. Because I was looking for the impact of London's rulers on overseas trade, I tried to raise as many doubts as possible in order to avoid overstating the case.

TABLE 5: OVERSEAS INVESTMENT OF THE RULERS

	Number of rulers who invested	Total company membership to 1604[4]	Percentage of members who were rulers
Muscovy Co., 1575-1600[1]	35	100	35
Venice Co., 1583-92	4	14	29
Drake venturers, 1587	5	21	24
Eastland Co., 1579	14	66	21
Levant Co., 1581-1603	24	133	18
Staple merchants[2]	3	18	17
Merchant adventurers[2]	34	269	13
Spanish Co., 1577	50	385	13
East India Co., 1599-1603	37	303	12
Company of Mineral and Battery Works, 1565-1604	10	77	13
Frobisher and Fenton venturers, 1576-82	13	121	11
Barbary Co., 1585-97	4	47	9
Company of Mines Royal, 1568-1605	4	57	7
Other ventures[3]	25	352	7
Privateers	24	389	6
Irish Co. (Munster), 1586-92	2	78	3
Gilbert venturers, 1578 & 1583	2	146	1
Northwest Passage Co., 1584	–	22	–
Cavendish venturers, 1586	–	4	–
Senegal Co., 1588	–	22	–
Gosnold venturers, 1602	–	5	–
Guiana Companies, 1594 & 1604	–	8	–
Totals and average percentage	290	2637	11

Footnotes on p. 106

charter was the only certain source for the Elizabethans. The dates for the Company of Mines and the Company of Mineral and Battery Works were extended slightly beyond the queen's death to accord with logical mileposts in the companies' development. But the Spanish Company Charter of 1604, with its large list of names, was avoided; distilling out the names of the rulers would have meant going far beyond the Elizabethan setting, since some would not have appeared in City politics until years later.

Most ventures launched before Queen Elizabeth's death were of interest to some of the rulers. But Table 5 shows that just over three-quarters of the investment was drawn to only one-third of the ventures (the seven with more than twenty rulers each). There may be a slight distortion here, in view of the incompleteness of records for the Venice Company, the Drake venturers and the Staplers Company. On the other hand incompleteness also characterizes the records of the Merchant Adventurers Company, the privateers, the miscellaneous collection of industrial enterprises (known as 'other' in Rabb's study), and to a lesser extent the Levant Company.[1] As a result, the concentration of investment among these already popular ventures may also be underestimated. The affiliation of the rulers with the Merchant Adventurers Company is almost certainly too low, since that link was traditional, and, before the 1570s, was one of only three overseas trading associations available to the rulers. John Strype asserted that there were 327 merchants in London at the time of Thomas Lodge's mayoralty (1562-3, not 1561 as Strype says), and even after allowing for the Staplers Company and the Muscovy Company a large number must have been merchant adventurers.[2] Strype named the twenty-two men considered to be the

1 Rabb, pp. 142-64 on completeness of the records.

2 *Survey of London and Westminster* (1720), vol. 2, bk. v.291; T.S. Willan estimated as many as 43 of the 201 charter members of the Muscovy Company were probably merchant adventurers also, whereas no more than 26 were ever associated with the Staplers Company; *Muscovy Merchants*, pp. 23-24.

Notes to Table 5, p. 105

1 Apparently the rulers were increasingly keen on the Muscovy Company with the passage of time, for of the 201 original members of 1555 only 47 (23 per cent) were or became rulers; Willan, *Muscovy Merchants*, pp. 75-132.

2 Since it was not possible to determine easily how many were members before 1604 and how many after, the figures here are for the entire 1575-1630 period, meaning that the percentage of Elizabethans alone is uncertain. Further uncertainty exists because the whole number of merchant adventurers and staplers is not established for the period.

3 For a description of these see Rabb, *Enterprise and Empire* pp. 163-4. As with the merchant adventurers and staplers, these figures are for the entire 1575-1630 period.

4 Most of the figures in this column are shown by Rabb, ibid pp. 104-6, 147-64; otherwise they are derived from the 'List of Names'.

greatest merchants of the time (twenty of whom were rulers), and from petitions to the crown in the *Calendar of State Papers Domestic* it is possible to identify most as merchant adventurers. Also suggestive of the great number of rulers trading as merchant adventurers is the charter of 1564.[1] It lists forty-nine members, and thirty-two (65 per cent) were or became London rulers. Twenty-four assistants were named to rule the company with the governor, John Marshe,[2] and sixteen of them (67 per cent) were or became rulers. Table 5 emphasizes formal trading companies and is mostly concerned with the second half of the Elizabethan period. After 1575 the appetites of a great many merchants for foreign venturing had been aroused, but in the earlier period the London rulers had an even greater impact. A very careful study of the early trade to Morocco, which began in the 1550s, shows that it was largely in the hands of London rulers, especially the cloth exporters.[3] Similarly, the Guinea venture of 1553 was undertaken by thirty-four men, at least twenty-one of whom (62 per cent) were London rulers.[4] These remarks suggest that the rulers' breadth of trading interests may be underestimated in Table 5.

Certain patterns in the rulers' investment emerge from a study of the table. The most popular companies, whether measured by company size or by percentage of rulers among the members, were mostly concerned with trade and trade only, not colonization. Nor did the rulers have much interest in exploration for its own sake, and still less in glory, national interest, missionary activity, or rivalry with Spain that

1 For the charter, George Cawston and Augustus H. Keane, *The Early Chartered Companies, A.D. 1296-1858* (1896), pp. 254-77.

2 Since I have just mentioned the difficulties involved in distinguishing namesakes, these can be illustrated here by the two John Marshes. Both of them were Spanish merchants in 1577 (Rabb, p. 338). One of them was a mercer and a merchant adventurer (and several times governor of the company) who also served as the common serjeant of London, 1547-63 (Rep. 11, fos, 320, 424; Rep. 14, fo. 186; Rep. 15, fo. 197b). It was probably the same man who was a charter member of the Muscovy Company, the governor of the Spanish Company in 1577, the MP (Willan, *Muscovy Merchants*, p. 112), and the undersheriff of London, 1563-6 (Rep. 14, fo. 201b). All these assignments are made on the assumption of a fairly significant age gap between the two Marshes: one died in 1579 (PCC 2 Bakon), the other was apparently still alive in 1609 as a member of the Virginia Company. This assumption is threatened by the discovery that one was also City solicitor, 1563-81 (CLRO, Research Paper, Box 4.23). I believe the identifications can be justified, however, along with the others made by Willan, if it is also assumed that after the older Marshe died in 1579 the City solicitorship was kept in his name for two more years, or given to his namesake for two years - not an inconceivable possibility at all, especially if the two Marshes were related, as they almost certainly were.

3 Thomas S. Willan, *Studies in Elizabethan Foreign Trade* (Manchester, 1959), pp. 94-162.

4 Willan, *Muscovy Merchants*, p. 27 n. 4.

did appeal more to gentlemen investors.[1] Nor were they as much interested in North America as one might expect.[2] They were not especially keen to rub shoulders with their social betters, the gentry, as is shown by their low membership in the ventures of great interest to gentlemen: Munster, Gilbert, Cavendish, Gosnold, and Guiana. With a few conspicuous exceptions, only a few promoted industrial companies. Within the 'for trade only' group, however, where they felt most at home, the rulers displayed great versatility. They traded from the Baltic to the Mediterranean, and from Spain to the Far East. The diversity of their trade was equally impressive, for they continued in the older lines with western Europe — largely exporting undressed cloths and importing wine — while simultaneously reaching out for the currants from the Levant, sugar from Morocco, naval stores of Russia, and spices of Asia. In the case of Russia especially they exported finished cloths for the first time on a large scale. They were not afraid to take great risks, and they seemed able to absorb losses. They were not a bit intimidated by company regulations which required members to devote themselves to an exclusive line of trade. In all these respects, except perhaps the lack of interest in North America, the rulers behaved in a fashion typical of other London and English merchants.

There are some differences, however, in the patterns of cross-memberships. Professor Rabb pointed out that almost half of the Eastland merchants traded to Spain, and nearly 40 per cent of the Muscovy merchants also traded to Spain.[3] Among the rulers these two rather surprising connections are even sharper: 79 per cent of the Eastland and 51 per cent of the Muscovy merchants traded to Spain in the Elizabethan period alone. Perhaps these figures reflect the greater novelty of investing before 1604, by comparison with 1604-30, and no doubt the greater flexibility of the London rulers. By comparison with other investors the Elizabethan rulers did have a greater penchant for the Spanish trade, especially those in the Eastland, Muscovy, or Merchant Adventurers Companies. Among the rulers in the Levant Company there was also a greater than average connection with the

---

1   Rabb, pp. 35-69 on motives.

2   No Londoner is known to have invested in the Newfoundland fisheries until 1610, and London merchants and ships had only a small part in this trade anyway; Gillian T. Cell, *English Enterprise in Newfoundland, 1577-1660* (Toronto, 1969), pp. 5-6, 55.   One ship was probably contributed to a joint colonization and walrus-fishing venture in the late 1590s by ruler John Watts, but it is not certain that he still owned the ship;   David B. Quinn, 'England and the St. Lawrence, 1577-1602', in *Merchants and Scholars: Essays in the History of Exploration and Trade,* ed. John Parker (Minneapolis, 1965), pp. 131-3.

3   P.108.

Merchant Adventurers Company, demonstrating again the continuing vitality of the latter. The Levant Company itself stands out rather differently, for, considering only the rulers, it was more inclined to consist of Eastland venturers and merchant adventurers, and less of Muscovy and Spanish merchants.

But there are more substantial points to be made about the uniqueness of the Elizabethan rulers as investors. Of the 273 rulers only 143 (or 52 per cent) invested at least once, and 108 (40 per cent) had more than one investment. Of the 143 investors 44 (31 per cent) were élite, 49 (34 per cent) were notables, and 50 (35 per cent) were leaders. The higher a man's political rank, the more likely he would be to invest: 69 per cent of the élite invested, 54 per cent of the notables, and 42 per cent of the leaders. The more prominent men also invested more often: 56 per cent of the élite, 40 per cent of the notables, and 31 per cent of the leaders invested in more than one enterprise.[1]

These figures suggest some interesting comparisons with those for all investors over the 1575-1630 period. In that period only 28 per cent invested more than once,[2] as against 40 per cent of the Elizabethan rulers. Considering only the merchants from the 1575-1630 period, the figure for multiple investment is still only 35 per cent. Considering the most prominent merchants, the multiple investments of the rulers are also more impressive: 82 per cent of the élite who invested were multiple investors, against 80 per cent of the merchant-knights over the period 1575-1630. It should be emphasized that the Elizabethans had fewer opportunities for multiple investing, since fewer companies were available.[3]

It begins to appear that the rulers had quite a dramatic impact on the overseas trade of England, despite lacking the same opportunities as those who succeeded them, and even though their investment preceded the period of most abundant investment.[4] Their contribution can be placed in even sharper perspective by considering just the Elizabethan

1 The figures can be summarized as follows:

	one investment	more than one
Elite	69%	56%
Notable aldermen	62%	42%
Notable Councilmen	44%	37%
Leaders	42%	31%

2 Rabb, p. 123.

3 Twenty-two of the eventual thirty-six categories of companies were available by about 1604 (Rabb, pp. 147-64). Nine of the thirty-six were only available before 1604, but fourteen only after; the others were available both before and after.

4 The greatest peak was the first fifteen years of James I's reign (Rabb, pp. 70-91).

period. It was in this early, formative period of investing that the contribution of the rulers was concentrated. Just over a quarter of the total investment for the period 1575-1630 was made in the years 1575-1603, and this initial push was provided mostly by the rulers of London.[1] This conclusion rests on the discovery that while the rulers represented a very small proportion of all the investing merchants (10 per cent at most), an assessment of their contribution — both qualitative and quantitative — shows that they were the single most influential group of investors.[2] If we assume, as we must in the

1 Rather more than a quarter of the total was invested before 1604 if the whole Elizabethan period is considered. Rabb, p. 70 estimates that there may have been as many as 500 investors before 1575 (8% of the total for 1575-1630); perhaps there were even more in view of the many uncounted merchant adventurers.

2 Rabb has identified the 3933 merchants and merchant-knights who invested in the period 1575-1630 (p. 27). Of the overall number of investers (6336), 1152 (18%) were not classified by status, and because half of them were MPs (Rabb, p. 178) I shall assume that 45% were merchants: the MP half, 15% merchants; the others, 76%. The 15% estimate is based on Neale (*Elizabethan House of Commons*, p. 147) and Douglas Brunton and Donald H. Pennington, *Members of the Long Parliament* (Cambridge, 1954), p. 53. Both list merchant MPs at about 15%. Assuming that 45% of the unclassified were merchants means adding in another 518. Next, some allowance must be made for the incompleteness of the data Rabb used; he suggests that one-quarter of the investors may not appear in his 'List of Names' (p. 11), which means, assuming that the unknown merchants constituted the same proportion of all investors as the known merchants (75.9, rounded to 76%), including a further 1605, for an adjusted total of 6056 merchants and merchant-knights. We can then assume that roughly half these were Elizabethan, or 3028. This is partly conjecture, but it is supported by comparable evidence: W.K. Jordan, *Charities of London* (1960), p. 50 showed that the number of merchant donors he studied between 1551 and 1600 (715) was practically the same as in the 1601-30 period (680). Finally, the most difficult correction of all is to estimate the percentage of London merchants from the English merchants. All the evidence suggests that most merchant investors had their principal headquarters in London, but what does most mean: 60%? 75%? 90%? I have chosen 80% on the grounds that London accounted for 80% of the entire English customs income at this time. (A.E. Millard, 'The Import Trade of London, 1600-40', Ph.D. thesis (Univ. of London, 1956)). This suggests there were approximately 2422 London merchants who were investing during the Elizabethan period. These figures suggest that the investing rulers constituted 6% of the London mercantile investors.

There is another way to estimate the number of investing merchants. Using annual admissions to trading companies as a guide to annual investment, Rabb suggests that around 1159 merchants were admitted between 1575-1603 (p. 72), and if an enlargement is allowed for the earlier Elizabethan period (based on Rabb's own estimate, p. 145) the corrected number would be 1459. In this case the 143 investing rulers would be 10% of the total.

A third estimate can be made from a contemporary's own guess: Sir Edwin Sandys in 1604 said there were between five and six thousand 'people free of the various companies in England' (Rabb, pp. 157-8). If, following Rabb's advice, we take the lower figure to compensate for Sandy's prejudices, then correct for merchants only (76%), and then for London merchants only (80%), we have 3040 London merchants. Assuming all of them invested in overseas trade, the rulers were 5% of the merchant investors.

The third estimate may be too low, since it rests on the assumption that all members of companies were also investors; the second may well be too high,

absence of fuller evidence to the contrary, that one investor equalled one share, then the rulers contributed no more than 10 per cent, on a per-company basis. But it has already been shown that the rulers were more likely than other investors to belong to more than one company. Moreover Table 5 showed that the membership of at least eleven different companies consisted of more than 10 per cent rulers. Then there is the evidence of their role in instigating such ventures as the Guinea and Barbary trades, the Muscovy Company, and the Merchant Adventurers Company.[1] At its origin the Company of Mineral and Battery Works was composed of 16 per cent rulers; the Company of Mines Royal had 14 per cent. The charter of the Spanish Company in 1577 showed 13 per cent; the Eastland Company charter of 1579 21 per cent; the second charter of the Levant Company in 1593 32 per cent; and the original members of the East India Company in 1599 were 20 per cent rulers.[2] Perhaps the most decisive evidence of all is their contribution as directors and governors of the various Elizabethan ventures. Here are the figures: Merchant Adventurers Company in 1564 64 per cent, Muscovy Company to about 1600 74 per cent, Mineral and Battery Works 60 per cent, Mines Royal 13 per cent, Spanish Company 50 per cent, Eastland Company 75 per cent, Levant Company to 1604 16 per cent, and East India charter members 40 per cent. As impressive as they are the statistics understate the rulers' contribution, because although only 13 per cent of the governors of the Mines Royal were rulers, the chief officer for many years was Alderman Lionel Duckett. In the Mineral and Battery Works Alderman Rowland Heyward was the governor for most of the Elizabethan period.

since records of admission are not complete and because it assumes all the investors were encompassed by official membership, leaving no allowance for the hidden investment of individuals or groups through broker-members. The first estimate may be faulty because of the notion that 80% of the Elizabethan merchant investors were Londoners. Had I figured Londoners as only 50% of that group, the rulers would have been 9% of the London merchant total; if 90%, then only 5%.

1 See above, pp. 105; 107, notes 1, 3, & 4.
2 Donald, *Elizabethan Monopolies,* pp. 71-2 and *Elizabethan Copper,* p. 242; for the Spanish and Eastland Companies see Table 5 above; the Levant charter is in Richard Hakluyt, *The Principal Navigations* (Glasgow, 1903-5), vi. 73-92. Even before the first charter of the East India Company in December 1599 there were 130 members affiliated together (from Rabb's 'List of Names') who must be seen as the instigators of the company. The 20% figure shown represents the proportion of rulers among this original group of 130. Among the 217 charter members the rulers still constituted a healthy 14%; Sir George Birdwood and William Foster, eds., *The Register of Letters, Etc. of the Governour and Company of Merchants of London Trading into the East Indies, 1600-1619* (1893), pp. 163-89. Because the names of the rulers were determined only for the period 1558-1603, the figures for the East India Company are probably too low because they do not allow for the original members who do not prove to be rulers until after 1603.

Nine out of eleven chief officers of the Muscovy Company were aldermen of London.[1]

Perhaps only the extent of their concerted involvement is very surprising, in view of the prominent position the rulers held in Elizabethan England. But it is worth insisting on this point in order to evaluate properly both the rulers' contribution as well as their motives for participating. It has been decisively shown by Professor Rabb that the gentry in England made a timely and significant contribution to the economic growth of England, that without their approximately one-quarter interest, which they mustered mostly during the time of James I, the future commercial and industrial supremacy of England might not have been realized at all, or certainly not as soon. As important as the gentry's contribution was, how much more vital was that of the 143 investing rulers of Elizabethan London. Their effort was under-taken in the earliest stages of development, before investment was fashionable enough to attract wide support from the landed classes. And if the gentry gave momentum to the whole movement, that was easy enough in the prosperous Jacobean years; risks were greater during the uncertain years of slump and recession which characterized the 1580s and 1590s.[2]

Why did such a few men take such an extraordinary interest in commercial investment, and what is the significance of their connection with the government of London? An answer to both questions has already been advanced by one writer, but he was not in a position to press his tentative insight to a conclusion. He noticed that among the charter members of the Muscovy Company of 1555 'at least 28. . . were or became aldermen of London and 16 of them reached the position of Lord Mayor.' But, he reasoned, 'this was perhaps less a sign of cohesion within the group than a sign of the wealth and standing of individual members of it.'[3] Yet it is precisely this 'cohesion within the group' that goes to the heart of the matter. It explains their greater than average interest in investment, their many overlapping connections in different companies, their consistent desire to initiate various ventures, and the indomitable spirit with which they managed nearly all enterprises. This concern for group cohesiveness suggests something rather different about the motives of merchant investment, something that went beyond simple gain, for gain alone need not be

[1] For Duckett see Donald, *Elizabethan Copper*, pp. 43-7 and *passim;* for Heyward Donald's *Elizabethan Monopolies*, especially pp. 35-9; on the nine Muscovy governors Thomas S. Willan, *The Early History of the Russia Company, 1553-1603* (Manchester, 1956), pp. 285-6.

[2] Rabb, pp. 68-71 for the background.

[3] Willan, *Muscovy Merchants*, p. 15.

pursued by cohesive groups. Certainly some gains are enhanced by co-operative effort, and the joint-stock company was an ideal instrument. But the rulers embraced both the joint-stock company and the traditional regulated company (in which indivuduals or partnerships traded with their own capital, instead of shared wealth as in the joint-stock organization). For the rulers gain was an initial requirement for the more distant goal of civic supremacy — a goal that was reached only after years of gathering wealth, building status and reputation, accumulating wide business and political experience, and, of course, the right sort of connections.

But the sixteenth century, in addition to being a time of commercial growth, was also an age of faith, though one punctuated by controversy. Having observed the rulers managing their material affairs, it would seem appropriate to notice their more spiritual concerns as well. Between the mundane and the spiritual spheres there was a profound harmony because in each the rulers acted upon similar assumptions, assumptions that reveal even more about their remarkable community. Perhaps no aspect of the rulers' lives excites as much curiosity as their religious attitudes. How religious were they? Was there anything in their religious beliefs and behaviour that was characteristic of all the rulers? To what extent were they separated by different creeds? To the first question more than one contemporary might have replied 'not very', and gone on to explain, in answer to the second, that the only shared element in all the rulers' experience was the desire for gain. 'London lickpenny' had long been a familiar figure and one readily recognized by Elizabethans. Speaking specifically of the rulers, Bishop Aylmer, vastly disappointed because the aldermen had rebuffed a scheme to dramatically increase (and pay for) the number of preachers in the City, said words to the effect that 'unless the Lords [of the Privy Council] wrote directly unto them, to let them know it was the Queen's pleasure, and theirs, little would be done in it, and so a good design overthrown by the might of mammon'.[1]

And yet there can be no doubt that these were religious men. Their testaments, for example, all begin in the same way, 'In the name of God, Amen', and go on to settle their accounts, spiritual and worldly, after the same pattern. 'First I commit and commend myself wholly unto almighty God, my merciful father, by and through the means of mine alone saviour, Jesus Christ. . .'[2] Perhaps it is unjustifiable to assume deep religious views from conventional statements, but such

---

1   John Strype, *Historical Collections of the Life and Acts of John Aylmer* (Oxford, 1821), p. 57.
2   Alderman Nicholas Backhouse (PCC 26 Arundell).

formulae may have been used precisely because they best embodied profound convictions. What was expressed concisely by one might be embroidered into an elaborate credo by another.

> First because my soul and spirit is the chief part of me and came from above I commend the same to the father of spirits, God Almighty, distinguished in three persons, to wit, father, son and holy ghost, but one in deity or godhead, most humbly beseeching the same god of his infinite mercy to pardon and forgive the infinite number of my sins, hoping and believing most assuredly in my heart that albeit my grievous offenses have deserved the intolerable curse of God and everlasting torments of hell, yet through and only through the obedience, bitter passion and death of my sweet saviour, Jesus Christ, I shall not only be fully and freely acquitted and discharged from all, both from the punishments and faults, but also I shall be reputed righteous through his righteousness layed and clothed upon me, and so finally I shall inherit the unspeakable joys of the kingdom of heaven, for he the lord of glory which knows not sin was pleased to be made the price and ransom for my sins. And like as my sins were laid upon him to his death, so his righteousness shall be imputed to me for my everlasting life and salvation. Secondly, for that my body is from beneath of the base substance of the earth whence it came and whither it must return, I therefore commit and commend it to the ground . . . where my said body shall remain a corruptable lump until the last day, at what time I believe it shall be raised up again a spiritual body joined again to my soul, clothed with incorruption and immortality and made like to the glorious body of my saviour, Christ, and my merciful redeemer shall then be my most gracious judge, and from thenceforth I shall be over with the Lord in the kingdom of heaven accompanied with his blessed angels and saints in such joys as the eye of man hath not seen, the ear of man hath not heard, the tongue of man cannot express nor his heart able fully to conceive, which unexpressable mercies and everlasting blessedness I most humbly beseech the Lord to grant me for his great name's sake, and for Jesus Christ's sake, my only saviour, Amen. . .[1]

The work of Professor Jordan on charitable giving during the early modern era in England has established an invaluable point of reference from which to examine all the attitudes of the Elizabethan rulers, especially the religious ones. In most respects both their impulse to charity and the tangible results that flowed from their inspiration were similar if not identical to those of the London merchants as a whole over the period 1480-1660. But their charitable giving elaborates on the uniqueness of the rulers in the context of the mercantile rank.[2] Their bequests reinforce what has been a central theme of this book, that the rulers took London to be the centre of their lives, and from London they drew both their existence and their identity. It is certainly proper to point out how national the scope of London's charity was; that just

---

1   Alderman William Romeney (PCC 42 Wood).
2   The remarks which follow take their point of departure from Wilbur K. Jordan, *Philanthropy in England, 1480-1660: A Study of the Changing Pattern of English Social Aspirations* (1959) and *The Charities of London*.

under a third of all benefactions in England came from London; that London sources probably provided as much as a quarter of what accrued to the counties beyond Middlesex and London, and that over a third of the greater and lesser merchants of London (37.8 per cent) gave outside London itself.[1] But there was a close relationship between these extra-Middlesex gifts and the birthplace of the donor, because, in cases where the birthplace is known, two-thirds of the donors supported the particular counties where they were born.[2] The importance of London emerges in the following comparison. Since most of London's merchants were not born in London (only 9.22 per cent), it is not surprising that nearly two-fifths of them should have given outside London; yet, although fewer than 10 per cent of the merchants were born in London, 69.05 per cent of their charitable giving was directed there.[3] Moreover, 95.15 per cent of their contributions to municipal betterments went to London, 90.22 per cent of what they gave towards religious purposes, 87.70 per cent of what went to social rehabilitation, 65.96 per cent of the educational donation, and 60.96 per cent of the wealth assigned to poor relief.[4]

Professor Jordan has suggested that the Reformation severely altered the charitable outpourings of London's merchants, that there was a shift in emphasis from personal piety and ecclesiastical support to such concerns as the relief of the poor, social rehabilitation, and education. These are important and probably incontrovertible conclusions, but when he distinguishes between the 'religious' and 'secular' applications of charity he draws a line that was not apparent to the sixteenth-century mind. Fasting, the frequency of praying, even outside church and especially at meetings of political assemblies; the continued recognition of saints and observation of traditional holidays; compulsory church attendance; festivals, triumphs, and public thanksgivings after deliverance from plague or foreign enemy; rates of interest; the often savage harshness of judicial punishments; the preponderance in printed books of devotional literature; the overwhelming interest in,

1 Jordan, *Charities*, pp. 308, 316. The figures taken from Jordan here and below are for the period 1480-1660.

2 Ibid. pp. 426-7.

3 Ibid. pp. 317-18, 308; the figure 9.22% is based on the approximate one-third whose place of birth is known. Because I have not calculated the rulers' donations by county, I am unable to suggest how they compared with all London merchants. An impression, based on samplings among the élite, is that the wealthier the ruler the more he was inclined to support London and other counties, but that in total amounts their charity was even more heavily devoted to London, that is, more than the 69% that was the contribution of all London merchants during the period 1480-1660. In that respect it may be significant that around 19% of the élite were born in London (see above, pp. 93-4), as opposed to 8.44% for all Jordan's greater merchants; see *Charities*, p. 316.

4 Ibid. p. 309.

and reference to, the Bible; a revitalized belief in witches and the resiliency of other popular superstitions; the general lack of credence for a Copernican cosmology, even among many scholars; the continued strength of theological and ethical studies at the universities and among the humanists; the proximity between physicians and priests, and the survival of teleology in history writing are all suggestive of how much of daily secular life was still invested with religious significance. It is difficult to see how it could be otherwise with charity. John Stow was certainly in no doubt about the intimate, though mysterious connection between religion and charity, and the vital stimulation given to both by such cities as London. 'At once the propagation of Religion, the execution of good policie, the exercise of Charity, and the defence of the countrey, is best performed by townes and Cities: and this ciuill life approcheth nearest to the shape of that misticall body whereof Christ is the head, and men be the members'.[1]

The religious posture of the rulers was based on an intricate blend of attitudes, not separable into distinct categories. There was a unity to their thinking and behaviour, an ineffable but acknowledged connection between civic authority, social rank, and responsibility, not to mention the mysteries of God and salvation. The religious implications are especially obvious in considering charity for educational purposes. Grammar schools enjoyed a phenomenal growth due to the benevolence of London merchants. Several rulers (and many other merchants too) made bequests in their wills for Oxford and Cambridge, occasionally specifying colleges, and nearly always the legacy was for 'poor divinity students'. In all likelihood their purpose was to help dispel ignorance in order to spread God's truth, especially in view of the well-known Puritan leanings of Sidney Sussex and Emmanuel Colleges, supported by a number of rulers. Indeed, what was the purpose of learning in Tudor England if not, in the broadest sense, religious? Regarding care of the poor the evidence is less explicit, but it is there nonetheless. Countless hundreds perhaps thousands of poor men and women gained relief at funerals, in the form of a mourning robe or a cash gift. Whether the prayers of two or three score paupers were quite as effective as those once offered by two or three chantry priests was perhaps uncertain, but the motivation of the merchant seems similar in each case. In addition to joining in prayers, the mourners were often treated to, and intended to be enlightened by, a burial sermon by 'some godly preacher' for whom the testator had left a bequest.

Poor relief itself is a topic that requires further study, not least because there would seem to be important religious feelings manifested

---

[1] *Survey*, ed. Charles L. Kingsford (Oxford, 1908), ii. 199.

in the act and manner of giving relief. Professor Jordan has pointed out the mixed and complicated motivations that stimulated charitable benevolence, stressing not only the greater resources available through mercantile wealth and the intensely greater need because of the obvious increase in poverty and its implicit threats to social order, but also' the greater sensitivity to poverty that manifested itself in what has been called the Protestant ethic, which consisted of a feeling of shame in the face of poverty, a sense of duty to help the poor by enlarging their opportunities, pride in having done so, and unashamed self-righteousness in besting the Romanists, whose evil ways contributed to poverty in the first place.[1] While we must defer for a moment an evaluation of the international Protestant Reformation as it affected the rulers, there can be no doubt that by the reign of Elizabeth Protestantism had made significant advances in London and among the rulers. And whatever else may be said about the Protestant impact on the rulers, their wills reveal their full consciousness of the doctrine of election. It would not seem unreasonable to argue then that the rulers understood that they were justified by faith alone, that they denied salvation depended either on good works, like charity, or on a man's worldly condition. If even prostitutes and vagabonds were redeemable in the sight of God, surely London's rulers could grant them no less respect.

But there are reasons for wondering whether such conclusions tell quite all of the story; in so far as they provide a general framework for understanding they have a claim on our attention, but to explain the rulers' charitable motives they plainly do not go far enough. Two things in particular require further amplification: the sort of people to whom the rulers gave their charity, and the rulers own understanding, in religious terms, of the significance of their giving. One thing that becomes clear after even a cursory look at Elizabethan society is that the poor who received charity were a rather special group, not what were later recognized as the 'hard-core poor': the masterless men, prostitutes, pimps ('bawds'), most beggars including some poor students and play actors, many prisoners, and the numerous classifications of vagabonds or rogues, from 'Abraham Men' to the 'Walking Morts'.[2] It was not on such ilk that the respectable munificence of merchant princes was expended.[3] These wretched folk were ignored, that is from the point of view of charity. Those deemed able to work were whipped if they were unwilling. Those unable to work because of bad health were sent to

---

1 Jordan, *Philanthropy*, ch. 6.
2 R.H. Tawney and Eileen Power, *Tudor Economic Documents,* 3 vols. (1924), iii. 407 ff.
3 Jordan made no attempt to classify the various groups of the poor, or to suggest which did and did not receive some form of charity.

one of the hospitals to recover; upon release either they worked or were whipped and sent on their way.[1] Lacking a thorough study of the lower ranks of London's society, one can be guided only by impressions, but it seems that the poor were the more likely to receive charity if they possessed some proximate link with the merchant donors. So often, when their anonymity drops away, the recipients of charity are householders (who, unlike the very poorest, were assessed for subsidies and other levies), merchants' servants, apprentices, artisans, the retailer down on his luck, debtors, orphaned children and unmarried daughters of London freemen, unsuccessful fellow guildsmen, and the aspirant merchants (the 'poor young men' who benefited from the loan funds established through the livery companies).

There is a very definite discrimination at work in all sixteenth-century poor relief, so obvious and acceptable to contemporary merchants as to preclude their mentioning it, but it was exercised and can be recognized in the clear (and statutory) preference for the poor who worked. Rarely the inherent bias was made explicit: Alderman Gourney provided relief for poor prisoners, but not those who held 'heretical' or 'superstitious opinions'; he also refused to support debtors.[2] Those who did work might find other opportunities awaiting them. Alderman Chamberlyn in 1562 successfully petitioned the Court of Aldermen to find three children in the poorhouses who might be bound as apprentices to one John Dawberie, to learn the ironmonger's craft.[3] On the other hand the drifters, unattached and unemployed, were considered a menace, and while the constables harried them out of the wards, the Court of Aldermen took recognizances of landlords (at £20 each) not to fill their vacancies with poor beggars.[4] The aldermen also supervised the vestry officers who were charged to visit abodes of the poor at least fortnightly to determine whether they could move on.[5] The increasing relief of poverty after the Reformation by means of the endowment may also have favoured the respectable poor, since endowments were usually administered through the guilds, hence by the greater merchants already so conscious of their own group and its mercantile associations. This haughty narrowness of the merchants was recognized by the popular writers; here is Robert Crowley speaking of almshouses (hospitals).

1   Tawney and Power, *Documents,* ii. 335-9 and E.M. Leonard, *The Early History of English Poor Relief* (Cambridge, 1900), pp. 22-40, 95-101.

2   PCC 35 Cobham.

3   Rep. 15, fo. 106.

4   Rep. 17, fo. 427[b].

5   Jour. 20, pt. 2, fos. 323-23[b].

A Marchaunte, that longe tyme hadde bene in straunge landis,
Returned to his contrey, whiche in Europe standes.
And in his returne, hys waye laye to passe
By a Spittlehouse, not farre from where his dwelling was.
He loked for this hospitall, but none coulde he se;
For a lordely house was builte where the hospitall should be.
Good Lorde (sayd this marchaunt) is my contrey so wealthy,
That the verye beggers houses be builte so gorgiouslye?
Than, by the waye syde, hym chaunced to se
A pore manne that craued of hym for charitie.
Whye (quod thys Marchaunt) what meaneth thys thynge?
Do ye begge by the waye, and haue a house for a kyng?
Alas! syr (quod the pore man) we are all turned oute,
And lye and dye in corners, here and ther aboute.
Men of greate riches haue bought our dwellinge place,
And whan we craue of them, they turne awaye their face.
Lorde God! (quod this marchaunt) in Turkye haue I bene,
Yet emonge those heathen none such crueltie haue I sene.
The vengeaunce of God muste fall, no remedye,
Upon these wicked men, and that verye shortelye.[1]

The discrimination is made even more unashamedly patent in a petition
by the City to the crown in 1552 for the possession of Bridewell
Hospital, where, it is specified, the following sorts of people will be
cared for.

And first, we thought to begin with the poor child, that he might
be harboured, clothed, fed, taught, and virtuously trained up,
which thing we have (God be praised) already begun. Next we
thought to take up out of the streets the miserable aged, sore and
sick persons (which also we have done) and the same to harbour,
and by physic and surgery to cure and make whole. Now resteth for
the third sort, an house of occupations, to be erected; wherein as
well the child, when he is brought up and grown to years . . . as also
the sore and sick when they be cured; who shall not be suffered to
wander as vagabonds, as they have been accostomed, but shall there
be exercised. And unto this shall be brought the sturdy and idle;
and likewise such prisoners as are quit at the sessions, that there
they may be set to labour. [2]

The bias towards the right sort of poor is also revealed in the ubiquitous
phrase, 'at the discretion of my executor'. Executors were invariably
family members or close friends or fellow merchants; all shared the same
aspirations and possessed the same prejudices about the 'poor'. One
seldom reads that a merchant supported the poorest people in London,
or even all the poor of his parish; instead one finds 'to ten poor
brethren of the mystery of ironmongers', or 'to five poor men and
women of Highgate parish, where I was born'. Where more comprehensive statements occur ('to the poor of St. Dunstan's, where I now
dwell') they are often explicitly qualified in favour of householders,
and probably all such sweeping bequests carried this limitation

1 Tawney and Power, *Documents,* iii. 405.
2 Ibid. ii. 307-8.

implicitly.[1] Professor Jordan has spoken eloquently of the 'enlightened aspirations' of the merchant donors, the 'national' scope of their charity and of the 'new society' they were forging.[2] All these judgements are fair enough, if taken as reflections in hindsight, but such liberal views were foreign to the rulers themselves. Particularly within London their charity benefited not only the poor but themselves, because of their intimate connection with every phase of London's life. Even beyond London it is questionable how often their charity was independent of some association which in turn was focused on the London ruling group. Alderman Wolstan Dixie, for example, left a provision in his will favouring certain residents of Leicestershire for divinity scholarships at Cambridge. His charity would seem to be 'emancipated from parochialism', until it is discovered that he asked preference for his own relations, and that the family of his father-in-law, Alderman Christopher Draper, were residents of Leicestershire.[3]

However narrow their focus, one cannot gainsay the extent of merchant contribution to poor relief, but the connection between benefactors and recipients hints at important religious feelings. Since the rulers, and other prominent merchants along with them, felt reasonably confident of their own ultimate salvation, as appears obvious in their wills, it was thought unfitting to their status as the elect (possibly even dangerous) to extend their charity to those whose election was less certain, and who turn out to be precisely those who were considered socially unredeemable. By withholding benefaction from the very lowest orders the merchants betrayed their assumption that charity, like salvation, was for the respectable few, or those who could be made respectable. It would appear then that in the rulers' minds salvation may not have been unconnected with worldly station.

Could the rulers have had any justification for such discriminatory behaviour, in particular any way of making their behaviour compatible with profound religious motivations? I believe they could, but to identify these feelings simply as Protestant does insufficient justice to the complexity and uncertainty that underlay even the deepest religious impulses. The abundant and exhortatory sermon literature on charity of the sixteenth and seventeenth centuries, which has been seen as fundamental to the charitable impulse, may only have come into existence because the English merchant's conscience, at which so much of the literature was directed, was so painfully divided against itself. For a practical man, sincerely seeking theological truth, there was much

1 Jordan (*Charities,* p. 98) cites explicit evidence of the bias at work in favour of 'worthy householders' or those 'of honest fame and most in need'.

2 See especially ibid. ch. 7.

3 PCC 1 Dixy and *DNB.*

to be doubtful about, as the history of religious activity in London in the generation between the Reformation and the accession of Elizabeth so well confirms. The wide fluctuations of royal policy in these years, both as to dogma and discipline, did nothing for a uniform religious consciousness in London, but even without the fickle example set by the crown the City had conflicts of its own.[1] One of the earliest patrons of William Tyndale in London was Humphrey Monmouth, who befriended the reformer in the 1520s and probably helped introduce Lutheran tracts from the Continent. Beaven is probably correct in calling him the first Protestant alderman.[2] But in 1528 under the threat of imprisonment in the Tower, and because suspicion of heresy had hurt his business, Monmouth was prepared to espouse orthodoxy outwardly while he was an alderman from 1534-7. Two other early Protestants who made their commitments during Henry VIII's reign, and who both became notable councilmen for the City, were the printer and chronicler, Richard Grafton, and the pious friend of Heinrich Bullinger, Richard Hills. But the prevailing mood, as evidenced by the patronage of the livery companies in City benefices, was one of diversity and uncertainty. The aldermen themselves were in no hurry to embrace reforms; a tract of 1542 claimed that most of the wealthy merchants refused to have the English Bible in their homes or allow their servants to read it — this several years after royal injunctions had ordered use of the same in parish churches. While most of the London parishes seemed willing to go along with the abolition of images, pictures, and the snuffing out of rood lights, they were far from unanimous on accepting the Prayer Book of 1549, and were even further apart on the nature of the Mass. In 1548 the aldermen took two firm stands for orthodoxy: they asked for a proclamation to keep fast days, and at the annual election of the mayor in September they ordered the singing of Mass. On the same occasion four years later, however, Holy Communion was dispensed with entirely and a sermon was preached. But in the very next year, Queen Mary having recently ascended the throne, the Mass was reinstated. Throughout the long reign of Elizabeth royal officials found it easy to become excited about the large number of Catholics said to be hiding in London, with the result that constant vigilance was urged on the aldermen, and regular searches. With this request the aldermen complied, though reporting priests, or catching those in the course of Mass, or rounding up a large list of poor folk was one thing; making life uncomfortable for fellow rulers of tender conscience was quite another. If the Privy

---

1 What follows is based on *The Victoria History of London* (Westminster, 1909), ed. William Page, especially pp. 245-339.

2 *Aldermen of London*, ii. 28, 169.

Council suspected that the aldermen were less than remorseless in their duty, we shall see that there was adequate reason for the suspicion.

Given the background, it is small wonder that in the early Elizabethan period (1564) the bishops should have reported to the Privy Council that among the JPs there were 431 who favoured the queen's established religion, 264 who were indifferent or neutral, and 157 who were opposed; or that in London Roger Cholmeley (formerly recorder) and Alderman Martin Bowes were said to be 'indifferent', while the then recorder, Richard Onslow, the former common serjeant, John Marshe, and the future town clerk, Anthony Stapleton, were all 'favourers'.[1] Referring to the London JPs as a group, which at this time included all the senior aldermen, the bishop of London captured the ambiguity of religious attitudes in his double negative: the London JPs were 'not to be misliked at this present'.[2] No matter what the rulers thought in private, as aldermen and councilmen they were themselves authorities, responsible for upholding the legal order. Mayor Christopher Draper, during an examination of several Protestant extremists in the summer of 1567, expressed very well the cautious pragmatism which guided the rulers in their official capacity; addressing these recalcitrant fellows Draper showed compassion, but he tried to suggest that private conscience can and must learn to live under the law.

> Well, good people, I would you would wisely consider these things, and be obedient to the Queen's Majesty's good laws, as I and other of the Queen's subjects are, that you may live quietly and have liberty, as my lord here and masters have said. And as for my part, I would you were at your heart's ease, and I am sorry that ye are troubled; but I am an officer under my prince, and therefore blame not me. I cannot talk learnedly with you in celestial matters; but I have a mother's wit, and I will persuade the best that I can. The Queen hath not established these garments and things for any holiness' sake or religion, but only for a civil order and comeliness; because she would have the ministers known from other men, as the aldermen are known by their tippets, and the judges by their red gowns, and sometimes they wear coifs; and likewise lords' servants are known by their badges ... Even so, when the ministers began to be despised, the Queen's grace did ordain this priests' apparel; but the people cannot be content and like it. Now what may the papists say? Some of them goeth to the court whispering, saying, that ye cannot be content that the Queen should command any thing in the church, not so much as a cap or a tippet; whereupon the Queen may have occasion to say: 'Will they not be content that I should rule in the church? I will restore that my forefathers have followed'; and therefore, masters, take heed.[3]

1 'Indifferent' was not intended to be flattering to Bowes, but it would be incorrect to assume that he was not deeply religious; he left a bequest for sermons in his will, among a number of other pious bequests.

2 'A Collection of Original Letters from the Bishops to the Privy Council, 1564', ed. Mary Bateson, *The Camden Miscellany* 9 (1895), especially 59-60.

3 William Nicholson, ed. *The Remains of Edmund Grindal,* The Parker Society Publications, 19 (Cambridge, 1843), 209-10.

Perhaps this reflects much more than an official posture. In times of severe doctrinal controversy, who else but higher authority was qualified to determine the faith? Some rulers doubtless asked this question and accepted its implications. Others doubtless were not content to place any authority above Scripture, or their reading of it. But, to return to the motives behind charity, there is good reason to suppose that not all the rulers took the same position on the critical issue of the nature of good works. To the self-conscious Protestants like Richard Hills, who had gradually and carefully worked out a systematic credo, there was little hesitation in declaring works to be the result or sign of grace, not the necessary prerequisite. But how many rulers endured the painful self-examinations that might, or might not, lead to certainty? In a time when controversy and doubt ran rampant among men, and remembering that it was within recent memory that such dissensions had sprung up, was it not prudent for the practical merchant to ignore troublesome theological implications of his charity and invest mightily, since, whether it was cause or result of his salvation, in either case charity was pleasing to God.[1] This level of pragmatism, bordering even on cynicism, was surely not beyond the aggressive and versatile men who paved the way for the British Empire. Yet if pushed too far this reasoning slips away from a point insisted on before, the essentially religious orientation of the Elizabethan rulers which was implicit in all their behaviour and all their attitudes. At the same time neither a Catholic nor a Protestant interpretation of good works will adequately explain the undoubted shifts in the kinds of charitable giving that Professor Jordan has so abundantly documented. There must be another explanation, one that takes account of profoundly religious motivations.

Reflecting on the life style of these men suggests what might be called the rulers' ethic. An articulation of the rulers' ethic would go as follows. By tradition aldermen and common councilmen assumed the rulership of London, a high but demanding dignity which determined that even the shape of their personal lives would be moulded by the London experience. Ruling London meant conferring with the greatest personages of the realm, even travelling far beyond the beloved City, but always being drawn back to London, the proper and perfect place for

---

1 Jordan says little on this difficult aspect of the problem of motivations, but he does notice it on p. 170 of *Philanthropy*. 'It will have been observed that even the most evangelical of these Protestant divines strayed very far indeed into those indefinable verges which delimit the doctrine of the necessity of good works. They were, it is true, carefully orthodox in their view that good works were the inevitable and demonstrable concomitant of a state of grace, but so insistent were they on the high necessity of charity that the lay auditor must have been more persuaded by the argument of works than the more intangible and subtle complexities of grace'.

men of their rank. In London they made their homes, found wives and raised children, built up wealth, and established lasting associations — mostly with other rulers and largely in the context of City government. London was also the chief recipient of their charity. They looked after virtually every physical feature of the City, from ditches to churches, and nearly all ranks of people within it, down to and including the reputable poor. Into their care were committed the ancient and nearly sacred privileges of the City, which went far beyond legal instruments to embody a unique way of life. Accordingly they should be clothed with broad and terrible authority, the kind that yields only to royalty and which itself is sanctioned by God. As upholders of a special order, they ought to be a recognizable and unified group; they should work together, not only to govern and protect the City but to perpetuate themselves. The two concepts were inseparable since there was no other group capable of ruling London. Thus it was inevitable, and expected, that the image of these powerful men would be impressed upon London, just as London in turn shaped their lives.

Being bred on this rulers' ethic, they were accustomed to thinking in terms of distinct groups in society; they had always done so, otherwise they could not have been the governing rank for so long. The discriminatory doctrine of predestination, the notion of an elect before God, did not come as any surprise to them. In view of their traditional stature in London, and because of the doctrinal uncertainties swirling around them, the rulers understood and accepted the doctrine of election not only in connection with ultimate salvation, but also in the practical context of their worldly rank. In short, how else to understand salvation without assuming their own election? It followed, in the temporal as in the spiritual realms, that the elect were not only the rulers but those respectable citizens who had some link with the rulers, and who therefore belonged to the exclusive community that was London. Now this rulers' ethic says something about the origins of the Protestant Reformation in England. It suggests that the Reformation took root there, at least among such men as the London rulers, not because the errors of Rome were exposed, nor because of anything as clear and decisive as a Protestant ethic, but because certain religious ideas inherent in Protestantism successfully articulated the implicit sense of a particular group and its community identity that for a long time had been characteristic of men like the rulers. Notions of distinct and chosen communities may have been reinforced and revitalized by Protestantism, but this deep sense of particular fellowship was also Catholic, but more than that, was fundamental to religious experience. The rulers' ethic antedated the Reformation, and helped make it possible. In that regard it is appropriate to refer to another recent study on charity.[1] Thomson shows, by reference to pre-Reformation wills, that the influence of Protestant teaching as a motive for the new socially oriented charity has been exaggerated, that this kind of charity had its start before the Reformation, that it grew from greater needs and greater sensitivities to need. Perhaps it is not too much to say that in London it grew because of the rulers' ethic.

In the years following the Reformation, especially during the time of Elizabeth, historians have found religious differences increasingly responsible for driving men into hostile camps, quite well-aware of rival dogmas and prepared to accept their consequences. Thus the highly charged campaigns against the papists. Thus the origin of a distinct Puritan movement within the established church itself. But within the fellowship, one might say brotherhood, of the London rulers, it is the similarity of religious attitudes that stands out. They were as aware as anyone of doctrinal collisions, but religious distinctions generated much less concern among them, because on the more fundamental questions of identity with London and acceptance of the rulers' ethic there was an abiding harmony. Up to a limit, therefore, and a broad one at that, there was room among the rulers for a variety of creeds and behaviour − on both ends of the religious spectrum. Alderman Monmouth, probably the first Protestant on the court, made no attempt to shun his Catholic brethren. Perhaps, being the first Protestant, he could not afford to, but it is significant that in the generation following the Reformation no interruption in the marriage pattern of the aldermen took place. Men on the rise politically continued to marry into other political families, with little or no apparent regard to religion, and the great men continued to marry their children off in the same fashion.[2] Once again it is appropriate to invoke John Stow, who so well illustrates the attitudes under discussion. In the exhaustive survey of his beloved London one has to read carefully between the lines to become aware that there was a Reformation in England. Dissolution of monastic foundations in the 1530s is noticed, but so are the surprising number of medieval precedents. The theme of Stow's labour of love is the glory of London, made famous through the ages by numerous individuals, some Catholic, some Protestant, but Stow is indifferent to this distinction. Exception must here be taken to Professor Jordan's characterization of Stow and his work: 'Stow's whole emphasis, his whole preoccupation, was intensely secular, but men could scarcely help reflecting that this almost staccato recital of the record of London's generosity was after all the

1   J.A.F. Thomson, 'Piety and Charity in Late Medieval London', *Journal of Ecclesiastical History* 16 (1965), 178-95.
2   Beaven, *Aldermen of London*, ii. 169-73 especially.

fruit of the reformed gospel'.[1] Hopefully the impression that Stow and the rulers were so 'intensely secular' has already been corrected; regarding the impact of the reformed gospel, let the reader turn over the pages of Stow's *Survey* and count the 'medieval' contributions.

Being a Catholic, or certainly thought to have been by his contemporaries, John Stow illustrates both the survival into Elizabethan times of older religious attitudes and the apparent acceptance of those attitudes by the rulers. A number of dedications of his works were offered to, and accepted by, the lord mayor and aldermen, and at least one to that redoubtable patron of Puritans, Robert Dudley, earl of Leicester. Stow was in the City's employ as a chronicler, was several times elected an aleconner, and was a collector in his ward. He was a member of the Society of Antiquaries, where he became friendly with such Protestants as Recorder William Fleetwood and the antiquary William Camden. He applied for a pension from the City and probably got it, but more interestingly he was specifically named as a recipient of Robert Dowe's charities, through the Merchant Taylors Company; Stow and Dowe were brethren of the company. Dowe was a leading common councilman, hence a ruler, of Elizabethan London.[2]

Given the legal disabilities, and the many obvious dangers, it is never going to be possible to say with assurance how many of the Elizabethan rulers were Catholic, or carried with them sufficient residual sympathy to be suspected of popish leanings. Alderman Thomas Whyte, the founder of St. John's College, Oxford, lived and probably died (in 1567) an avowed Romanist.[3] Yet Whyte was associated with the Puritan, Richard Hills, in the foundation of the Merchant Taylors School, and in his will he warmly remembered his deceased friend and fellow alderman, Rowland Hill, another firm Protestant.[4] Alderman David Woodroffe was remembered with venom by the martyrologist John Foxe, because of his supposedly harsh treatment of Protestants at Smithfield, suggesting that he may have been a Catholic.[5] If he was,

1 *Philanthropy*, pp. 234-5.

2 Kingsford's Introduction to Stow's *Survey*, especially pp. vii-xxviii. Kingsford mentioned Stow as an aleconner in 1584-5, but Stow repeated in 1585-6, 1588-9, 1589-90, and 1595-6 (Jour. 21, fos. 371[b], 465[b]; Jour. 22, fos. 189[b], 302[b]; Jour. 24, fo. 22[b]). For Camden see the *DNB*; for Fleetwood, a notorious enemy of Catholics, but not of Stow, see P.R. Harris, 'William Fleetwood, Recorder of the City, and Catholicism in Elizabethan London', *Recusant History* 7 (1963), 106-22.

3 On his Catholicism see *DNB*; W.J. Loftie, *A History of London* (1883-4), i. 325-6; A.G. Dickens and Dorothy Carr, *The Reformation in England to the Accession of Elizabeth I* (New York, 1968), p. 127.

4 F.W.M. Draper, *Four Centuries of the Merchant Taylors' School, 1561-1961* (1962), ch. 1; PCC 36 Stonarde.

5 *Book of Martyrs*, ed. G.A. Williamson (Boston, 1965), p. 452.

that may be part of the reason why his fellow aldermen eased him out of the court, though their delicacy is worth noting.[1] In any case, no corruption of the blood ensued, for Woodroffe's son, Nicholas, rose through the ranks to become mayor in 1579. It is unsafe to assume much about religion from family relationships at this time, but Alderman John Whyte was the brother of the Catholic bishop of Winchester, also named John, who preached the sermon at Queen Mary's funeral. If Alderman Whyte leaned at all towards the traditional faith through habit, he also showed newer inclinations because he left money for sermons in his will. In 1578 one of secretary Walsingham's spies, one Davie Jones, submitted a list of some very prominent persons in London who were said to be 'papists'.[2] Among them are Lady Champyon, probably the widow of Alderman Richard Champyon, who died in 1568, and three attorneys of Guildhall. Two other names are supplied − 'Buckland of Paternoster Row' and 'Mr. Loe, vintner, the Mitre, Cheapside . . .' − which are the names of notable councilmen, Richard Buckland and Thomas Lowe. Now if the list truly was drawn up in 1578 (it may have been earlier), the two councilmen were probably not intended, since both had been dead for some three and four years respectively. But the likelihood of identical families is very strong: Richard Buckland was a parishioner of, and was buried in, St. Michael le Querne, which was at the head of Paternoster Row; the 'Mr. Loe, vintner' had an address in Cheapside, and so did the councilman, also a vintner, who paid the subsidies of 1559 and 1572 in St. Mary Colechurch, and was buried in the Mercers Chapel, directly adjacent to St. Mary Colechurch. But Davie Jones also trawled for bigger fish: 'Alderman Cooper' and 'Sir Thomas Offley' are included in his list of suspected Catholics. Alderman 'Cooper' can only have been John Cowper, fishmonger, alderman 1558-70, retired but alive in 1578 and still entitled to the courtesy title of alderman; there was no other knight in England named Thomas Offley at the time. It should be recalled that for over ten years Offley was perhaps the most influential man on the court, and that his family connections with other political families were wider than those of any other alderman.[3]

As there was little or no discrimination against Catholic rulers by their Protestant brethren in the early part of Elizabeth's reign, so later on there was little fuss made between the more orthodox Anglicans and their Puritan fellows. There is no evidence, for example, that Puritan rulers arranged their children's marriages exclusively along lines

---

1 Woodroffe was one of those who left the court rather than serve the mayoralty. His brethren on the court gave him over three years to consider his decision.

2 *CSPD, Addenda* (1566-79), vol. 25/118.

3 See p. 102.

of religious conscience, or that young Puritans were either favoured or
discouraged in rising politically on account of religion. One is struck by
the latitude of belief and enthusiasm that was considered tolerable, the
similarity of thought and feeling that ran deeper than denominational
affiliations. Is this an Anglican, Puritan, or Catholic speaking?

> First and before all things I utterly renounce and forsake this
> wretched world and commit me to the infinite mercy of Almighty
> God to whom I give and bequeath my soul most humbly, beseeching
> my maker and redeemer to take me to his mercy and grace and that
> I may [be] partaker of his joys everlasting which he hath ordered
> for me and all mankind, my sinful body to be buried within the
> choir . . . with as much convenient speed as may be possible after
> my decease . . . without pomp or vain glory.[1]

It is the Catholic, Alderman Thomas Whyte. It is noticeable that he
speaks out against 'vain pomp', usually thought to suggest Puritanism,
and by that standard many rulers were Puritan. On the other hand
Alderman Whyte, and most other rulers, provided a number of mourning
robes for friends. Many other rulers arranged to have charity dispensed
to the poor who attended their funerals. Both these practices were
criticized as superstitious by Puritan writers of the period.[2] At the
same time sabbatarianism in London has been said to indicate the
advance of Puritan preferences, though it is difficult to know how much
Puritan initiative to assign to the rulers in this respect, since most
violations of the sabbath also threatened good order. In any case the
Privy Council even more than the rulers led the attack on 'sabbeth
breakers'. But these are not very satisfactory measures; besides, what
are we to make of the not insignificant number who refer reverently to
the saints?[3] Again it is the similarity of attitudes cutting across doctrinal
lines that is observed. Asceticism and modesty may have been part of
the spirit of the times, but not overlooking the requisites of rank. Alderman Duckett wrote a very pious will and asked to be buried without
pomp, 'but yet nevertheless in a decent and comely order in respect of
my calling in the commonwealth'. Decency required dispensing thirty
funeral robes to various poor men, at a value of twenty shillings each, as
well as gowns for Recorder Fleetwood, his daughters-in-law and their

---

1 PCC 36 Stonarde.

2 Keith Thomas, *Religion and the Decline of Magic: Studies in Popular
Beliefs in Sixteenth and Seventeenth Century England* (1971), p. 66.

3 Article 22 of the Thirty-Nine Articles (1563) called worship of the saints 'a
fond thing, vainly invented, and grounded upon no warranty of Scripture, but
rather repugnant to the word of God'. Nonetheless, if worshipping saints was
prohibited, revering them was not, and how many understood where to draw
the line? This rather ambiguous distinction can be found in the writings of
seventeenth-century divines; see Paul E. More and Frank L. Cross, *Anglicanism*
(Milwaukee, 1935), pp. 524-40.

husbands, two cousins, and all of his servants.[1] Alderman John Garrarde went so far as to ask for no funeral, yet he rejoiced in his lavish collection of silver and carefully bequeathed it piece by piece.[2] Alderman Roger Martyn perhaps best illustrates the blend of piety and magnificence that was so typical of the rulers. Though supporting the poor in the very Puritan parish of St. Antholin's, and providing £20 for sermons in the Mercers Chapel, at the same time he left money for dinners in his memory at the Mercers Company and the Waterbearers Company. He left memorial cups to the Mercers Company, the Merchant Adventurers Company, the Staplers Company, as well as to his own ward. And he ordered seventy rings to be given to his friends.[3]

All this is sufficient evidence of the difficulties involved in trying to identify a 'Puritan' element among the rulers, especially when the term probably meant little to the rulers themselves. Nevertheless, with these warnings in mind, it may be worth making 'a mirror into men's souls' if only to get an approximate idea of how large an opposition group, or potential one, was growing within the ranks of the London rulers. Some men can pretty certainly be called Puritans because of their patronage of known Puritan preachers, like Richard Hills, who asked that Robert Crowley, vicar of St. Giles Cripplegate, preach at his burial, or, failing him, the more moderate John Bateman, parson of St. Martin Vintry.[4] Others can be called Puritan for various reasons. Thomas Heaton and Richard Springham had been Marian exiles.[5] William Craven deliberately encouraged lectures at one of the more radical parishes, in this case St. Antholin's. Henry Billingsley, Wolstan Dixie, and John Harte supported Emmanuel or Sidney Sussex at Cambridge. William Quarles and James Harvye supported the Dutch or French churches in London.[6]

1   PCC 9 Rutland.

2   PCC 53 Clark.

3   PCC 1 Martyn.

4   PCC 36 Drury. By this measure probably Andrew Palmer, Nowell Sotherton, and Nicholas Wheeler were also Puritans. On the other hand when it is possible to identify the intensity of a preacher's zeal most of those supported by the rulers were quite orthodox Anglicans, not Puritans. In sorting out Puritans and Anglicans I have been greatly aided by Paul S. Seaver, *The Puritan Lectureships: The Politics of Religious Dissent, 1560-1662* (Stanford, 1970).

5   C.H. Garrett, *The Marian Exiles* (Cambridge, 1966), pp. 182, 292-3.

6   Here I have used wills and the information on charitable donations in the Parliamentary Papers, beginning with *Index to the Reports of the Commissioners for Inquiring Concerning Charities in England and Wales,* vol. ix, pt. 2 (1840). In addition to the above named, the following rulers can be called Puritans with fair certainty: Thomas Aldersey, Henry Anderson, Nicholas Backhouse, William Elkyn, Anthony Gamage, William Glover, Richard Goddard, Richard Gourney, James Hawes, Baptist Hicks, John Ryvers, William Romeney, Stephen Slanye, Thomas Smythe and Humphrey Weld. I deliberately avoided assuming that a man was a Puritan if the only reason for thinking so was a family tie or a friendship with another Puritan; these ties were too common among rulers of

The overall number was around twenty-seven.[1] Though he reached the Court of Aldermen, one of the most prominent Puritans of the time did not choose (perhaps was not encouraged) to stay on and become a member of the élite; this was Thomas Smythe. At the same time it is interesting that of the eleven Puritan councilmen among the rulers only three were ever nominated to rise to the court. On the other hand it is difficult to attribute their failure to religion, or at least not solely, since only two of the eight not nominated were of appropriate wealth. There was clearly no attempt to keep Puritans down, for Craven, Billingsley, and Dixie, for example, did join the élite, and Gamage, Gourney, Romeney, and others only failed because they died before their turn as mayors.

A minority group of Puritans in the City government, even if they amounted to only 15 or 20 per cent of the rulers, would have been an important faction, had they chosen to create one. But in calling some men Puritans it was in most cases only because they gave rather more signs than their fellows of being keen on encouraging the spread of God's word, by patronizing preachers and colleges, founding lecture-ships, providing for sermons. Yet to keep this in perspective it seems that the rulers' support of preaching, though important, was far outweighed by such congenialities as dinners and rings and mourning robes for their friends, and gifts of silver and other things to their livery companies. Exact figures are not available, but it would seem that the rulers spent far more in connection with their funerals than they did on sermons and lectures. Moreover, an interest in good preaching was not uniquely Puritan but was shared by a number of rulers, including orthodox Anglicans, and attests again the deeply religious spirit of the times.[2] What is not found among the Puritan rulers is any hint of an opposition group, either as private men or City officials. Not surprisingly the few with more advanced religious feelings frequently mentioned each other as close friends, but such connections do not seem based exclusively along lines of religion, or exclude other men of less zeal.

At the same time the patronage of the rulers underlines their respectable moderation. During the Elizabethan period the mayor and

quite different faiths. Perhaps, for one reason or another, a few more rulers can be counted as Puritans, but very few more.

1   I have been unable to find appropriate documentation for most of the leaders to decide on their religion; among the notables I have been more curious about the councilmen than the aldermen. Therefore 27 Puritans is on the basis of 141 rulers, or 19%.

2   Seaver, *Puritan Lectureships, passim,* has documented the Puritan contribution to the lectureship, but he points out that the institution had wide appeal among Anglicans. Among the approximately 200 rulers for whom appropriate sources were found, thirty-two left provisions for lectures and sermons.

aldermen presented to four City livings, but less than half the incumbents were Puritans.[1] The pattern was little different in the early Stuart period, for in the then five benefices under City control no Puritan was appointed. Of the preachers appointed by the City to give annual sermons on Midsummer Day, and at four other set times, only a minority were probably Puritans.[2] Being concerned to encourage sound preaching, the rulers were as willing as most to sponsor lectureships. By 1603 nineteen of the thirty parishes (63 per cent) favoured by the rulers for residence had established lectureships; by 1630 twenty-nine of the thirty had done so.[3] Yet, despite the undoubted strength of Puritanism in London, it is suggestive of the moderation among the rulers that most corporate towns and boroughs in England, London excepted, sponsored lectures for their communities, while the only successful type in London was the parish lecture, which enjoyed no official sponsorship from the City government.[4] Therefore it should not be surprising that when the Privy Council in 1581 tried to impose some organization, and outside controls, on the development of London lectureships, the rulers balked.[5] It was not only crown interference that the rulers were wary of. In the early Stuart period the City took the decisive step for seven or eight years during the 1620s of contributing directly to lectures at St. Antholin's. Yet opposition over sponsorship developed with the very Puritan feoffees for lay impropriations. The aldermen tried to make continuance of their support conditional upon nominating lecturers; when the feoffees would not accept this, the aldermen withdrew their support.[6]

Finally, it is appropriate to draw attention to the rulers' residence in London. Not counting the suburbs or the liberties, or the ward of Bridge Without (Southwark), there were 111 parishes in Elizabethan London.[7] The rulers chose to reside in only seventy-one of them.[8] Twenty parishes were the preferred residence of no less than 59 per

[1] Parish pressures were responsible for these appointments: H.G. Owen, 'The London Parish Clergy in the Reign of Elizabeth I,' Ph.D. thesis (Univ. of London, 1957), pp. 241, 265-8.

[2] Dorothy Ann Williams, 'Puritanism in City Government, 1610-40,' *The Guildhall Miscellany* 1 (1955), 10-11.

[3] Seaver, *Puritan Lectureships*, pp. 304-5. For the rulers' preferred residences see note 1, p. 132.

[4] Ibid. pp. 83-4.

[5] Ibid. pp. 121-3 for the details.

[6] Williams, 'Puritanism in City Government', pp. 1-8.

[7] Seaver, *Puritan Lectureships*, pp. 301-2. Stow's count was 110 (*Survey*, ii. 138-42).

[8] In their wills they usually named their parish and others of which they had been members.

cent; 74 per cent chose to live in only thirty parishes.[1] Glancing at a map of contemporary London shows that the rulers preferred to live within the City walls, and that they disdained the parishes that were large and doubtless crowded with people. None of the preferred thirty were in the wards of Bishopsgate or Aldersgate, nor in the riverside wards of Baynard Castle, Queenhithe, and Dowgate. But there was no particular section of the City that was more favoured than another, for the thirty parishes spread from St. Michael le Querne in West Cheap to St. Andrew Undershaft in Aldersgate Street; from St. Michael Bassishaw (Basinghall) in the northwest to St. Magnus by the Bridge in the southeast. About half were north of the line made by Cheap-Poultry-Lombard-Fenchurch, and exactly half were east of Walbrook. The intramural parishes traditionally had been considerably smaller than those beyond the bars, and the preferred thirty were among the wealthier ones in the City.[2] Of the thirty favourite residences of the rulers only two were among the nine most radical or Puritan parishes of London.[3] That no organized opposition developed within the City's government can be attributed first to the deep pride with which the rulers viewed their own traditional position as authorities, and secondly to the fierce sense of independence they so frequently manifested — both of which confirm their unshakeable loyalty to the rulers' ethic.

1 The thirty favourite parishes of the rulers were as follows: Allhallows Bread Street, Allhallows Honey Lane, St. Andrew Undershaft, St. Antholin Budge Row, St. Bartholomew Exchange, St. Benet Gracechurch, St. Benet Sherehog, St. Dionis Backchurch, St. Dunstan in the East, St. James Garlickhithe, St. Lawrence Jewry, St. Magnus the Martyr, St. Martin Orgar, St. Martin Outwich, St. Mary Aldermary, St. Mary at Hill, St. Mary Magdalen Milk Street, St. Mary Woolnoth, St. Michael Bassishaw, St. Michael Cornhill, St. Michael le Querne, St. Olave Jewry, St. Pancras Soper Lane, St. Peter le Poor, St. Peter Westcheap, St. Stephen Coleman Street, St. Stephen Walbrook, St. Swithin, St. Vedast Foster Lane, and Tower Ward. The last, Tower Ward, is not a parish, but this was as closely as the rulers defined their residence. Professor Jordan noted that the London merchants in his study were concentrated in 22 parishes, of which 14 appear in the above list; see *Charities*, p.52.

2 In 1547 the Chantry Commissioners reported that there were only three intramural parishes with over 800 communicants, but outside the walls there were only a few with less than 800 (*Victoria History of London*, pp. 287-8). The wealth of these parishes might be inferred from their location, and the residence of the rulers within them, but it is confirmed by their proportionate assessments towards the various subsidies.

3 Seaver, *Puritan Lectureships* p. 199 on the most radical parishes.

8

LONDON AND THE CROWN

While governing in London the rulers had always to keep in mind the sovereignty of the queen, even though they were left free, indeed encouraged, to administrate by themselves. Yet so autonomous had their authority become, and so nominal the supervision of the crown, that in the second half of the sixteenth century the aldermen were more than custodians of the queen's authority, they were the de facto sovereigns of the City and had been for the past two hundred years. By the opening of Elizabeth's reign a century and a half of disputed successions to the throne, of intermittent domestic rebellion and foreign war, and finally a generation of religious division had left the monarchy in no position to dispute the aldermen's sway. As a result, while Londoners poured out ever greater treasure and supplies on behalf of the crown, the rulers were able to extract in return a continuing reaffirmation of the City's venerated traditions and liberties, which helped secure the hold of the mayor and aldermen.

To perpetuate their virtual supremacy the rulers relied upon the habits sanctioned by tradition and on continuous communion with the crown. Tradition meant authoritative aldermanic rule, of which the crown was warmly in favour. Communion might seem an inappropriate description of City-crown relations, since it conflicts with the convenient notion of Tudor paternalism. But the two enjoyed a relationship that is not well conveyed by the term paternalism. There was mutual respect based on awareness of the resources and prerogatives of each; there was intimacy and sharing because of their need of the other.

The City assisted the Privy Council with the complaints, petitions, and claims concerning London which poured in from every part of the realm, from every department of government, and all ranks of society. The size of business emanating from London was small indeed considering its preponderance in the nation's affairs. Although the City had its own administrative machinery through the Court of Aldermen, some of the petitions coming from London bypassed the mayor and aldermen. Certainly the Dutch ambassador to England, who had rented a London house in 1600 only to find the water turned off, might have felt entitled to appeal directly to the Privy Council.[1] Since they respected the City's jurisdiction, privy councillors normally

1 *APC,* xxx. 588.

returned such cases to the mayor and aldermen, instructing them to satisfy the suitor or to send information so that they might take further action. Petitions that received an unfavourable hearing from the aldermen sometimes reappeared in Westminster. In the summer of 1573 the Privy Council wrote to the rulers asking them 'to permit liberty to certain Italian players to make show of an instrument of strange motions', then wrote again in five days marvelling that they had not yet complied. [1] The rulers were reluctant to allow the assembling of potentially noisy and troublesome crowds. The Italian instrument must have been marvellous indeed, for the Privy Council usually shared this hesitation about crowds; it often wrote to the City on the subject of suppressing plays, and on one occasion even wrote to ask on what grounds the City refused to allow certain plays so that these arguments might be used at an appropriate time. [2] In cases where a petition was obviously occasioned by the aldermen's previous refusal, great care was taken to return the matter to the aldermen. If the matter could be handled by the City, privy councillors did not pre-emptively end it and let the City wonder why; they might make suggestions or give a gentle chiding, but they did not ignore the aldermen's jurisdiction.

The Privy Council also assigned suits at law to particular courts in the City. Of course, this was the exceptional practice, for City courts heard most of their cases without waiting for special direction from royal officials. The majority of such suits were actions for debt, and most concerned London merchants. These cases were heard in the Mayor's Court or one of the two Sheriff's Courts. Also the Privy Council might halt proceedings in these cases pending further advisement.[3] To hear appeals in error from these courts the crown granted commissions to royal justices. [4]

Of greater concern to the City were the Privy Council's general orders. The most important concerned borrowing money, raising troops for the queen's armies, their supply, and provisioning the City with adequate materials and foodstuffs, particularly corn. Many of these orders concerned business the privy councillors knew perfectly well lay within the jurisdiction of the City, and they came as reminders of duty, or because the councillors had reason to believe that the City was lax. The aldermen were often reminded to count the number of aliens in the City and to drive from the wards those who refused to partake of

1 Ibid. viii. 131 and 132.
2 Ibid. p. 215.
3 Ibid. xxii. 428-9 and 53.
4 *CPR* (1563-6), pp. 490-2.

any form of divine service.[1] Other frequently recurring topics, and the ones which dominate the councillors' correspondence with the mayor and aldermen, include: setting prices in the City, licensing taverns, arresting vagabonds, suppressing plays, controlling beggars, and enforcing regulations dealing with plagues. There was sometimes occasion to scold the civic authorities, however, as in 1597 when the mayor was rebuked for not adequately enforcing rules for the observation of Lent, in particular the ban on eating flesh.[2] Similarly, in August 1600 the Privy Council wrote complaining that troops recently sent by the City to Ireland were not raised by a proper levy at all, but by a search for rogues and vagabonds; the scoundrels had deserted, and the City was ordered to send more men.[3] Sometimes it was best to summon individual aldermen to Westminster for a firsthand report, as in January 1593 (a time of serious plague), when six aldermen reported on their compliance with orders for the plague.[4] Though there is a hint of displeasure in this instance, a summons to Westminster was not reserved for upbraidings, since face-to-face assemblies best settled much business.

Most of the business directed to the City or to individual aldermen was not a part of the recognizable routine, but it was an integral part of government as understood by privy councillors and aldermen. It was through these extraordinary assignments that the aldermen showed their versatility and proved their value as local governors. The Privy Council often summoned Londoners before it; in order to insure that these citizens appeared the mayor could rely on aldermen, common councilmen, or any number of guild or parish officers who might know the people involved and who could see that they received and carried out appropriate orders.[5] The mayor was asked in 1575 to assist the bishop of London in handling alien Anabaptists in the City.[6] The co-operation of the temporal and spiritual powers that resulted produced cruel persecution of these people and sent two to the stake.[7] In a more charitable mood the Privy Council ordered the mayor and sheriffs to take up collections at the annual Spital Sermon for redeeming prisoners in Algiers.[8] The mayor might even supervise

---

1 *APC,* xxx. 135.

2 Ibid. xxvi. 520-1.

3 Ibid. xxx. 620-1. The use of rogues, masterless men, and other undesirables, however, was sometimes specifically called for.

4 Ibid. xxiv. 21-3.

5 Ibid. viii. 345.

6 Ibid. pp. 369, 370, 389, 398 and 402.

7 Ibid. p. xxi.

8 Ibid. xxx. 157. In around 1593 a merchant had pawned some of his crew in Algiers for money to purchase essential supplies. The merchant died before

the paying of certain royal officers, or check up on certain captains suspected of mustering and taking men abroad without the queen's licence, or investigate those exporting grain without a licence.[1] With their numerous interests in shipping and naval stores, and their wide jurisdiction over the Thames, and all sorts of supplies moving through the port of London, the aldermen's assistance was crucial during times of war. Since London was the assembly centre and embarkation point for troops going abroad, additional burdens occasioned by war were common for the rulers. The City authorities wrote to the Privy Council in December 1596 to complain that in recent years (going back to the time of the Armada) they had spent 100,000 marks on naval affairs alone. [2]

So important was the disposition of London to the welfare of the realm that the Privy Council used its extensive authority to help London in a number of ways. When faced with periodic wheat shortages, London could count on privy councillors to authorize additional grain supplies from the counties, by writing to local mayors, deputy lieutenants, sheriffs, and justices of the peace. [3] Particularly in wartime this higher demand was not easy to meet in view of the natural jealousy of Londoners in other counties. It was useful to have the Privy Council step in, too, when London was involved in disputes with other jurisdictions. But privy councillors did not always favour London. The City complained in 1595 about the rising cost per unit of Newcastle coal, and its inferior quality of late. In this case the Privy Council can hardly be seen as the honest broker, because the queen had been leasing certain of these lands and their mines from the bishop of Durham since 1582. Eventually she assigned the lease to the earl of Leicester, who in turn gave it to his secretary, Thomas Sutton; he later delivered it to Sir William Riddell and others for the mayor and burgesses of Newcastle. The higher prices London complained of had been rising steadily with each transfer of the lease since 1582. [4]

If the City became involved in jurisdictional disputes with a branch of the central government, or even among its own rulers, recourse to the Privy Council was possible. In 1591 the City and the lord admiral disputed the right to coal metage, which the City held by ancient

restitution was made; his creditors made difficulties for other merchants trading there in hopes of forcing them to pay the old debts.

1 Ibid. viii. 127, 77, and 19.
2 HMC *Calendar of the Salisbury MSS,* 6 (1895), 534-6.
3 Not infrequently supplies were requisitioned from as far away as Lincolnshire and Yorkshire.
4 *APC,* xxvi. 27-8; *Remembrancia,* pp. 78-81; and John Brand, *The History and Antiquities of Newcastle upon Tyne* (1789), ii. 268-9.

custom. The mayor wrote to Lord Burghley, as aldermen often did in such cases (he was referred to as the City's 'good friend'), and eventually the admiral retracted his claims.[1] Burghley had earlier come to the City's aid in an unpleasant personal dispute involving one Edward Skeggs. He had been disenfranchised by the mayor and aldermen for certain offences, but as was normal for minor infractions, he regained his privileges later on. Determined to take revenge on the aldermen, Skeggs, under pretence of carrying out his duties as a purveyor for the queen, stole twelve capons intended for the mayor's table; to make sure of provoking a quarrel he was insolent to the mayor. His trump card was the earl of Arundel (himself a privy councillor and at the time lord steward) to whom he wrote a distorted report of the incident claiming that he had been interfered with in his duties. The lord steward, who did not ascertain the soundness of Skeggs's claim, and who apparently was ignorant of his motives, wrote harshly to the mayor promising punishment as soon as the plague then ravaging the City should subside. The mayor wrote his side of the story to Burghley, who quietly resolved the matter without involving the City again.[2] In a series of suits involving two former sheriffs, a keeper of the Wood Street Compter, and one alderman, the Privy Council ordered the lord keeper to keep the disputes out of the common law courts and settle them by equity.[3] While not much explicit evidence of it is found during the relative tranquility of Elizabeth's reign, the Privy Council was strongly in favour of maintaining the ruling oligarchy of the City and its traditional practices of government. In October 1628 the councillors wrote to the mayor, recorder, and aldermen complaining that at the recent mayoral elections 'the Commons, misled by some few popular and turbulent spirits, had endeavoured to introduce some innovation in the election'. The aldermen were reprimanded for their lax enforcement of discipline and asked for the names of the ringleaders so that punishments could be made.[4] In this case the aldermen were glad to comply.

The close bond between the City and the crown consisted of much more than their mutual interest in good government for London. Perhaps the most dramatic example is London's contribution of men and arms to the queen's service. Between 1585-1602, when several thousand troops were raised each year in England and Wales, and a total for that period of 105,810, the contribution of London alone was

---

1 W. Maitland, *History of London* (1756), i. 274-5. The City's rights in the matter were upheld by the first Charter of James I (20 August 1605).
2 Ibid. pp. 255-6.
3 *APC*, xxiv. 42-3. A debtor had escaped from the compter, and his creditors initiated action against the sheriffs, who in turn sued the keeper and his sureties.
4 *Remembrancia*, pp. 208-9.

9,515.[1] If coupled with the 1,045 from Middlesex for the same period, London and Middlesex supplied a full 10 per cent. England's population in around 1600 has been variously estimated at between three and five million; London's was around a quarter million. Even the low figure for England (London then accounting for 8 per cent of the realm) shows that London's troop contribution was disproportionate to its population. London surpassed all other counties in total numbers supplied, only ten of which sent over 2,000 men; the next largest contributor was Kent with 4,600.

Less dramatic, though of greater importance to the crown, were the grants and loans of money. Without calculating all grants resulting from acts of Parliament or Common Council, the major loans portray the extent of the crown's dependence upon London. Between 1575 and 1598 the queen borrowed from the City five times to the total sum of £120,000.[2] But official loans from the City, raised in the livery companies on a scale set down by the Court of Aldermen, do not fairly represent the financial support provided by various merchant-rulers. A group of Londoners lent £30,000 to the queen in or around 1560.[3] Then in 1569 several merchant adventurers lent £16,000, most of them paying £1,000 each; of the fifteen participants all but five were then aldermen, another soon became an alderman.[4] In 1589 a loan of £15,000 was raised among 128 merchants of London, among whom were aldermen and prominent common councilmen.[5] But the City's financial support did not stop there. Loans from foreign merchants to the queen were usually arranged so that the City stood bound as a surety for the queen's credit. Obviously with the City behind her, the queen's credit was much better.[6] London merchants helped in soliciting, collecting and carrying foreign loans.[7] Because of their wide connections in commercial centres, London merchants, again including the prominent political leaders, also carried and delivered money abroad for the crown.[8]

1 Charles G. Cruickshank, *Elizabeth's Army*, 2nd ed. (Oxford, 1966), pp. 290-1.

2 R.R. Sharpe, *London and the Kingdom* (1894-5), i. 519, 546, 549 and 560.

3 *CSPD* (1547-80), vol. 19/2 and *CPR* (1558-60), p. 353.

4 John Strype, *Survey of London and Westminster* (1720), vol. 1, bk. i. 283.

5 BL Lansdowne MS 60, no. 18.

6 *APC*, xvii. 419-20 (23 July 1589). The loan was £60,000 from German merchants. Many other such examples are in City records, especially in Reps. 14 and 15. See also *APC*, viii. 53-60 which itemizes some debts of the queen in 1571. City merchants acted as sureties for these debts, and of the fifty-nine bonds drawn up all but fifteen were held by London aldermen.

7 *CSPD* (1547-80), vol. 105/69-74 and 506. The four principal merchants spoken of in this case were all active in City politics: Richard Martin, Thomas Aldersey, Andrew Palmer, and Edmund Hogan were all common councilmen at the time (1575); Martin later became an alderman.

8 Ibid. (1595-7), vol. 251/95.

Because they were the leading political and economic figures in London, the crown relied on aldermen and common councilmen to carry out a number of miscellaneous assignments through special commissions. The mayor for the time being was most often relied on in these respects. Mayor Cuthbert Buckle was one of several special commissioners (including two other aldermen, the earl of Essex, the lord admiral, Lord Buckhurst, Lord Rich, and Robert Cecil, among others) who sat at Guildhall on 28 February 1594 to try one Dr. Lopez, suspected in a plot against the queen's life on behalf of 'popish' interests.[1] The mayor and at least two other senior aldermen were included on the Commission for Uniformity of Religion, set up first in 1571 to enforce the acts of Uniformity and Supremacy.[2] The mayor in 1574 joined the master of requests and two other crown appointees to examine certain letters patent and settle a dispute, concerning importing barrelled fish, between a serjeant of the queen's catery and one William Hunt.[3] The mayor was often asked to look after visiting foreign dignitaries, which might mean punishing those who were rude to Danish gentlemen, or finding lodgings for the French ambassador.[4]

Other London rulers had their share of special commissions as well. A commission established for Ludgate Gaol in February 1559 to hear and settle prisoners' grievances included the bishop of London, the dean of St. Paul's, some crown justices and attorneys, the mayor, both London sheriffs, the recorder, two senior aldermen, four junior aldermen, and three common councilmen.[5] The mayor and six aldermen were included on a commission in 1570 to 'survey all grounds within two miles of the city and suburbs of London heretofore used for archery and to cause them to be reduced to the same state for archers as at the beginning of the reign of Henry VIII'.[6] Not all assignments required an official commission, and not all concerned the interests of the crown; personal requests from distinguished individuals were also dealt with. In November 1574 at the supplication of the earl of Leicester, the mayor and five other aldermen heard a dispute between an old blind man, in whose favour Leicester had written, and two others. Having done so, they agreed that his case was just and wrote to Leicester to say so, then wrote to the master of the Court of Requests praying him to hear the case as well.[7]

1   Ibid. (1591-4), vol. 247/103.

2   *CPR* (1569-72), p. 440 and *APC*, viii. 173.

3   *APC*, viii. 233.

4   *CSPD* (1581-90), vol. 229/1 and *APC*, xxx. 258-9.

5   *CPR* (1558-60), pp. 29-30. The commission had power to summon witnesses, hear evidence, and punish creditors; they were to meet at least four times a year.

6   Ibid. (1569-72), p. 29.

7   *CSPD, Add.* (1566-79), vol. 23/70-71.

But most of the special commissions given to the aldermen and councilmen concerned trade or finance. One Dr. Hectour, apparently a crown attorney or friend of a privy councillor, fell into debt, and to save him embarrassment the Privy Council appointed the mayor, the master of the rolls and Dr. Wilson to speak with Hectour's creditors and try to persuade them to wait two more years for their payment.[1] Most aldermen and the greater councilmen arbitrated commercial disputes from time to time. Alderman George Barne and the judge of the Admiralty Court settled a dispute between a foreign merchant and one Colclouth, perhaps the common councilman Mathew Colclouth. Alderman Barne and Alderman Ratclyffe examined Spanish prisoners captured in 1588, because they spoke Spanish.[2] Councilmen Thomas Aldersey, Andrew Palmer, and Alderman Richard Martin in around 1582 investigated illegal gold exports.[3] Sometimes these commercial activities involved the rulers in matters of state. The government in the Netherlands under the duke of Alva had confiscated goods belonging to English merchants there, a step that invited retaliatory measures from England. Special commissioners determined the extent of English losses and assured their compensation out of the proceeds realized by selling the confiscated Spanish goods.[4] The danger from Spain became a familiar one thereafter, especially as the Dutch began to organize their resistance, for this meant the flow of men and arms from Spain was increased. The Privy Council in September 1574 asked the mayor and the Merchant Adventurers Company to join with the lord keeper and the chancellor of the duchy of Lancaster to plan the outfitting of a fleet to observe the movements of the Spanish in the Channel.[5]

Of equal interest is the part played by City rulers in the queen's diplomatic service. The governors of the Muscovy Company offered a useful link between the tsar and the queen, one that had advantages for the queen and the merchants. In 1583 Alderman James Harvye, knowing his opinion was worth considering, sent along his views on a proposed trading treaty with Russia.[6] Eight years later Aldermen George Barne and John Harte and other governors wrote directly to Lord Burghley to warn the queen of the tsar's suspicions that his letters were not reaching the queen; they suggested that the queen

---

1 *APC,* viii. 128.
2 Ibid. 325 and xvi. 210-11.
3 *CSPD* (1581-90), vol. 157/58.
4 *CPR* (1569-72), pp. 353 and 355. Of the forty English merchants named in these two commissions at least twenty-four were active in City politics.
5 *APC,* viii. 290.
6 *CSPD* (1581-90), vol. 158/20.

should do something to dispel his suspicions.[1] London merchants also contributed substantially to the maintenance of foreign embassies. In 1591 a group of nineteen merchants trading to Turkey (including four aldermen, two common councilmen later to become aldermen, and a third future alderman) petitioned the crown for incorporation as the exclusive traders to Turkey, in order to keep out the dishonest traders. Among the arguments used to persuade the crown, they claimed to have spent a total of £40,000 for the cost of ambassadors, consuls, and agents for the queen.[2]

The City also offered the crown a sizable recruiting ground for royal officers. A number of justices and lawyers graduated from legal positions in the City to those in Westminster. This was especially true of the Elizabethan recorders, all nine of whom progressed to some higher position.[3] Onslow, Bromley, Coke, and Flemming became solicitors-general; Fleetwood and Drew became queen's serjeants, Croke a king's serjeant; Cholmeley became a serjeant-at-law, and Wilbraham an attorney of the Court of Wards — to name but a single position attained by each man. Three recorders became speakers of the House of Commons, two chief justices, and one lord chancellor. In view of his important role as legal adviser to the aldermen and his frequent journeys to Westminster on behalf of the City, the recorder was a central figure in City-crown relationships. The crown might be expected to influence appointments to this office. On the occasion of one vacancy the lord keeper wrote to the aldermen to know the candidates for the position. The City protested that the recordership was in its gift — which the crown never disputed — and indicated that James Altham of Gray's Inn (later a baron of the Exchequer) was its choice.[4] Something happened to change the aldermen's minds, however, for Altham was not chosen and never was recorder of London. It has been said that William Fleetwood owed his advance to the recordership to the earl of Leicester, and that Lord Burghley was instrumental in the rise of Edward Coke.[5] If the crown tried to influence the appointment of the recorder, the City tried to keep ex-recorders in a friendly disposition by granting them pensions and annuities.[6]

1   Ibid. (1591-94), vol. 240/65 and 70.
2   Ibid. vol. 239/44.
3   A.B. Beaven, *The Aldermen of the City of London*, 2 vols. (1908-13), i. 289-90 has summarized the careers of all but two of them, Edward Coke and Thomas Flemming, for whose subsequent positions see *DNB*.
4   W. Maitland, *History of London* (1756), i. 279-80.
5   *DNB* for both.
6   Richard Onslow surrendered his recordership on 27 June 1566 and on 21 November, in view of his renouncing a previous reversion to an undersheriffwick, he was granted by the aldermen an annual pension of £40 (Rep. 16, fos. 138b-39).

Though the problem of conflict of interest suggests itself, it is unlikely that this presented much of a problem to Elizabethan recorders. If they owed their rise in office to the patronage of an influential privy councillor, that was hardly unusual since patronage of one sort or another accounted for nearly all promotion in the sixteenth century. It would be a mistake to assume that officeholders usually discharged their duties in accordance with a patron's wishes, as a way of thanking the patron for his favour. Favours were usually done for the patron before an appropriate reward was made, if at all. Particularly in the case of Elizabethan recorders it is very hard indeed to demonstrate open conflict of interest. It was commonly recognized that while recorder of London a man worked for the interests of the City, regardless of his patron. He would not have sat in the Court of Aldermen and been assigned important City business if it were otherwise. Similarly, once the recorder left the City's service he was the queen's servant, despite his pension or his annual gifts from the City. Such gifts and pensions as the recorder received after he entered the crown's service were not meant to secure favour so much as simple attention to normal business. Such remuneration was normally paid to royal officials by those having frequent recourse to them; it was an essential source of their profits from office.

While the crown and the City were heavily dependent upon each other, their interdependence was one that brought fruitful rewards to both. Their intimate relationship also profited individuals. Some of the rulers held crown offices. Martin Bowes was master of the Mint from 1533 to 1544, and under-treasurer from 1544 to 1551, receiving the first position three years before becoming an alderman. Though he owed the king £10,000 upon retirement, he was allowed a continuation of an older pension of £66-13s-4d and was granted an annuity of 200 marks as well.[1] Richard Martin, like Bowes a goldsmith, became master of the Mint in 1581, three years after becoming an alderman and held the post until his death.[2] Another goldsmith, Councilman Andrew Palmer, was comptroller of the Mint from 1583.[3] Alderman Henry

Onslow was also speaker of the House at the time. Thomas Bromley was granted an annuity of £10 for good service and as a New Year's present shortly after he became solicitor-general (Rep. 16, fo. 460b). The same excuse was given for granting Thomas Wilbraham £13-6s-8d after he became an attorney of the Court of Wards (Rep. 17, fo. 141). In 1580 William Fleetwood, then recorder, was granted £40 'towards his charges in being made a serjeant-at-law', and other serjeants-at-law were granted £10 (Rep. 20, fo. 119b).

1   John Strype, *Ecclesiastical Memorials*, 3 vols. (Oxford 1822), vol. 2, pt. 1:425 and Beaven, *Aldermen of London*, ii. 29.

2   Beaven, ii. 40.

3   *Remembrancia*, pp. 277-8.

Billingsley was a collector of customs from 1589, for which in one year (1591) he received £400 by way of salary alone.[1] Other rulers were customs officers, including Alderman Richard Saltonstall, Alderman William Ryder, Councilman Richard Young, and Councilman Robert Dowe (Dove).[2] But in general only a few of the rulers held such royal offices, and most if not all had other supporting enterprises, particularly domestic or foreign trade. The rulers' lack of great interest in royal offices was not unique, for during the years 1600-24 the aldermen held few crown offices, and only rarely invested as customs farmers.[3]

A few of the rulers had special positions which enabled them to supply goods to government departments, particularly cloth for the Household. Baptist Hicks, councilman for a time (and briefly an alderman for five days in 1611), was the queen's mercer for many years, a position he is said to have obtained through his brother, Michael, the secretary to William Cecil.[4] As the queen's mercer he had some very lucrative contracts indeed. For one particular sale of goods he received £5,390-18s-0½d, and that was only a part of one year's business.[5] Councilman Walter Fisshe was the queen's tailor for over twenty-five years.[6] Councilman Henry Campion was the queen's brewer.[7] These royal contracts were carried out in such a way that they did not interfere with political careers in the City. By 1579, one of the years when he was the queen's brewer, Henry Campion had been a leading common councilman for at least eight years. He had served on a number of ad hoc committees appointed by the Court of Aldermen, and had been a member of the Grain Committee in 1578, a semi-permanent committee that continued to meet during 1579. He had served as a governor of Christ's Hospital during the years 1575-7 and of St. Thomas's Hospital during the years 1578-9; later he served for Bridewell Hospital from 1579-81. He had been on the vestry of

1 *CSPD* (1591-94), vol. 238/71.

2 Ibid. (1598-1601), vol. 269/25 and (1595-97), vol. 254/3 and (1591-94), vol. 239/89, and *DNB* for Ryder.

3 Robert G. Lang, 'Greater Merchants', D. Phil. thesis (Oxford Univ. 1962), especially pp. 309-18.

4 He continued as the king's mercer under James I. He was also a contractor for crown lands in 1609; see *DNB*.

5 PRO [L]ord [C]hamberlain's Department 9/93/57. Throughout volume 93 of these accounts (Great Wardrobe), Hicks is noticed: see also fos. 8b, 32-3, 40-2, 57-59b and 75b (year: 44-45 Elizabeth). For more on Hicks's extensive crown connections under James I, see Robert Ashton, *The Crown and the Money Market, 1603-40* (Oxford, 1960), *passim*.

6 See the same series (LC 9) mentioned in the last note for records of his accounts, especially the volumes which cover the first half of Elizabeth's reign.

7 *CSPD* (1547-80), vol. 132, p. 636 of the Calendar; and Jour. 21, fo. 370b where he is exempt from serving as sheriff in 1584 because of being in the queen's service.

Allhallows the Great since at least 1574 and in 1577-8 was an auditor of the churchwardens' accounts — for the second time. He was to be an auditor again in 1581-2 and 1584-5, and was churchwarden in the parish between 1585 and 1587. In his livery company, the Mercers, he had been a liveryman since 1555 and a member of the court of assistants from 1568. By 1579 he had served as warden of the company twice, the second time in 1578-9.[1] Yet Campion was not an exceptionally active councilman. He was a leading one to be sure, but the diversity of his activity is typical of many councilmen, including all of those mentioned above with some royal office or contract. In fact Richard Young, Andrew Palmer, Robert Dowe, and Walter Fisshe were all rather more active than Campion, as were each of the aldermen mentioned.

Few London rulers enjoyed any special position or office with the crown, but a number were able to profit by supplying goods. For the expenses involved in her coronation the queen turned to a number of London merchants to advance loans and provide cloth for the thousands of robes and gowns that were specially prepared for the occasion. A list of London merchants lending money for this purpose includes two aldermen and eight men then on the Common Council. Eight others were later councilmen; two of these became aldermen. Councilman Francis Pope advanced £1,396-0s-10d for coronation cloths of various types, Councilman Thomas Ackworth £1,089-18s-1d, and Alderman William Hewet £722-17s-2½d.[2] Similarly, for Elizabeth's funeral Alderman William Craven supplied cloths worth £599-15s-7½d, Councilman Robert Jenkinson £472-10s-2½d.[3] These examples are but selections, and a more thorough search would doubtless disclose that many civic leaders were crown suppliers on at least a part-time basis.

In a number of other ways various rulers prospered because of their relations with the crown. On loans to the crown creditors took interest.

---

1 For his committees in 1577, for example, Rep. 19, fos. 247 and 273; for the Grain Committee: Jour. 20, pt. 2, fos. 434-35b, 442 ff; as a hospital governor: Rep. 18, fo. 431, Rep. 19, fos. 241b, 369b and 495b, Rep. 20, fo. 114b; for the positions in his vestry see the VM (MS 819 at the GLMR) under the appropriate dates. For the livery company offices see the court of assistants minute book under the appropriate dates: entry of 15 February 1555 for the livery, the years 1568-9 and 1578-9 for his wardenships, the attendance lists from 1568 for membership of the court of assistants. In addition he may well have been the same Henry Campion who was captain of the London Trained Bands in 1588, the year of his death; Leslie, 'A Survey, or Muster', *Journal of the Society of Army Historical Research* 4 (1925), 62-71.

2 PRO LC 2/4 (3)/146-47. The itemization of these totals are in various other folios of the volume.

3 LC 2/4(4). Unfortunately this volume has no folio numbers for the appropriate references.

There were statutes against usurious rates of interest, but it was the practice in these cases to grant a dispensation allowing 10 to 12 per cent.[1] It was customary to have crown lands assigned to creditors as security for repayment of loans; or, for the loan of 1604 to James I, the jewels, pearl, treasure, and merchandise captured in 1592 from the Spanish and Portuguese carracks.[2] For the financing of his expedition to the Netherlands the earl of Leicester turned to the City for a loan of £25,000. Eighteen months later, in April 1587, he sent an urgent plea to the queen that unless he was paid soon, the mortgages he had given on his properties to various merchants would be beyond redeeming. Among the five named mortgagees are Councilman Henry Campion, who was enjoying a lease in Kent worth £6,000 in return for having lent £2,300; Councilman Thomas Aldersey and others enjoying lands worth £7,000 for a loan of £2,000; and Alderman William Webbe holding lands in Warwick for his loan of £1,500.[3]

It is sometimes clear that favours granted by one party called for reciprocation by the other. The loan of around 1560, mentioned before, was largely subscribed to by members of the Merchant Adventurers Company. In November 1563 the queen granted them a licence to·export certain cloths and to make up the money owed them by taking relief from customs payments.[4] In the case of one alderman at least, Thomas Lodge, the crown was prepared to do much more than merely reciprocate favours. Lodge was one of the several merchants who had lent money to Elizabeth in 1560. He had also been one of the sureties for redeeming Sir Henry Palmer in 1558, while the latter was a captive in France.[5] Possibly as a result of this favour and in anticipation of his share in the 1560 loan, Lodge was granted on 11 April 1559 the wardship and marriage of John Machell (son and heir of the deceased alderman, John Machell), and a special licence to export seventy sarpliers of wool on 22 June of the same year.[6] Possibly, too, the licence granted him in December 1560 to have base monies brought to the Mint for refining into bullion (and the subsequent commission of 25 November 1561 to take up lead, sulphur, coal, and other materials for the melting and refining of the metal) was connected with the queen's continued efforts to favour Lodge.[7]

1   *CSPD* (1547-80), vol. 19/2 and vol. 14, p. 111 of the Calendar.
2   *CPR* (1558-60), pp. 431-7; *Remembrancia*, p. 187 and note, and Sharpe, *London and the Kingdom*, ii. 13.
3   *CSPD* (1581-90), vol. 182/49 and ibid. *Add.* (1580-1625), vol. 30/24.
4   *CSPD* (1547-80), vol. 31/9.
5   Ibid. vol. 13/54.
6   *CPR* (1558-60), pp. 35 and 93.
7   *CSPD* (1547-80), vol. 14/55 and *CPR* (1558-60), p. 73. He was buying up lead as early as 1546, possibly with the Mint scheme already in mind. See Charles

But there may have been no connection between these events. By 1563, when there is no strong evidence Lodge was still owed favours by the queen, he was still receiving them. Towards the end of that year he may have spent some time in the Fleet Prison, for debt. The lord treasurer took up his cause and, with the help of other privy councillors, succeeded in having an advance of £6,000 made to him. Furthermore, it was suggested he be allowed to ship goods without custom's dues for six years.[1] Despite the intervention of the Privy Council on his behalf Lodge's respite was brief, and by 3 December 1566 for reasons of debt he had given up both his place on the court of assistants of the Grocers Company and his place as an alderman.[2] It would appear that Lodge enjoyed great favour with the queen or several of her leading officers, but regardless of favour there were contributing reasons for helping Lodge in 1563. That November he finished his year as mayor, which was known to be a heavy expense. In supporting him the crown may have had no other motive than maintaining the dignity and authority of the mayoralty itself, which was the right arm of the crown in England's largest city.

The crown could also be of direct aid to the London rulers in their business careers. On one occasion £31,619-15s-10d was loaned to certain merchants, among them several rulers.[3] Also in making claims against the merchants of a foreign country the assistance of the Privy Council was invaluable. After receiving a petition from several London merchants complaining that certain Frenchmen had seized their goods, the council wrote to the Admiralty to investigate the complaint, 'to the intent that their lordships [the privy councillors] may either cause the French ambassador to be dealt with for their restitution, or else take some other order as they shall think agreeable with law and justice'.[4] As in the case of Spanish merchants in the late 1560s and early 1570s, the crown occasionally took reprisals in favour of English merchants. It was particularly in connection with the chartered trading companies that the crown could do the most useful favours for the London rulers. That the prosperity of these companies depended in no small part upon propitious relations with the crown — to obtain the right to associate in the first place, to be given monopoly rights, or to gain licences for exporting or importing contrary to established law — does not need demonstration. It is worth repeating, however, that a large

J. Sisson, *Thomas Lodge and Other Elizabethans* (Cambridge, Mass., 1933), p. 16, n. 2.
1   Sisson, pp. 16-21 and 162-3.
2   Ibid. pp. 33-4.
3   *CSPD* (1581-90), vol. 173/44.
4   *APC,* x. 267-8.

majority of the rulers took part in foreign trade and understood very
well the need for continued royal favour. Many rulers also took part in
domestic trade or industry. The Company of Mineral and Battery
Works, chartered in 1568, was under the co-governorship at its
inception of Aldermen William Garrarde and Rowland Heyward; the
treasurer was Anthony Gamage, then a common councilman and later
an alderman. Among the shareholders of the company were two other
aldermen, Thomas Offley and William Bonde; two future aldermen,
George Bonde and Richard Martin; one common councilman, George
Barne (also a future alderman); and two future councilmen, Andrew
Palmer and William Bonde, junior.[1]

Good relations with the crown were especially important to the rulers
because compensation for political office did not amount to a great
deal, certainly not as much as the costs of exercising some offices. This
is not to say that aldermen had no opportunities for valuable financial
benefits. It was the intentional practice of the Court of Aldermen to
favour its own members in the leasing of City houses.[2] Even if he chose
not to live in it, the alderman might grant the lease to others. It was true
of leases granted by the City, and by livery companies and parish
churches, that aldermen and councilmen held a considerable share of
the available property – in many cases only after they came into some
City office. Yet, considering the wealth they usually had before
assuming high civic office, these favours had more to do with maintaining the dignity and position of the rulers than with compensation.
Aldermen also had authority over orphanage money, which they sometimes borrowed on their own account. But the aldermen did not collect
fees for specific services rendered, as did the horde of clerks, nor did
they receive any salary, annuity, pension, or any other form of direct
and regular remuneration. They were meant to be wealthy men before
they came into office, and this was an obvious deterent to bribery.
Against these various favours was the fact that aldermen frequently
paid outstanding bills for the City, or advanced loans to the Chamber,
and were reimbursed later when it was practical. And every alderman
covered from his own pocket the cost of his robes, of the periodic
dinners he might give for his ward officers or his livery brethren, and a
number of other expenses; he even paid for a dozen buckets in his ward,
to be kept in readiness in case of fire.[3] In the latter half of the
seventeenth century it was thought by one contemporary that the fine
paid to avoid serving the office of alderman was only one-third of the

1   Maxwell B. Donald, *Elizabethan Monopolies* (*1961*) pp. 35-9, 43-7 and 58.
2   Rep. 13, pt. 2, fo. 452b.
3   Rep. 4, fo. 124.

charges connected with the office.[1] If that ratio has any meaning for the Elizabethan period, the average expense of an aldermanry would have been around £1,200-1,500.[2]

To promote and preserve that benign disposition in the crown and its officers which was so essential to the rulers' private business activities and the City's constitutional stability, the Court of Aldermen acted as a nerve centre for distributing favours. There were routine disbursements of cash to the petty officials who periodically handled civic petitions or performed minor services for the City. These recipients were the clerks of the Exchequer, clerks of the Privy Council, clerks of the House of Commons, the serjeant-at-mace of the House, and so on. But higher officers also collected their fees for helping the City in particular issues. The comptroller of the Household under Queen Mary received £20 in 1553 'for his friendship and lawful favour heretofore shown and hereafter to be born and shown unto the same [the City] in their lawful pursuits and affairs'.[3] Similarly, in May 1560 committee members appointed by the Court of Aldermen to see the lord treasurer and the chief baron of the Exchequer concerning the City's right to appoint the measurer of woollen cloth were instructed 'that they shall gratify either of the said lords therefor [for their favour] in such sort at the said City's charge as they by their sad discretions shall think meet and convenient'.[4] There are more ambiguous references, such as the following: 'Item, it is ordered that Mr. Chamberlain [the City's chamberlain] shall presently pay and disburse the sum of £250 to certain noble personages which have moved and procured Her Majesty's most gracious favour and royal assent in a cause greatly importing the benefit of this City'.[5]

The following miscellaneous favours are all from the year 1562; each is very typical. The earl of Bedford wrote in favour of one Robert Dicons, a tailor, for the lease of a City property; the court granted it for thirty years without raising the rent and agreed to bear the maintenance charges — usually borne by the leasee. Richard Sackville (under-treasurer of the Exchequer and chancellor of the Court of Augmentations) wrote requesting that the clerk of the Bridgehouse, a master mason and carpenter of the same, should come down on the following Monday to Rochester

1 John R. Kellett, 'The Causes and Progress of the Financial Decline of the Corporation of London, 1660-94', Ph.D. thesis (Univ. of London, 1952), p. 195 referring to a contemporary pamphlet: BL London and Middlesex Pamphlets, 10350 g11 (no. 12).

2 The average fine in both periods was between £400-500.

3 Rep. 13, pt. 1, fo. 77. I am grateful to Mr. Robert Braddock for this reference.

4 Rep. 14, fo. 335.

5 Rep. 24, fo. 225.

in Kent to advise on a bridge there; he was told that the appropriate officers were unavoidably occupied that day, but this kind of request was not always rejected. The queen wrote asking for the freedom of the City to be granted to one Steven Fulwell; the court agreed. Both the earl of Shrewsbury and the earl of Sussex were also granted the freedom, and the fee was waived.[1] A final example concerns William Cecil, granted on 15 April 1561 a diversion of the City's water to his house in the Savoy. Not every house in London had its own water supply. When one of Cecil's servants carelessly wasted some of the water, Cecil himself was quick to apologize and promised to dismiss the man if he could be discovered. He agreed to allow the aldermen to fence off and lock up the area around the water pipe and keep the keys; but after all, he kept his water rights.[2]

Certainly the most sought after plums at the City's disposal were the many offices in its gift. There were perhaps five hundred at any one time, a large number being at the disposition of the mayor and the two sheriffs. Included were the members of the mayor's household, the sheriffs' serjeants, yeomen, and assistants, a number of special legal advisors, and, most numerous of all, weighers, measurers, inspectors – scores of positions to do with the markets and economic regulation.[3] The Court of Aldermen granted most offices by means of a reversion, but it was not at all unusual to grant more than one reversion for the same place. Most candidates understood this. When the vacancy developed one candidate took the office, the others either held onto their claim in anticipation of the next vacancy (since often places were filled according to the oldest reversion), or surrendered them in return for some other consideration – usually money or another reversion. Candidates could also sell their reversions, therefore a reversion was a general indication of favour but not necessarily the key to an office.

Sometimes a reversion was offered a man, even though the City had no intention of allowing him to hold the office concerned. One John Dewell, a former servant of the lord chancellor, had been granted a reversion to the office of water bailiff; in 1592 the vacancy developed but another took the office. The Privy Council wrote on Dewell's behalf demanding explanations. The aldermen replied that he was not a suitable candidate and had never been seriously considered as the future water bailiff; his grant was a mark of favour to the lord chancellor, and Dewell himself was offered £40 to renounce his claim. The Privy Council finally replied that Dewell was content not to have

1 Rep. 15, fos. 43b, 61b, 64b, 68 and 69b.
2 Rep. 14, fo. 470 and Rep. 16, fos. 239b-40b.
3 For more details on the number of offices see Appendix 2.

the office, but since it was worth £100 a year he should be given that much at least.[1] It was not always so expensive for the City to reclaim reversions.

If the City granted a large number of petitions from the queen, privy councillors, and other courtiers, the aldermen also knew how to say no. It was easy to refuse a petition if the candidate was not a freeman of the City, or if a promise had already been made to another. At other times the court stalled for time, knowing that it did not want to grant a particular office, and hoped meanwhile to find some other way of satisfying the petitioner. On 8 December 1562 the court refused the queen's suggestion for a freedom, on the grounds that not enough aldermen were present (one more than the quorum attended) and a later answer would be given.[2] Since aldermen sometimes did more serious business with fewer present, this was patently an evasion; so was their plea on another occasion that the Common Council had to grant freedoms, that therefore the aldermen could not accept requests directed solely to them.[3] It was true that the Common Council did control freedoms at the time, but had they wished the aldermen could have summoned the councilmen with no delay, as they did on occasions when it was important to do so.

Sound reasons existed for not always co-operating with those who sought civic offices. In the first place the aldermen could brook no interference in the places open exclusively to the rulers themselves: the offices in the livery companies, the wards, the parishes, the hospitals, and the positions of councilman and alderman. It was through these elected positions that the rulers governed the City. But obviously patronage over the other appointive places was crucial to their leadership, and had they lacked the gift itself they would have been abandoning an essential bargaining tool in their continual dialogue with the central government. They were quick therefore to repel the occasional royal attempts to recapture the patronage of a particular office. In defending their rights to patronage, the rulers, and in particular the aldermen, were upholding the ancient privileges and immunities which constituted London's political independence. Simultaneously they were looking after their own personal advancement, for if they could offer freedoms, leases, pensions, services, and offices to the crown and its friends, they had reason to expect that the crown would return the favour. Of course City-crown relations did not proceed only in accordance with 'deals'. Nor were the interests and

1   *APC,* xxii. 269-70 and 521 and *Remembrancia,* p. 283.
2   Rep. 15, fo. 158b.
3   *Remembrancia,* p. 155.

desires of either party always predictable, for individual privy councillors sometimes worked against others to gain a City office for different candidates. In the same way individual merchants made petitions directly opposed to the interests of other merchants, who happened to be their brethren on the Court of Aldermen. The essence of the greatly interdependent relationship between crown and City was that at many points opportunities arose to do each other favours; these were often followed up in the mutual recognition that continued relations would be smoother as a result.

The granting of offices, perhaps better than any other form of the City-crown communion, demonstrates the reciprocal nature of that intercourse. Neither party was always satisfied. Yet the interdependence of the two and the general success of both parties in compromising with one another encouraged an atmosphere of harmony and mutual trust. In no small measure the basis of this harmony was the willingness of the crown to treat the City with great respect, both by repaying its considerable debts with reasonable promptness, and by recognizing and supporting London's ancient liberties. The more the relationship continued, the more it was fruitful to the crown's power, the City's autonomy, and the rulers' own prosperity. As the rulers became more deeply entrenched in the City, the crown contented itself with their rulership, just as the rulers were increasingly royalist as the crown extended its favour and protection. Charles I did his best to trample on the tacit understandings that crown and City had built up over generations, but so deep was the bond between them, and so basic to the continued welfare of both, that even through the period of the Civil War many of the rulers remained loyal, and after the frenzy of the puritan interlude the Restoration brought back a monarch and a group of rulers devoted to the traditional communion.

9

THE TRIUMPH OF STABILITY

London in 1600 was, by any measure, one of the great cities of Europe, even if London is taken to mean the traditional City of twenty-six wards. A number of comparisons with other early modern European cities suggest themselves, though there are certainly some difficulties in indulging in this sort of analysis. No very extensive comparison is possible here, even among other English cities. Any remarks about other cities would have to be based on a sampling of secondary literature. More serious, the categories used would emerge from an understanding of just one city, in just one period, but employing these rather peculiar criteria may distort or hide the uniqueness of other cities. Nonetheless, in concluding this study it may be possible to accentuate the uniqueness of Elizabethan London by referring to several other Renaissance cities. It is particularly tempting to do so because of the work of Gideon Sjoberg. [1] Sjoberg, a sociologist, has uttered a timely and gentle reminder to historians that their pursuit of the unique and the particular has often blinded them to the broader patterns of general similarity. Using his study as a model shows that, indeed, there are a number of important respects in which early modern London was a rather typical urban entity of pre-industrial vintage.

London was like other pre-industrial cities for most of the period under examination in that it enjoyed only a slow growth in population: from thirty or forty thousand in the late fourteenth century to perhaps ninety thousand at the accession of Queen Elizabeth. It was only during the second half of the sixteenth century that in this respect London began to behave most uncharacteristically, by expanding to roughly a quarter of a million by the early seventeenth century. Whether growing gradually or rapidly, its population, typically of pre-industrial cities, was sustained by depending upon, if not subjecting, the surrounding rural lands. In the case of London it seems that virtually the whole country was called upon, in one degree or another, to sustain the behemoth on the Thames. Sjoberg has emphasized the implications for class structure of urban domination, suggesting that the cities spawned a parasitic class that was supported by the lower ranks beyond. But in England most of those who constituted the highest social group lived largely outside London and other cities. The extent to which urban groups held sway over rural peoples in England has not been determined and would seem to be worth exploring. Suffice it to say that a more

---

[1] *The Pre-Industrial City: Past and Present* (Glencoe, Ill., 1960).

appropriate way of explaining the English situation would be to recall how London both dominated and stimulated economic growth in the counties, for example in the shipping industry and in coal extraction.[1] Within the City itself economic practices reflected a wide similarity to Sjoberg's model. It was difficult to maintain standardization in prices, in the kind of goods produced, or in their quality. In fairness to the rulers, though, it must be said that they desired and worked hard to enforce certain standards. Also the City's economic base had a limited ability to expand, in part because it lacked standardization, but even more because of the restrictive practices of the guilds. Yet while the guilds restrained more enterprising industrial growth, they also had a vital part to play in looking after the spiritual and social needs of their own members. They had a direct influence on many aspects of personal life, and in this they were like other traditional guilds. Similarly on the subject of family, London provides abundant testimony to the prevalence of nepotism in making all kinds of personal and professional choices. Moreover, many of the attitudes found in London were remarkably like those in other pre-industrial cities. A deep religiosity is perhaps the most common, also an abiding regard for rank as reflected in dress, manners, and elaborate rituals; even religious practices and beliefs were not untouched by consciousness of social station. This awareness of rank helped in determining, on the one hand, whom to exclude from citizenship, and, on the other, whom to accept as the prime movers in political and social life. This urban group of Sjoberg's is much like London's rulers: they composed a kind of class or separate rank within the city. Not only did they govern, but they enjoyed most of the privileges and amenities that were available to urban dwellers. They commonly lived in the heart of the city, and they controlled recruitment to their exclusive group by co-option. As governors they exercised their authority by reference to tradition, and to certain absolutes that were based on respect for personal qualities and rank. In all these respects Renaissance London conforms closely to the model of Sjoberg's pre-industrial city.

Yet it is especially in the composition and behaviour of London's rulers that some important dissimilarities are found. In the pre-industrial model the élite were the social leaders of the country, but they were not especially qualified to govern in cities except in so far as they deliberately introduced themselves there and governed by virtue of their greater power and traditional rank. In England and Western Europe, however, the only people who fit this description of an élite were the landed powers, yet they were not the ones who held power in

1 Ralph Davis, *The Rise of the English Shipping Industry* (1962); John U. Nef, *The Rise of the British Coal Industry,* 2 vols. (1932).

London. It is apparent that Sjoberg was talking about the traditional aristocracy as the élite, for he says that they spurned trade, indeed they considered all but the wealthiest businessman to be among the outcaste groups. London's merchant-rulers were like Sjoberg's élite in that they were an oligarchic class, but the whole basis for their solidarity was vastly different. They were mostly members of the twelve chief livery companies of the City, and 70 per cent of the top political men were from only six companies. Membership in the companies was usually through apprenticeship, but apprenticeship often initiated more lasting results. Business and marriage connections were common among the rulers, and guild associations were often at the base of each. Through business and marriage ties, high standards of wealth were maintained; all London's rulers were men of the first rank in this respect. Even the social backgrounds of the rulers were largely similar: most were sons of prosperous Londoners, the middle rank of gentry, or provincial tradesmen.[1] Such common bonds were made stronger by the deliberate way in which the rulers went about choosing and advancing men of their own standing to positions of political leadership in the City. At the same time it is remarkable, considering the potential business schemes they might have developed, how much of their activity was focused on London. Individual rulers displayed versatility in deploying their time and resources, to be sure: Alderman Thomas Leigh and members of his family bought and sold leases to coal lands;[2] Aldermen William Romeney and John Watts were involved in different projects to drain fens in the Midlands;[3] Aldermen Thomas Cordell, Robert Chamberlain, and Richard Staper all invested in shipbuilding.[4] Considered as a group, however, the rulers were reluctant to engage in much that did not have a direct bearing on the City. The extent of their participation in the business of their own guilds is not known, but it was probably large. A number of rulers involved themselves in the grain trade in order to keep London properly supplied; others traded in wood and coal directly for the City.[5] Even their most ambitious ventures, those in foreign trade, were developed for the benefit of a particular group of men who lived in London. Considering also their rather meagre interest in crown offices, and their preference for marriage ties with their own group, the rulers were overwhelmingly bound to London. Because of these deep social, economic, and political ties, and because of their

---

1 See the works cited, p. 156, n. 1.

2 Nef, ii. 38.

3 William Dugdale, *The History of Imbanking and Draining* (1664), pp. 352, 383, 387.

4 *CSPD* (1595-97), p. 351; vol. 269/34.

5 Rep. 14, fos. 516b-17; Rep. 15, fos. 2, 24, 24b, 93, 323b, 433-33b; Rep. 16, fo. 333b; Rep. 21, fos. 537, 537b.

shared assumptions about government, the traditional community of London's citizens, even the poor, and above all because of their abiding loyalty to each other, the rulers constituted a highly self-conscious and cohesive class.

Within the very fluid and competitive world of London mercantile society, the rulers had created a kind of haven, one that gave purpose to their lives and from which they controlled the restless world around them.[1] Though the pressures of change were increasingly evident over the half century of Elizabeth's reign, what changed most among the rulers was not their response to these pressures, nor even their understanding of them, but rather there was a growing pride in the special character of the ruling group itself. To meet the challenge of crisis and change they found strength by looking within themselves. No group of men can ever stand entirely still, but at a time when such forces as humanism, the Reformation, Puritanism, parliamentary self-aggrandizement, sharp social mobility, and inflation were all bringing about fundamental transformations in England, the rulers of London marched to a different tune. It was not that they were indifferent to these developments, but what shaped their religious experience, for example, was not the Puritan movement itself, not the parliamentary pressure for reform, not the radical clergy's dream of a nation united in glorifying God, but the need for spiritual solace, especially within their own lives, and by extension the lives of their fellow rulers and the community of London. What guided them was the rulers' ethic. It was this ethic that shaped their many activities: the way they governed the City, their relations with the crown, and their initiative in overseas trade. Their whole style of living was governed by an attempt to perpetuate a traditional ideal. Factionalism seems to have made no inroads among them. During informal encounters in the privacy of their own homes, the aldermen doubtless voiced varying opinions on any of the matters before them, but on the fundamental concerns — the nature and purpose of the ruling group — there was a basic harmony. Were it otherwise, there could have been no convenient separation between practical action in the Court of Aldermen, and policy discussion outside. If some were discontent, or if conflicting ideologies separated individuals, there would have been no enthusiastic participation by all in the tedium of government, no dependable procedures, no formal routine, no accepted ruling élite.

1 While no doubt competitive, London merchants exhibited their rivalry most often by striving to live up to the standards established by the greatest men, that is the rulers. The style of the political leaders was aped over and over: in business, in marriage, in charitable donations. Of the 201 charter members of the Muscovy Company in 1555, 144 were described as 'merchants of London'; 68 were or became involved at some level of City politics. Of the other 76, at least 36 had the last name of a political family.

Another way in which the rulers differed from their counterparts in the pre-industrial model was their mobility. A continuing fact of life from the fourteenth to the seventeenth centuries was the great fluidity of the merchant class in London, and the failure of individual families to perpetuate themselves in positions of leadership for longer than three generations — at most. The necessary result was a constant injection of new blood. The steady stream of new men represented all social groups, save the very highest and lowest, and came from virtually all corners of the realm, not just London.[1] The very fluidity of the merchant class was part of the reason why the greatest merchants of the City developed such strenuous and nearly total devotion to London. Lacking any distinctive regional, class, or familial origins, the rulers found their particular role in the one thing they alone could do, rule London. The more they did so, the more their political capacity came to influence other aspects of their lives. In order to maintain this group of rulers it became necessary to protect and expand their financial power; to select their successors not only on the basis of wealth and the right sort of connections, but primarily on their willingness and ability to serve; and ultimately to formulate, even if unconsciously, an ideology that gave the rulers a sense of identity in the context of civic government. It was from this political commitment that they built a feeling of unity and continuity, which was otherwise not available to them. It followed from their political engagement that they did determine status mostly on the basis of achievement, not birth. In all these respects they are quite unlike the élite of the pre-industrial model.

The other ways in which they differ from that model can be attributed to their self-consciousness as London's rulers. Their perception of themselves as an integral, governing community made it easy for the crown to co-operate with them in a number of ways, and to establish a partnership which produced great benefits for both. The City performed considerable services for the crown, not least the supply of money and troops. By adjudicating trade disputes and working on royal commissions, the City rulers relieved the crown of the expense and difficulty of maintaining a larger central government. The City also distributed valuable favours to the crown and its officers in the form of offices, leases, fees, and freedoms. The crown had a direct interest in preserving and protecting the ruling class of the City which granted it so many favours and relieved it of so much tedium. This was done first by supporting the traditional institutions and privileges of the City through

---

[1] Thrupp, *The Merchant Class of Medieval London* (Ann Arbor, Mich. 1962), ch. 5; Wilbur K. Jordan, *Charities of London* (1960), especially pp. 316, 426-7; Lang, 'Greater Merchants', pp. 1-79.

which the rulers exercised their leadership, and second by encouraging the personal business ventures of the rulers. Though the queen did not favour only the merchants who happened to be associated with civic government, she had good reason to provide the political leaders with their share. City politics, mercantile enterprise, and royal favour were closely related. Therefore while civic activity was burdensome and time-consuming, for the few who held supreme power in London it was also profitable; accordingly, it was approached not with reluctance but with dedication and enormous energy. In the pre-industrial model the purposes of government were said to be to supply services, to maintain order, to exact tribute for the expenses of government, and to underwrite the rule of an élite. All that can be justly said of London, too, if it is understood that government was indistinguishable from a way of life for the rulers. Unless that was preserved all government would collapse.

The rulers also differed from the pre-industrial pattern with regard to education and religion. The rulers exercised only an indirect control over the organization of religion and education, through patronage of schools, colleges, libraries, sermons, and lectureships. For the rulers, moreover, educational institutions were not the means of sustaining their religious norms, nor did formal institutions play much part in the most essential aspects of the rulers' education. Both their religious norms and their education were forged by the London experience itself, especially ruling. The members of the typical pre-industrial élite were virtually the only ones with access to formal education, and they protected their positions by withholding such privileges as wealth and education from others. By contrast the London rulers could not have monopolized wealth and education had they wanted to, for there was a broad base of prosperity and literacy in London beyond the circle of the rulers. While the rulers certainly had a greater number of advantages than other groups, they also shouldered more arduous responsibilities. The other prominent citizens of the City were content to let the rulers have the lion's share of both the privileges and the responsibilities; the less fortunate ranks would not have conceived of taking either into their own hands.

In turning to some actual cities of the early modern period, the greatest similarities are found in considering other English communities. Most if not all English cities were, and traditionally had been, governed by an oligarchic élite of merchants, an élite which was recruited by continual introduction and amalgamation of new men who represented a variety of social backgrounds and a number of different places of origin. As civic governors all these élites seem to have mustered the same admirable devotion to matters small and large, and to have taken a comprehensive and paternalistic view of their duties. In methods of governing, each city had its particular features, but broadly the dominance of an executive council or court by the greatest merchants stands out as a parallel. In most English cities there seems to have been a close relationship between a central executive court and the lesser authorities in the neighbourhoods; further research is needed to discover how unique the link was between London's aldermen and common councilmen, on the one hand, and the vestry councils and courts of assistants in the guilds, on the other. In most cities it seems that the merchant-rulers were the key political figures, not the legal officers or bureaucrats whom the rulers subordinated and supervised. There was usually a close connection between political power, wealth, economic activity, family, and guild. Some élites reflected a rather narrower band of connections; for example, the rulers of Bristol were largely merchant adventurers,[1] and those of Newcastle were mostly men who monopolized control of the coal fields (the hostmen).[2] The priority of particular connections varied from place to place too. In Newcastle the Mercers Company was the dominant guild because of its traditional tie with the hostmen; in Bristol, family connections were apparently more useful than those of guild.

In all the English communities the most notable similarity is that in the century and a half preceding the Civil War there was a marked continuity and internal harmony in political affairs, and a predominance of local interests over national. Whether a city's economic fortune was in decline, as in the case of Lincoln,[3] or on the upswing, as in London or Exeter,[4] the recruiting of the élite and their manner of governing followed traditional lines. No doubt this relative tranquility in political development was due to the disposition of the sovereign, and the many legal grants and practical circumstances which enshrined local autonomy. At the same time no English city had to undertake the perils of carrying out its own foreign policy, the results of which on the Continent often had profound, and shattering, effects on civic political practice.[5] Even such a potentially disruptive force as Puritanism did not by itself disturb the prevailing calm. In Newcastle Puritans managed to

---

[1] Patrick McGrath, *Merchants and Merchandise in Seventeenth Century Bristol,* Publications of the Bristol Records Society, 19 (Bristol, 1955).

[2] Roger Howell, Jr., *Newcastle-Upon-Tyne and the Puritan Revolution* (Oxford, 1967).

[3] J.W.F. Hill, *Tudor and Stuart Lincoln* (Cambridge, 1956).

[4] Wallace T. McCaffrey, *Exeter, 1540-1640: The Growth of an English County Town* (Cambridge, Mass., 1958).

[5] Gene Brucker, *Renaissance Florence* (New York, 1969); E. William Monter, *Calvin's Geneva* (New York, 1967); William J. Bouwsma, *Venice and the Defense of Republican Liberty* (Berkeley and Los Angeles, 1968).

sustain a minority group in the city's leading offices, but they were not a dogmatic party, for they divided on such issues as ship money and monopolies. Even during the Civil War a substantial group of the rulers, as in London, remained loyal royalists. In Exeter the extent of Puritanism is less clear, but on the eve of the Long Parliament the rulers there accepted royal leadership and sought to preserve the integrity of their own small group – again, remarkably like the rulers of London.

The respects in which London stands out from other English cities seem, in large part, attributable to its greater size. Size and a rather special set of arrangements with the crown is a better way of putting it. No other city enjoyed the sort of reciprocal relations with the crown that London did, no other city could buttress and supplement royal authority in the way that London did, and no other community of civic governors was so carefully protected and nourished by the crown as the London rulers. No other group of rulers had so much cause for profound loyalty to the crown. Also no other English city could have had a comparable impact on the realm, or its commercial expansion. The great predominance of London doubtless gave her rulers greater confidence; they were in a unique position to make the most of their opportunities. But it was a consequence of these close ties that the crown was relentless in keeping the rulers up to the mark: it seemed implicitly understood that its flow of favours depended on satisfactory discharge of civic duties.

In looking at some leading continental cities it is not unusual to find great merchants of international stature who simultaneously realized in civic politics the core of their being. The rulers of Nuremberg,[1] Strasbourg,[2] Florence, and especially Venice seem to have shared something like the rulers' ethic. By comparison with these cities what was unique for London was, once again, its close reciprocal relationship with a sovereign power, especially the reinforcement of stability and tradition which resulted from that relationship. Geneva, thanks to its Calvinist zeal, revitalized its economic strength and earned great influence because of its religious exports, but to achieve these results Geneva had to break with its past and its traditional overlord. Strasbourg and Nuremberg, like other imperial free cities, could not long maintain their independence in the face of ambitious territorial princes and consolidating nation states. Florence fathered the Rennaissance, but it developed no fondness for stability and continuity; nor did its independence long endure. Venice, of all the continental cities

---

1 Gerald Strauss, *Nuremberg in the Sixteenth Century* (New York, 1966).
2 M.U. Chrisman, *Strasbourg and the Reform* (New Haven, 1967).

mentioned the most like London, kept its independence longer than most, but it enjoyed no sponsorship from a benign patron. Paris did have a tie with her sovereign more like London's, though there the embrace of the monarchy seems to have suffocated the city. Also there were profound differences in the nature of its ruling élite, or actually the lack of one.[1] Socially the leaders of Paris were not the great merchants, or not exclusively, because there were also lawyers, crown officers, and the nobility. No particular group had ever unified itself into a ruling class in Paris, and subsequently imposed its identity on the city. There was no communal ethic that bound the prominent together; jurisdictionally there were separate powers both for the burghers at the Hôtel de Ville, and for the crown's officers at the Châtelet.

If stability is a virtue, Elizabethan London must be acclaimed a paragon. But there was a price to pay. From an internal point of view the only price was to lose flexibility, not a very heavy charge, to be sure, unless there were threatening circumstances that demanded change. There were not. There were some signs of strain in the fact that the ancient ward inquest simply could not keep up with the growing abuses in the ward, yet the slack was taken up by vestrymen, as well as by the Common Council and the Court of Aldermen. The livery companies were no longer able to provide an adequate supply of corn, but private dealers largely filled the gap. No great food scarcities developed in London, at least among the citizens. The great burdens of civic government were met, with extraordinary success, by widening the base of participation to include more common councilmen. London was growing at an alarming rate, and the rulers could not cope in parishes where they had no control over the vestry, or over individuals not associated with the guilds. But, with the exception of a few 'outliberties' which they were forced to absorb, the rulers were successful in disassociating themselves from expanding London, and, to their eternal relief, they successfully resisted the crown's scheme to reorganize and rationalize government for the whole metropolitan region. Because no fundamental adjustments were made in the face of the enormous physical expansion of London, which began during Elizabeth's reign, the City — traditional and beloved by her rulers — became 'the City', no longer synonymous with London. That was doubtless a source of satisfaction to the aldermen. Well might they congratulate themselves, for in a time of upheaval they had survived unscathed, unchanged because they adhered to a cherished ideal.

1 Orest Ranum, *Paris in the Age of Absolutism* (New York, 1968); Leon Bernard, *The Emerging City: Paris in the Age of Louis XIV* (Durham, 1970).

But if the uniqueness of London was mostly in its association with the crown, that very link was to exact a heavy price. So stable had the ruling élite become, and so dependent upon the crown to reinforce it, that gradually, imperceptively, the rulers became unable to change. Under the first two Stuarts the crown interfered more in civic government, it openly tried to influence some elections, it wrangled with the rulers over the suburbs and tried to involve them more than the rulers desired, it extracted greater amounts of money, and it quibbled over certain civic rights formerly guaranteed by charter. Even worse, the crown strained the reciprocal relations with the rulers by challenging the right of the livery companies to their Irish estates, and by pressing investigations into 'concealed' lands of the companies.[1] In the face of these attacks the aldermen had little choice but to comply; they had become royalists without wanting to, really without knowing it. They suffered temporary eclipse with the star of Charles I when the parliamentary radicals thrust them aside.

But traditions are more difficult to remove than men. Despite the boldness of the radical leadership in London in the early 1640s, it is interesting how in most important respects they embraced the approach of London's rulers. Though as new men they differed from their immediate predecessors in social and economic background, that had been true of new men coming into the rulership since the early fourteenth century. It was in their lack of family and business ties with the previous rulers that they differed the most. What remained similar was their behaviour once in power. They showed great respect for ancient City privileges and traditions, and particular liking for an oligarchic method of ruling. Not only did these radicals use tactics reminiscent of the aldermen, they were also reluctant to bring about any reform of the legal constitution which might threaten their own rule. The political engine of the City was ideal for their purposes, offering as it did both the devices with which to control London and the means for resisting detestable royal policy.

The City, in other words, continued to live a life of its own, and it went on influencing the lives of those who controlled its institutions. In concluding this book on the men whose destiny was most closely joined with the City's — the rulers — several points about merchants and their place in the wider scheme of things suggest themselves. Hopefully sufficient emphasis has been placed on the uniqueness of London's political élite for merchants no longer to be considered a homogeneous group within the comfortable but still subservient upper

1 Valerie Pearl, *London and the Outbreak of the Puritan Revolution* (1964), ch. 3.

regions of the third estate. For three centuries preceding the Stuart accession, the rulers of London had been a fiercely independent community who would have refused to stand and be judged on the middling terraces of society where some historians have consigned them. They did not maintain their existence by filling the belly of the Exchequer, or by serving the convenience of the sovereign. To what meagre, inglorious station would the crown have been reduced, one wonders, without the backing of the City and its rulers? The rulers' support of royal government was mandatory and comprehensive, to be sure, but it was not gratuitous. In return for co-operating with the crown the City preserved its political autonomy, and the rulers enriched themselves through royal favours. The rulers exhibited no fondness for social climbing, nor did they abandon their own urban ways for those of rural gentility. Even as they invested in county estates, even while they shared in business enterprises with the gentry, even when a few of their relatives married into the nobility, the rulers continued to live in the City. Their lives were centred on the City and the overlapping ties of kinship and fraternity they had created there. They fashioned some of the boldest and most profitable ventures known to Europe, but profit was not their goal. Profit was a necessary condition to stay in business, but the purpose of all their enterprise was to preserve their own unique way of life. That was achieved largely through civic politics, and for that reason every ruler participated actively in the often tiresome details of civic government. Through a clear understanding of themselves and what was best for them, the rulers saw that the world around them, and their future too, must be utterly in harmony with their past. Thus they fashioned and refined the politics of stability. Thus, by the end of the sixteenth century, the rulers of London were traditionalists to the core, not so much by policy or design as by birthright and instinct.

APPENDICES

1

LIST OF RULERS

This appendix lists the various rulers according to the categories mentioned throughout the text; lists of other influential men in City politics are also included.

A. The élite. The élite are the sixty-four aldermen who were mayors; seven were mayors before Elizabeth's accession and ten succeeded to the mayoralty only after the queen's death, but all are considered Elizabethans. For details on their years of service consult Beaven, *Aldermen of London*, ii. 29-48. The élite are listed in the order in which they came to the Court of Aldermen; the year of their mayoralty is shown.

Martin Bowes, 1545-6
Rowland Hill, 1549-50
Thomas Whyte, 1553-4
John Lyon, 1554-5
William Garrarde, 1555-6
Thomas Offley, 1556-7
William Hewet, 1559-60
Thomas Curtes, 1557-8
Thomas Leigh, 1558-9
William Chester, 1560-1
Thomas Lodge, 1562-3
William Harper, 1561-2
John Whyte, 1563-4
Richard Malorye, 1564-5
Richard Champyon, 1565-6
Christopher Draper, 1566-7
Roger Martyn, 1567-8
Thomas Rowe, 1568-9
Alexander Avenon, 1569-70
William Allen, 1571-2
Rowland Heyward, 1570-1, 1591
Lionel Duckett, 1572-3
John Ryvers, 1573-4
James Hawes, 1574-5
Ambrose Nicholas, 1575-6
John Langley, 1576-7
Thomas Ramsey, 1577-8
Richard Pype, 1578-9
Nicholas Woodroffe, 1579-80
John Braunche, 1580-1
James Harvye, 1581-2
Thomas Blanke, 1582-3

Edward Osborne, 1583-4
Thomas Pullyson, 1584-5
Wolstan Dixie, 1585-6
George Barne, 1586-7
George Bonde, 1587-8
Richard Martin, 1589, 1594
Martin Calthorp, 1588-9
John Harte, 1589-90
John Allott, 1590-1
William Webbe, 1591-2
William Rowe, 1592-3
Cuthbert Buckle, 1593-4
John Spencer, 1594-5
Stephen Slanye, 1595-6
Henry Billingsley, 1596-7
Thomas Skinner, 1596
Richard Saltonstall, 1597-8
Stephen Soame, 1598-9
Nicholas Mosley, 1599-1600
William Ryder, 1600-1
John Garrarde, 1601-2
Robert Lee, 1602-3
Thomas Bennett, 1603-4
Thomas Lowe, 1604-5
Leonard Holliday, 1605-6
John Watts, 1606-7
Henry Rowe, 1607-8
Humphrey Weld, 1608-9
Thomas Cambell, 1609-10
William Craven, 1610-11
James Pemberton, 1611-12
John Swynnerton, 1612-13

B. The notables. The fifty notable aldermen are listed first, in alphabetical order, followed by the forty-one notable councilmen. In the lists that follow, the livery affiliation and the approximate dates on the Common Council are shown for councilmen. If anything, the inclusive dates shown understate the actual length of tenure, because once elected councilmen often served for life, but their names appear in the records usually only when they became officeholders or joined committees.

James Altham
Henry Anderson
Nicholas Backhouse
James Bacon
Edward Bankes
Benedict Barnham
Francis Barnham
Humphrey Baskerfeld
Paul Bayning
Henry Beecher
William Bonde, Sr.
Francis Bowyer
William Boxe
Robert Brooke
John Catcher
Richard Chamberlyn, Sr.
Roger Clarke
John Cowper
William Dane
William Elkyn
Richard Foulkes
Anthony Gamage
William Glover
Richard Goddard
Richard Gourney

Edward Gylbert
Robert Hampson
Robert Hardyng
John Hawes
Christopher Hoddesdon
Edward Holmedon
Peter Houghton
Robert Howse
Edward Jakman
William Kympton
Richard Lambert
William Masham
John More
Henry Mylles
Hugh Offley
John Oliff
Henry Prannell
Anthony Ratclyffe
William Romeney
Thomas Smythe
Thomas Starkye
Robert Taylor
William Thwayte
Ralph Woodcocke
David Woodroffe

Thomas Aldersey, haberdasher, 1571-99
Thomas Bacon, salter, 1547-71
Thomas Banks, barber surgeon, 1583-96
Thomas Bannyster, skinner, 1553-72
Richard Barnes (Baron), mercer, 1558-71
Richard Bowdler, draper, 1583-99
Thomas Bramley, haberdasher, 1577-99
Richard Buckland, haberdasher, 1558-71
Anthony Cage, salter, 1559-83
Florentins Caldwell, haberdasher, 1593-1602
Mathew Colclouth, draper, 1571-83
Thomas Fettiplace, ironmonger, 1589-1601
Walter Fisshe, merchant taylor, 1573-1581
William Gibbons, salter, 1558-77
Richard Grafton, grocer, 1553-61
John Harbie, skinner, 1578-1610
John Harryson, goldsmith, 1558-71 (alderman, 9 September-21 October 1574)
Richard Hills, merchant taylor, 1558-73
Roger Jones, dyer, 1589-1604
John Kyrby (Kyrkby), grocer, 1575-8

William Leonard, mercer, 1560-73
Nicholas Luddington, grocer, 1565-89
John Mabbe, goldsmith, 1573-77
Robert Offley, haberdasher, 1558-93
Andrew Palmer, goldsmith, 1577-93
William Peterson, haberdasher, 1558-65
Hugh Pope, haberdasher, 1559-60
Thomas Pygot, Sr., grocer, 1558-65
John Pynder, vintner, 1589-99
Blaise Saunders, grocer, 1574-77
George Sotherton, merchant taylor, 1582-99
Nowell Sotherton, merchant taylor, 1589-1608
Richard Staper, clothworker, 1577-1600 (alderman, 14-17 October 1594)
William Towerson, Sr., skinner, 1561-83
Geoffrey Walkedon, skinner, 1555-71
Thomas Ware, fishmonger, 1560-89
Roger Warfeld, grocer, 1577-89
Christopher Wase, goldsmith, 1589-1603
Nicholas Wheeler, draper, 1561-83
Lawrence Wythers, salter, 1559-73
Richard Young, grocer, 1561-83

C. The leaders. From the total of 118 leaders thirty-six were selected for study in various comparisons with notables and the élite. These thirty-six are indicated by an asterisk (*).

William Abrahm, vintner, 1576-84
Thomas Ackworth, merchant taylor, 1559-61
John Alderson, vintner, 1593-9
Richard Arnold, haberdasher, 1593-9
Robert Aske, goldsmith, 1583
Thomas Audley, skinner, 1573-89
John Baker, mercer, 1559-65
Roger Bansted, embroiderer, 1561-?77
Thomas Bayarde, clothworker, 1575-9
Cuthbert Beston, girdler, 1559-?66
William Beswicke, draper, 1558-61 (alderman, 5 October 1564-10 July 1565)
John Blounte, clothworker, 1583-97
William Bodnam, grocer, 1571-5
William Bonde, Jr., haberdasher, 1593-1602
Simon Bourman, haberdasher, 1589-99
Edmond Bragge, haberdasher, 1571-83
*Edward Bright, ironmonger, 1559-74
Bartholomew Brookesby, skinner, 1558?-73
Richard Browne, merchant taylor, 1558-73
William Bulley, fishmonger, 1560-5
John Cage, salter, 1589-99
John Calthorp, draper, 1558-63
Robert Cambell, ironmonger, 1579-99 (alderman, 19 January-1 February 1597)
Henry Campion, mercer, 1571-7
Robert Chamberlain, ironmonger, 1599 (alderman, 29 July-October 1596)
*William Chelsham, mercer, 1558-71
William Chester, Jr., draper, 1589-1600
Nicholas Chowne, haberdasher, 1555-61
William Cockyn, skinner, 1573-89
*Robert Coggan, clothworker, 1589-99
Thomas Cordell, mercer, 1590-9 (alderman, 11 February-27 November 1595)
William Coxe, grocer, 1560-73
Thomas Cranfeld, mercer, 1573-83
George Crowther (Crowder), vintner, 1574-89
Henry Dale, haberdasher, 1577-83
Thomas Daunster, girdler, 1571-83
William Denham, goldsmith, 1576-7
Richard Denman, grocer, 1589-99
*Bartholomew Dodd, haberdasher, 1560-77
*Robert Dowe, merchant taylor, 1565-93
Robert Duckington, merchant taylor, 1559-61

*Baldwin Durham, mercer, 1589-1602
John Edmonds, fishmonger, 1571-93
Robert Fletton (Flecton), grocer, 1599-1600
*George Forman, skinner, 1558-75
*John God, merchant taylor, 1559-71
Richard Gore, merchant taylor, 1601-11
*John Gresham, Jr., mercer, 1560-76
Richard Hale, grocer, 1583-99
*Edward Hall, haberdasher?, 1561-76
Thomas Hall, salter, 1573-9
*Thomas Heaton (Eaton), mercer, 1560-71
*William Hewet, Jr., clothworker, 1574-93
James Hewyshe, grocer, 1576-89
*Baptist Hicks, mercer, 1589-1603
John Highlord, skinner, 1589-1603
Robert Hilson, mercer, 1574-83
*Edmund Hogan, mercer, 1565-93
Roger Hole, fishmonger, 1583
*Humphrey Huntley, ironmonger, 1583-95
Godfrey Isbard, haberdasher, 1576-83
Henry Isham, mercer, 1576-93
John Jackeson, founder, 1558-71
*Thomas Jennins, fishmonger, 1555-71
Clement Kelke, haberdasher, 1573-84
John King, tallow chandler, 1560
*Thomas Kyghtley, leatherseller, 1559-67
John Lacie, clothworker, 1558-83
Edward Lee, merchant taylor, 1558-63
John Loves, mercer, 1559-60
*Thomas Lowe, vintner, 1558-71
Emanuel Lucar, merchant taylor, 1559-61
*John Lute, clothworker, 1559-86
Arthur Malby (Manby), fishmonger, 1574-89
Thomas Medcalf, goldsmith, 1559-?74
William Meggs, draper, 1576-99
*William Merycke, merchant taylor, 1559-71
*Richard Morris, ironmonger, 1561-83
John Mynore, draper, 1560
Gabriel Newman, joiner, 1589-99
Gregory Newman, grocer, 1559
*John Newman, grocer, 1583-99
William Norton, stationer ?, 1583-93
Thomas Offley, Jr., merchant taylor, 1559-60
William Parker, draper, 1559-61

John Peyrce, fishmonger 1565-9
Nicholas Pierson, skinner, 1589-1603
Richard Plott, brewer, 1571-83
Francis Pope, merchant taylor, 1559-61
Richard Poynter, draper, 1558-61
Richard Procktor, merchant taylor,
 1589-1602
*John Quarles, Sr., draper. 1559-73
*William Quarles, mercer, 1589-93
 (alderman, 6 September-8
 November 1599)
*Richard Reynolds, goldsmith, 1561-73
Thomas Riggs, haberdasher, 1573-83
*Francis Robinson, grocer, 1558-73
William Sherington, haberdasher,
 1573-83
*John Skott, salter, 1560-83
Gregory Smythe, merchant taylor,
 1593-7
Robert Sole, salter, 1561-83
*John Sparke, merchant taylor, 1560-73
Nicholas Spencer, merchant taylor,
 1571-93

*Richard Springham, mercer, 1559-65
*John Stone, haberdasher, 1589-1600
John Storer, baker, 1589-1603
Edmund Style, grocer, 1558-61
*Oliver Style, grocer, 1599 (alderman,
 19 October-14 December 1596)
Christopher Swaldell, barber surgeon,
 1589-93
Thomas Taylor, goldsmith, 1583-9
Robert Thomas, draper, 1599
Richard Thornhill, grocer, 1569-71
*John Wetherall, goldsmith, 1559-76
John Whitehorn, clothworker,
 1559-65
William Widnell, merchant taylor,
 1574-8
*Thomas Wilford, merchant taylor,
 1561-99
*John Withers, salter, 1577-91
*Richard Wright, ironmonger,
 1583-99
*Robert Wythens, vintner, 1573-93
 (alderman, 18-20 June 1590)

D. The other aldermen. Of the 138 Elizabethan aldermen twenty-four were neither élite nor notable aldermen; they served less than a year, usually only long enough to arrange a discharge. Several of them have been listed before as notable or leading common councilmen.

Bartholomew Barnes
Lancelot Bathurst
William Beswicke
Hugh Brawne
Robert Cambell
Robert Chamberlain
Peter Collett
Thomas Cordell
John Dent
Edward Fisher
Giles Garton
Gerard Gore

Philip Gunter
John Hardyng
John Harryson
John Hayden
Henry Heyward
Richard Humble
William Quarles
John Robinson
Richard Staper
Oliver Style
William Thorowgood
Robert Wythens

E. Other common councilmen. The names of 492 other men who were probably on the Common Council follow below. Their names were gathered partly from among certain officeholders and committee-men in certain select years; see p. 13, n. 3. In addition whenever I found evidence in parish, ward, or livery records — and other places in civic records, such as the Repertories and Journals — of a man's member-ship on the council, I added him to this list. However it has never been my intention to identify all councilmen. Indeed that is no longer possible given the scanty survival of election records, and the fact that names in the City's minute books are only those of officeholders and committeemen. It is not therefore a complete roster of Elizabethan councilmen, though it does represent a list of the most active ones, who held offices and served on committees. Once again, dates shown are an indication of the active years as committeemen and/or office-holders, not the whole span of tenure on the council. Where no date follows the name, or where only one year is shown, the man was noticed only once as either a committeeman, a hospital governor, or as a surety for civic bonds. Because men could change livery affiliation, it is possible that some men are shown more than once, for example, the two Thomas Allens may be the same man. Lacking sufficient evidence to distinguish such possible duplications, I have listed both.

Henry Adams, cutler
Richard Adams, ?, 1575
William Albanye, merchant taylor, 1561-76
John Alden, grocer
Anthony Alderson, clothworker
Francis Allen, clothworker
Thomas Allen, haberdasher
Thomas Allen, skinner, 1571-91
Robert Allison, brewer
George Allyn, skinner, 1558-61
Richard Allyn, haberdasher, 1558-9
John Alsoppe, haberdasher, 1576-7
James Anston, ?, 1595-1601
Robert Appowell, ?, 1576
John Archer, fishmonger, 1583-9
Richard Ashbye (Asby), embroider, 1588-95
Edward Atkinson, ?, 1575-9
Gyles Atkynson, merchant taylor, 1558-60
James Awstin, dyer

William Babham, grocer, 1575-83
Nicholas Bacon, ?, 1561
Thomas Bagshaw, fishmonger
William Bailley, ?, 1559-73
John Baker, ?, 1577-88
    Baker, scrivener
    Ballett, goldsmith
William Bancks, skinner ?, 1576
Edward Barkeley, mercer
Christopher Barker, ?, 1584-8
Francis Barker, ?, 1558
William Barnard, draper
John Barnes, haberdasher, 1572-4
Richard Barnett, mercer
Thomas Barnham, draper, 1573
Richard Barrett, mercer
George Basseforde, ?, 1559-60
Thomas Bateson, mercer, 1589-99
John Bayworth, clothworker
William Beareblock, goldsmith
Aunsell Becket, haberdasher, 1571-6

Harry Beecher, Jr., haberdasher, 1583
William Benedick, ?, 1596-1614
William Bennett, fishmonger
Francis Bennison, haberdasher, 1570-1
Hugh Bennye, ?, 1571
William Bery, ?, 1559
John Best, ?, 1571-6
George Biship, stationer
John Blackman, ?, 1571
Michael Blagne, tallow chandler
Thomas Blunte, mercer, 1561-73
John Bonde, ?, 1560
Thomas Bonde, ?, 1561
John Boorne, leatherseller, 1580-5, 1596-8
Thomas Bowcher, haberdasher
William Bower, haberdasher, 1559-61
George Bowles, grocer
Richard Bowser, ?, 1583-6
Thomas Boxe, grocer, 1599-1600
Thomas Bradshaw, mercer, 1577
Cuthbert Brand, clothworker
Thomas Brasy, haberdasher, 1573-4
Robert Braunche, ?, 1559
George Braythwayt, draper, 1565
Robert Brette, merchant taylor, 1576-83
Peter Bristowe, ?, 1560-2
William Brokebancke, grocer
Thomas Bromfield, leatherseller
John Brooke, draper ?, 1571-3
Bartholomew Broskerby, scrivener, 1558
Humphrey Browne, girdler
John Browne, ?, 1576
Thomas Browne, haberdasher, 1558-76
Henry Buckfeld, girdler, 1558-61
Clement Buckle, draper
Thomas Bullman, ?, 1571-3
James Bullye, fishmonger, 1560
Anthony Burbage, ?, 1581-6
Edmund Burbon, ?, 1560
John Burnell, clothworker

Edward Burton, clothworker, 1565-74
Simon Burton, wax chandler, 1571-3
Henry Bushe, skinner, 1558-9
Christopher Busher, ?, 1559-60
    Bussell, haberdasher
Henry Butler, draper
Thomas Bygges, blacksmith, 1561
John Byley, ?, 1576
William Byrde, mercer, 1559-60

Lawrence Caldwell, vintner, 1597-1611
Henry Callyce, girdler, 1559
Anthony Calthorp, ?, 1571-3
Bryan Calverley, draper, 1571-87
Abraham Campion, clothworker
Alexander Carlyle, ?, 1559
William Carowe, draper
Robert Carrell, ironmonger
Thomas Castell, draper, 1558
John Cater, vintner, 1559
    Chaire (Chare), ?
Richard Chamberlyn, Jr., ironmonger,
    1599
John Cheeke, mercer
Francis Cherry, vintner
William Chyvall (Chevall), draper,
    1558-9
Owen Clayde, salter
William Clayton, grocer
John Clerke, clothworker, 1575-83
Henry Cletherowe, ironmonger
William Cocks (Coxe), grocer
William Coggan, clothworker, 1589
Roger Coise, ?, 1569-72
Robert Cokayne, clothworker
John Colby, clothworker
William Coles, grocer
John Collett, ?, 1600-3
Zachary Collisar, clothworker
John Colmer, grocer, 1571-7
Richard Colmer, grocer, 1576
Thomas Colshill (Colcell), ?, 1561-78
Gabriel Colsten, grocer, 1577-80
Henry Colthurst, grocer
James Colymer, haberdasher
John Comes (Combe), ?, 1598-
    1609
Edward Cooke, ?, 1558-59
Robert Cooper, draper
Thomas Corbett, skinner
Clement Cornewall, ironmonger,
    1558
John Cosworth,?, 1559-61
William Cosworth, ?, 1559
Richard Cotton, ?, 1583-9
John Cowper (Cooper), ?, 1601-9
Richard Cowper, dyer
    Coxe, clothworker
John Craiford, tallow chandler
John Craythorne, cutler, 1558

Henry Crele (Crede), ?, 1560
Ralph Crewe, mercer, 1599
Geoffrey Croume, ?
Richard Crowche, sadler
William Crowche, ?, 1594-1606
Henry Cryde, ?, 1559
Richard Culverwell
William Curtes, pewterer, 1558-9
Robert Cutts, ironmonger

Arthur Dawbenny, merchant taylor,
    1575
Oliver Dawberry, tallow chandler,
    1565
James Deane, draper
Robert Dickenson, draper
Thomas Ditchfeld, salter, 1559
Thomas Dixon, clothworker
    Dobbs, skinner
Francis Dodd, haberdasher, 1576
George Dodd, vintner
Philip Dodd, ?, 1573-6
Richard Dodson, clothworker
William Dodworth, merchant taylor
Mathew Dolman, haberdasher
Allen Downer, ?, 1598
Giles Duncombe, leatherseller
Edward Dycher, clothworker,
    1559-76

Robert Easte, ironmonger
Christopher Edwards, ?, 1571
John Edwards, draper
John Edwards, vintner
Thomas Egerton, mercer
Edward Elliott, vintner
James Ellwicke, mercer
Edward Elmer, grocer, 1559-76
Henry Elsing, baker, 1567-81
Jeffrey Elwayes, merchant taylor
James Emery, salter
John Essex, ?, 1559-60
Mathew Eyeld, ?, 1576

Nicholas Farrar, skinner
Richard Farrington, clothworker
Thomas Farrington, vintner
Henry Faux, grocer
James Feake, goldsmith
    Feltham, vintner
Humphrey Ferfax, grocer, 1577
Richard Ferror, grocer, 1558
Mathew Field, mercer, 1571
Cornelius Fishe, skinner, 1599
Thomas Fisher, skinner
Ralph Fitch, vintner
Thomas Forman, skinner
Richard Foulkes, clothworker, 1560-1
    (alderman? 19 January 1557-6
    August 1560)

Edward Fowler, grocer, 1559-61
Richard Fox, clothworker
John Foxall, mercer, 1574-5
Robert Frier, goldsmith

Robert Gabbett, haberdasher
Richard Gadbury, ?, 1594-1601
William Gale, barber surgeon, 1590-1607
Thomas Garden
Christopher Gardener
Thomas Gardener, ?, 1587-90
        Gardiner, goldsmith, 1573-4
John Gardner, mercer
Simon Gardner, fishmonger
Thomas Gare, ?, 1571
Anthony Garrarde, mercer, 1576-7
William Garraway, draper
Henry Gele, ?, 1559
William Gifford, ?, 1558-62
James Gonnell, stationer,
        1579-93
John Goodwyn, ?, 1560-1
William Gore, merchant taylor
Lawrence Gough (Goffe), draper
Richard Grace, goldsmith, 1558
Richard Granger, ?, 1571-6
John Gravage, haberdasher
Thomas Green, cutler
Lawrence Greene, cutler, 1573-5

Nicholas Hacker, fishmonger
Richard Hacket, dyer, 1571
Thomas Haies (Hayes), draper, 1603
John Haldon, ?, 1560
John Hall, draper, 1589-93
Robert Hall, grocer
John Halson (Hulson), scrivener,
        1558-9
William Hanbury, baker
George Hangar, clothworker
William Harding, clothworker
John Hare, mercer, 1556-61
John Harrison, stationer
Sebastian Harvye, ironmonger, 1602-3
John Hawes, Jr., clothworker, 1593
Paul Hawkins, vintner
Robert Hawys (Howse), merchant
        taylor, 1576-89
Thomas Hayt, ?, 1571
Thomas Heardson, draper, 1577
Folke Heathe, skinner
John Heathe, cowper, 1571
Francis Heaton, goldsmith, 1576-7
Richard Heckes, poulterer
Hugh Hendley (Henley), merchant
        taylor
George Heton, merchant taylor,
        1558-9
Edward Hewer, ?, 1559-60
Thomas Hewet, clothworker, 1561-71
Edward Heyward, draper, 1559-61

Anthony Hickman, ?, 1565
Thomas Hickman, haberdasher
Anthony Higgens, skinner
William Higges, mercer
Francis Higham, draper
Thomas Hill, haberdasher, 1599
John Hilliard, goldsmith, 1576
Edmund Hills, woodmonger, 1571
John Hitchens (Hutchens), 1584-99
William Hobson, haberdasher, 1576
Richard Hodge, ?, 1571-4
William Hogeson, merchant taylor
George Horde, baker, 1559
William Horne, grocer
Simon Horspoole, clothier, 1590-2
Charles Hoskyns, merchant taylor,
        1565
Robert Howe, salter
Miles Hubbard, clothworker
Thomas Hunt, fishmonger
Thomas Hunt, skinner, 1558-77
William Huson, draper
Richard Hutton, armorer

John Ingram, baker, 1571
John Ireland, salter
John Isham, mercer, 1571

Arthur Jackson, clothworker
John Jackson, clothworker
William James, merchant taylor, 1558
Robert Jenkinson, merchant taylor,
        1598-1615
John Johnson, merchant taylor, 1599-
        1600
Richard Johnson
Thomas Johnson, merchant taylor,
        1598-1626
William Judd, ?, 1558-60

John Kead, baker
Hugh Keale (Keyle), goldsmith
John Keale (Keyle), goldsmith
William Keltridge, ?, 1580-98
William Kerwyn, freemason
George Kevall, scrivener, 1597-1601
Anthony Keye, ?, 1595
Robert Keyres, ?, 1576
Edmund Keys, salter, 1559-65
Warner King, fishmonger
Edward Kympton

William Lambe, clothworker, 1573-5
John Lamberd, ?, 1565-71
Francis Lambert, ?, 1571
John Langley, draper
Thomas Lawrence, goldsmith
Garrard Lee, draper, 1558
Henry Lee, draper, 1559

Peter Leggat, ?, 1587-8,
    1589-93
Henry Leigh, ?, 1558-61
William Lorymer, innholder, 1561
Nicholas Love, ?, 1565
Richard Loxon (Lockson), armorer
John Lucas, skinner

Anthony Mabb, ?, 1573
Randall Manning, skinner
Anthony Marlor
John Marshe, Sr., mercer, 1559-61
Robert Marshe, grocer
Thomas Marston, haberdasher, 1558
John Martin, ?, 1589-98
Mathew Martin, brewer
John Martyn, ?, 1594-8
Thomas Masham, ?, 1559
James Maston
Richard May, merchant taylor
Thomas Maye, vintner
Lawrence Mellowe, clothworker
Leonard Milnes, haberdasher
Miles Mordyng, skinner
Thomas More (Moore), ?, 1559-60
Hugh Morgan, grocer, 1575-83
James Morley, ?, 1561
William Mortymer, carpenter, 1558
Thomas Mustyan, ?, 1559-76

Henry Naylor, clothworker, 1558
    Nedham, ?, 1573
Harry Nelson, ?, 1566-7
John Newberry, stationer
Guy Newman, goldsmith
Robert Newman, vintner
Clement Newse, mercer, 1559-61
John Newton, mercer, 1598-1600
Thomas Nycell, goldsmith
Thomas Nicholson, ?, 1561
John Noble, ?, 1571

John Oldham, clothworker
William Onslowe, scrivener, 1573-93
Richard Onver, dyer
William Orneshaw, grocer, 1575
Roger Owfiele, fishmonger

William Page, ?, 1573
Lawrence Palmer, clothworker
John Park, pewterer
    Parkhurst, draper
John Parkins, mercer
Nicholas Parkinson, clothworker,
    1571-4
John Parr, embroiderer, 1587-1603
Robert Payne, grocer
    Payne, fishmonger
Henry Payton, mercer
Robert Pecok, salter, 1559
John Pelsant, grocer, 1583

Thomas Person (Pyerson), scrivener,
    1558-9
Edmund Piggot, grocer, 1587-95
Thomas Piggott, ?, 1598-1608
Edward Pilsworth, clothworker
Richard Platte, dyer, 1589-99
Walter Plummer, merchant taylor
John Pollard, embroiderer
John Pont, merchant taylor, 1576
John Pookye, ?, 1601-7
Thomas Pope, merchant taylor
John Porter, fishmonger, 1599
Robert Powell, haberdasher, 1576
Anthony Prior, draper, 1573-6
William Pryce, merchant taylor
John Purvye, embroiderer
William Pyreson

John Quarles, Jr., draper, 1586-99
Bartholomew Quinie, clothworker

John Ranse, ?, 1560
John Reade, baker, 1593-5,
    1599-1619
Nicholas Revell, ?, 1573
William Reynolds, ?, 1559
Henry Richards, ?, 1559-62
John Richmond, barber surgeon
William Ridgeley, ?, 1558-69
Peter Robinson, salter
William Robinson, baker
John Rogers
Richard Rogers, goldsmith
Robert Rogers, leatherseller
Oliver Rowe, merchant taylor
John Royce, mercer, 1559
Thomas Russell, clothworker, 1589-99
Thomas Russell, draper, 1583
Morgan Rychards, ?, 1571-87
    Ryland, cutler
James Ryley

William Salte, ?, 1586-7, 1588-93
Andrew Sares, salter, 1577
Thomas Sares, haberdasher,1573-9
Thomas Saywell, salter
Richard Scales, salter, 1596-1603
Richard Scarlet, ?, 1600-7
Stephen Scudamore, vintner
Richard Selbye, ?, 1592-3
Richard Sharpe, wax chandler
Robert Shaw, cowper·
Richard Shepham, merchant taylor
Thomas Shotsham, ?, 1571
John Sibthorp, ?, 1592-5, 1597-8
John Sikelmore, ?, 1571
Anthony Silver, leatherseller, 1559
Thomas Simons, skinner
William Skadamore (Scudamore),
    ironmonger

172

Oliver Skinner, salter? or ironmonger?
Richard Skyppe, mercer
Rowland Sleforde (Slyford),
    clothworker
John Sloker, ?, 1559
Richard Slyford (Sleforde),
    clothworker
David Smith, embroiderer, 1578-87
John Smith, mercer
Henry Smythe, mercer, 1573-1600
Robert Smythe, merchant taylor,
    1599
Anthony Soder (Soda), grocer,
    1598-1619
John Southall, clothworker, 1575-89
George Southurk, grocer
Thomas Sponer, goldsmith, 1558-65
William Squyer, ?, 1584-90
Thomas Stacey, mercer, 1559
Anthony Stanlake, mercer
James Stapper, skinner
John Stephens, ?, 1588-93
John Stevenson, ?, 1571
George Stockmeade, grocer, 1576-7
George Stoddard, grocer, 1571
John Stokes, fishmonger
William Stone, haberdasher, 1586-8
    Stones, mercer
Richard Stookbrydge, mercer, 1558
Humphrey Strete, ?, 1595-1626
William Strete, ?, 1559
Nicholas Style, grocer, 1605-6
Stephen Swingfeld, fishmonger
William Sylliard, ?, 1565

Henry Taileford (Taylefoor),
    clothworker
John Tatton, ?, 1572-7
John Tayllor, haberdasher, 1576-97
Lawrence Tayllor, cutler, 1558
Richard Tayllor, grocer, 1558-61
Thomas Thomlinson, merchant
    taylor, 1589-99
Thomas Thomlinson, skinner, 1593
George Thornton, ironmonger, 1561-2
Anthony Throckmorton, ?, 1560-1
Thomas Tirrell (Terrell), ?, 1586-97
Richard Totehill, stationer, 1558
William Tracye, ?, 1559
Richard Traford, salter
John Traves, merchant taylor, 1558
Raph Treswell, ?, 1600-17

Thomas Trott, ?, 1576
William Tucker, grocer, 1560-5
Edward Turfett

John Vauxe, merchant taylor
Richard Venables, merchant taylor
Richard Vyollet, fishmonger

Richard Waar, dyer
Thomas Wade (Waad), ironmonger
Thomas Walker, vintner
John Ward, leatherseller
Thomas Ward, fishmonger, 1589
Lawrence Warner, skinner
Mark Warner (Warmer), ?, 1573
Nicholas Warner, skinner, 1585-96
John Watson, goldsmith
William Watson, ?, 1559
John Weaver, mercer, 1587-98
Thomas Webb, haberdasher
Henry Webbe, merchant taylor,
    1586-98
John Westwray, ?, 1601-4
Thomas Wheeler
John Wheler, ?, 1591-2
Christopher Whichecott, ?, 1582-3
John White, haberdasher, 1583
William Whitle
William Widgington, ?, 1573-6
John Wight, draper
Thomas Wight, draper, 1606-9
Thomas Wight, stationer, 1599
Roger Wilcox, clothworker
John Wilkenson, ?, 1571
Richard Wiseman, goldsmith
Richard Woare, dyer, 1593-4
Thomas Wood, pewterer
Robert Woode, fishmonger, 1558-69
Gamaliel Woodford, ?, 1591-8
John Woodward, ironmonger
Richard Wright, merchant taylor,
    1589-99
    Wright, vintner
William Wrothe, ?, 1571
Richard Wyatt, woodmonger
Robert Wygge, goldsmith, 1558
Robert Wynche, haberdasher, 1577-8
Roger Wythey, ?, 1558
John Wytton, ?, 1565-6, 1569-82

Gregory Young, draper
Gregory Young, grocer
Robert Young, ?, 1559-61

2

LIST OF CIVIC OFFICES

Because of the connection between City offices and patronage, both civic and royal, it becomes of interest to know how many offices there were in the City's gift. The list below includes 170 offices that were held by approximately 479 men at any one time. For two reasons, however, this list cannot claim to be a complete one. Inadvertently, some places have undoubtedly been overlooked. Secondly, even a faultless search would not disclose the many places not discussed or itemized in any City record. It is known, for example, that the garbler of spices had a number of assistants, but how many, by whom they were appointed, how paid, and how long they served are questions that may never be satisfactorily answered now. The clerk of the Chamber also had his own clerks. Indeed, a cursory glance at this list will suffice to suggest the high number of officers who almost certainly did have assistants of one kind or another. Only rarely is there some record which throws light on the number of subordinates under a particular man. (See below p. 177 n. 1 for those under the keeper of Blackwell Hall for example.) Also uncertain is the whole number of searchers and sealers of any particular product. There were often six for tanned leather and a dozen for wine, but the number varied.[1] The same goes for any office shown here in the plural.

The list shows the names of the principal appointive offices in the City's gift around 1600-60. With the possible exception of those marked with an asterisk (explained below) the list would be the same at the earlier part of that period as at the later. It should be remembered that none of the elective offices in the wards, parishes, companies, hospitals, or those in the City administration itself have been included here.[2]

The two principal sources for this list are the Elizabethan Oath Book[3] and *The City Law*, printed in 1647.[4] The former gives the oaths of the officers who commonly took an oath at their entry into office.

---

1 See Rep. 14, fos. 347 and 100^b-101 respectively.

2 These have been discussed in chapters 2-4.

3 This is a manuscript volume at the CLRO. An entry of 12 July 1580 in the Repertories refers to the fact that a new copy of the Oath Book was needed; one of the clerks of the Mayor's Court was commissioned to do the job (Rep. 20, fos. 92^b-93). From internal evidence the volume was drawn up between 29 April 1584 (the latest date referred to in the text of any oath) and 23 March 1602 (the date

Continued on next page

4 See pp. 63-6 in that work.

The latter is a list of seventy-one places said to have been in the mayor's gift, though this meant in the gift of the Court of Aldermen and the mayor, for a number of the places included were actually awarded by the whole court. The reason why the places in *The City Law* list were said to be in the mayor's gift is that during his year as mayor each alderman was entitled to receive at least a part of whatever money was collected upon awarding them, or in some cases for actually selling them. The list is far from complete for what it attempts to cover. Three other sources were used to determine how many places were in the gift of the mayor. In 1596 it was determined that all offices to do with 'weighing, measuring, packing, gauging, garbelling, and sealing of leather, and the government, oversight and correction of them' belonged to the mayor.[1]

On the practice of venality, there is a hint that it was known at least as early as 1452.[2] It was, of course, the mayor and the two sheriffs who profited most from selling offices. It is not known how many places were venal in the late sixteenth century, but the number grew as the Chamber's needs grew. In 1696 a list was drawn up showing that seventy-nine offices, involving over 230 men, were for sale.[3] This list was drawn up through unofficial sources, possibly hostile to the civic authorities, but even an official list in City records of about the same time (1703) showed that sixty-nine were venal.[4]

These last two lists were also used in making up the list below. They are especially useful because they show the actual number of officeholders at a particular time. These numbers must be treated cautiously, however, because the number may have inflated over the century after Elizabeth's death. A number on the list below, therefore, can be taken as accurate for the late sixteenth century; a number in parentheses is the number on either the 1696 or 1703 list. Some of the places shown on these two lists may not have existed in 1600. Two offices were not counted for that reason: the collector of the duty on coals for orphans, and the collector of the duty on wines for orphans. A number of other places, commonly grouped among the artificers of the City, have an uncertain origin. They may have existed before 1640, but because they are not on the 1647 list, or earlier ones, an asterisk is placed before them. The names of several officers not on either the

of a marginal alteration on folio 40). A few oaths towards the end of the volume (after folio 62[b]) were entered only after Elizabeth's death. There are earlier collections of oaths in City records (see *Cal. Let.-Book D*), but they contain no officers not also on the list here. For drawing my attention to the Elizabethan Oath Book I am grateful to Mr. David Bernstein.

1   Rep. 22, fos. 89[b]-90 and 98-98[b] (1589), and Rep. 23, fos. 522[b]-523 (1596).
2   *Cal. Let.-Book K*, p. 346.
3   Broadsheet 8.109 at the GLMR.
4   Jour. 53, fos. 714-15.

1694 or 1703 lists, which did exist after 1660 and may have been created even before 1600, have been added.

For the officers in the mayor's Household there are two lists, both nearly the same: MSS 90.12 at the CLRO, and a list in Stow's *Survey,* ii. 187-8. For the slight differences between the lists see above, p.85, n. 2.

For comparison with a later period, Richard Hayes, *An Estimate of Places for Life* (1728), pp. 8-10 has been consulted. Only five offices on that list are not included below: the hall keeper, the City measurer, the rent gatherer, and the same two omitted from the 1696 and 1703 lists (the collectors of duties on coal and wines for orphans).

Finally, for the few offices in the gift of the whole Common Council see above p. 17.

4	Aleconners[1]
	Alnegors, searchers and sealers of woollen cloth
	Attorney in Chancery
	Attorney in Exchequer
	Attorney of Guildhall
4	Attorneys in the Mayor's Court (also called clerks of the Mayor's Court)[2]
8	Attorneys in the Sheriffs' Courts
	Auditor of the City

Bailiff of Billingsgate
Bailiff of Edelmonton[3]
Bailiff of the hundred of Oswalston (Osalston)
Bailiff of Queenhithe
Bailiff of Southwark[4]
* Bargemaster of the City's Barge
(18) * Bargemen of the City's Barge
Beadle to the Court of Requests
Bellman
* Bricklayer of the City
Bridgehouse: offices under bridgemasters
    Baker
    'Boteman'
(2) Carpenters
    Clerk
    Comptroller
    'Dawber'
    Labourers
    Mason
    Masters of the masons and carpenters
* Paver
* Plasterer
* Plummer
2 Porters

1 Before 1564 aleconners were elected by Congregation.
2 The junior one of these was the clerk to the Court of Common Council.
3 *Calendar of the Salisbury MSS,* pt. 4:615 (19 September 1594).
4 The bailiff had around ten assistants (Johnson, *Southwark,* p. 305).

```
           * Purveyor
             Renter
             'Shotsman'
             'Tydeman'
             'Tylor'
             Under masons
   22   Brokers ¹
```

Carpenter of the City
Carroom holders
Chamber: offices under chamberlain
        Comptroller
        Clerk
        Renter
        Under chamberlain
Chronicler of the City (also called Chronologer) ²
* City crier for things lost and found
Clerk of Bridewell
Clerk of the commissioners for the enlargement of prisoners in the King's Bench
Clerk of commissioners for the enlargement of prisoners in execution in the compters
Clerk of the Court of Requests
Clerk of the works
* Clockmaker of the City
Collector of scavage
Collector of wheelage on London Bridge
Common carriers of Hadleigh
Common controller
* Common outroper
Common packer
4 Common pleaders
Common porter
Common serjeant
Common weigher
Coroner
Coroner of Southwark ³
Feodary of London
* Founder of the City

Garbler of spices
* Gardener of the City
Gauger of barrels of saltfish, salmon, and eels
Gauger of wines and oils
* Glazier of the City
* Gunner of the City's Barge

Hosts to merchant strangers

* Joiner of the City
Justice of the Bridgeyard ⁴

Keeper of Bay Hall

---

¹ There were twenty-two of these in 1560 (Rep. 14, fo. 422).
² Apparently the office originated only in 1620; it was abolished in 1668 (*Remembrancia,* p. 305, n. 2; Sharpe, *London and the Kingdom,* ii. 439).
³ Johnson, p. 120.
⁴ Ibid. pp. 151 and 229 ff.

Keeper of Blackwell Hall [1]
Keeper of Bothlen
2 Keepers of the compters [2]
Keeper of the compter in Southwark
Keeper of the conduit at Newgate
* Keeper of the Green Yard
Keeper of the Guildhall
Keeper of the justice hall in the Old Bailey [3]
Keeper of Leadenhall
Keeper of Ludgate
Keeper of the markethouse in Newgate Market
(2) * Keepers of the Moorfields
Keeper of the New Burial Place
Keeper of Newgate
* Keeper of the Pest House
Keeper of the Sessions House
Keepers of wood and coal for the poor
Keeper of Worsted Hall

Marker of fustians
2 Marshals
Marshal for Southwark [4]
Mason of the City
Mayor: household of
Common crier (also formerly called serjeant-at-arms) [5]
Common hunt
Foreign taker
3 Meal weighers
3 Serjeant carvers
3 Serjeants of the chamber
Serjeant of the channel (also called serjeant of the markets)
Swordbearer
Under waterbailiff
Waterbailiff
Yeoman of the channel (also called yeoman of the markets)
2 Yeomen of the chamber
4 Yeomen of the waterside
2 Yeomen of the woodwharves
6 Young men [6]
Measurers of bayes
4 Measurers of charcoals
(10) Measurers of corn (probably same as measurer of grain)
(4) Measurers of fruits
Measurer of linen cloths and silks
Measurer of sack cloths
(4) Measurers of salt
Measurer of woollen cloths and cottons

1 The keeper had five clerks under him in 1560 (Rep. 14, fo. 423), and six porters in 1563 (Rep. 15, fo. 190[b]). There was also a keeper of the storehouse in Blackwell Hall.

2 Each keeper had a clerk.

3 Rep. 14, fo. 339[b] is the reference for this officer who does not appear on any of the lists used in making this appendix.

4 Johnson, p. 325.

5 This officer was the one who carried the City's mace before the mayor.

6 They were assistants to the four chief household officers, who, in order of importance, were the swordbearer, common hunt, common crier, and waterbailiff.

Meters of onions [1]
Meters of oysters
(15) Meters of seacoals

8 Overseers of the Thames watermen

* Painter of the City
* Paver of the City
* Plasterer of the City
* Plummer of the City
Porter of Billingsgate
Printer of the City [2]
* Printer of the sessions paper to each lord mayor

Recorder
Remembrancer
Renter of Finsbury [3]

Searchers and sealers of boots, shoes, and leather goods
Searchers and sealers of hopps and soap
Searchers and sealers of oil & vinegar, salt & butter
Searchers and sealers of tanned leather
Searchers and sealers of wines
Second 'biriship'
Sheriffs: Offices under [4]
   2 Clerks of the papers
  (8) Clerk sitters
   2 Prothonotaries
   2 Secondaries
 (36) Serjeants
   2 Undersheriffs (also called judges of the Sheriffs' Courts)
 (36) Yeomen
* Smith of the City
Solicitor of the City
* Stationer of the City
Steward of Finsbury
Steward of Southwark [5]

Town clerk (also called the common clerk)

Under escheator [6]

4 Viewers

Waiter at the waterside
* Waits of the City

---

1 'Meters' were measurers. A number of the officers here called measurers are often referred to as meters and vice versa.

2 The earliest holder of this office I have identified is John Wolfe (1591). See *DNB* under Reyner Wolfe.

3 In the Elizabethan period there was a 'farmer' of Finsbury, but this was probably the same officer as the renter.

4 There were also various 'stewards, butlers, porters, and other[s] in [the sheriff's] household many' (Stow, *Survey,* ii. 188).

5 He appointed clerks and attorneys to assist him, usually three attorneys (Johnson, p.285).

6 The escheator for London was the mayor.

Waterdrawer of the Dowgate Conduit
Watermen of the Thames
Weigher at the Iron Beam
Weigher at the King's Beam
Weigher at the Small Beam
Weigher at the Steelyard
Weigher of hopps
Weighers of meat
Weigher of silk (probably same as weigher of raw silk)
* Wireworker of the City

3

SIZE OF THE COMMON COUNCIL

What was the size of the Common Council in the Elizabethan period? Stow listed 200 or 202 common councilmen, depending on whether Cornhill Ward was counted as having four or six representatives.[1] It is correct to name six there because the Wardmote Book of Cornhill, dating from 1571, shows six not four. Cornhill had six councilmen at least as early as 1533[2] and probably even in the middle of the fifteenth century.[3] It also had six in 1549.[4] If 202 is the more accurate number,

---

1 *Survey*, i. 200.

2 Rep. 9, fo. 42.

3 Letter-Book D, fo. 72[b] and fos. 75 and 76. The discussion of three fifteenth century lists of councilmen is in the footnote below; on each Cornhill had six councilmen.

4 This list of 'around 1549' survives today only through a printed copy made in 1840 by the then town clerk, who was making a report to the Common Council of the number of times in the past the size of the council had changed. (See the list and others in *Minutes of the Proceedings of the Court of Common Council*, 23 Jan. 1840, pp. 15-18). The town clerk missed at least three other lists, however, of the mid-fifteenth century. (See them in Letter-Book D, fos. 70[b]-76[b]). The first one is clearly dated for 1458-59 and lists 190 names under their respective wards; the second one is below the first and may be for the succeeding year. Many names are erased or crossed out but the total is 189 names. The third list, for the council of 1460-1 ('Ano 39' is written at the top, and the thirty-ninth regnal year of Henry VI was 1460-1), is really two lists: first a table showing the number of councilmen from each ward, then the listing by names under ward headings. The table shows 187 councilmen but there are 190 actual names. This confusion and the many erasures prompted Dr. R.R. Sharpe to say the list's importance was 'problematical' (*Cal. Let.-Book D*, p.179). Curiously, the number supplied by the table, 187, and the breakdown by wards it shows correspond exactly to the list of 'around 1549', which was found in 1840 in another place entirely 'Jour. 16, in the beginning', where it no longer is). There is no reason to doubt that there was once a manuscript list of around 1549, but it is not known whether it was merely a copy of the older 1460 list or whether it actually reflected the number and distribution of councilmen in 1549.

By the middle of the sixteenth century the civic authorities were aware of London's growing size and appropriately greater need for more councilmen. It would seem they searched their records — exactly as the town clerk did in 1840 — and found that at the last official reckoning there were 187 allotted to the various wards. In view of all the other erasures and crossouts the small discrepancies between the table and the three lists of 1458-60 may be due to nothing more than a clerical error — forgetting to cross out a few more names. Or there may have been disputes between various candidates, or perhaps one man resigned and an extra name is that of his successor. Whatever the reasons for the discrepancies, apparently there was a need for a definitive statement concerning how many representatives each ward should have. It was provided in the table. There was no point in drawing up a table showing how many councilmen each ward actually had, for that was a matter of common knowledge to contemporaries of any period. Since London was quadrupling her population during the sixteenth century, it is not surprising that a new evaluation was needed, indeed there may have been more than one. The older list of 1460, therefore, was probably copied

there is a further adjustment required to Stow's figures, for in neither of
the two editions of his *Survey* for which he was personally responsible
(1598 & 1603) is there any number for Billingsgate Ward. The Kingsford edition supplied the number seven, in brackets, which is also the
number given in the 1633 edition by Anthony Munday,[1] as well as in
the encyclopedic edition of 1720 by John Strype.[2] It is not known how
Munday arrived at the number seven, but apparently Strype and
Kingsford copied him, for there is no indication in City records that
Billingsgate ever had seven councilmen. On the 1460 list and the similar
one of 1549,[3] the number is ten; other lists of councilmen by wards,
including several from 1675-1758,[4] all show Billingsgate with ten
right up to the year 1838.[5]

In the sixteenth century wards were not represented on the basis of
population; that in 1840 the town clerk was asked to outline the
numbers for each ward over previous centuries suggests tradition still
exercised considerable weight in the nineteenth century. Had population
been the sole criterion, the civic authorities would have had to keep far
more accurate demographic figures than they did. Also, representation
only according to population is a rather abstract idea, embodying a
logical but oversimplified view of things. To the aldermen of the sixteenth century a ward might need more representatives as it grew larger,
but since these representatives sat on the Common Council of the City
their number had to express something of the relative dignity, age, and
perhaps wealth of the various wards. It was over such matters that
disputes could arise, and every ward's leaders doubtless sought to retain
their highest traditional number, as a matter of principle. Therefore,
Billingsgate can be assigned ten councilmen because no City record
shows a different number for the ward any time during the period
1460-1840. This makes the membership of the Common Council
during the Elizabethan period 212.

around 1549, not as an indication of current ward representation, but as a basis
for studying revisions. As a result of these adjustments new tables were probably
drawn up, and though none survive in City records there is a table in John
Stow's own handwriting among the papers he collected (BL Harley MS 539,
fo. 183b), doubtless copied from the City records to which he had access as a
'Fee'd Chronicler' as early as 1595 (*Survey*, vol. i. p. xxiii). His manuscript table
shows the same number of councilmen and the same breakdown by wards as that
eventually published in his book, except that in the book he showed Cornhill
with four or six instead of just four as in his list.

1   Anthony Munday, et al., *The Survay of London* (1633), p. 229.
2   *Survey of London and Westminster* (1720), vol. 1, bk. ii. 173.
3   Letter-Book D, fo. 75. For a discussion of these lists see note 4, p. 180.
4   See them in 'List of Aldermen, Deputies and Common Councilmen, 1675-
1783' at the CLRO, shelf 40 C.
5   *Minutes of the Proceedings . . . . ,* 23 Jan. 1840, pp. 15-18.

With regard to the whole number of Elizabethan councilmen it is not possible to be precise because records of election — the surest source — do not survive from every ward. Even counting the names that occur in City records in every year for forty-four years would prove inconclusive, since those councilmen who were never noticed in the records would be omitted — that is, those who never held an office, served on a committee, or acted as a surety for a civic bond. Nonetheless, an estimate of the whole number can be made. [1] All holders of the higher kind of City office from hospital governor on up were also members of the Common Council. [2]

Next, by examining one of the offices with a large number of councilmen — hospital governors, whose number toward the end of the reign approached that of the Common Council itself — it is found that in three pairs of select years the average number who repeated as governors the next year was 85 per cent.[3] This does not include the aldermanic governors, of course. In order to reappear as a governor a man needed to be re-elected to the council, therefore it may be said that in spite of standing annually for election at least 85 per cent of all councilmen were returned each year. It is important to say at least 85

1   The size of the council for the forty-four years of Elizabeth's reign cannot be strictly comparable to other periods of equal duration for the reason that attitudes towards office and external political pressures made some difference in how long men served. For example, the much shorter period of 1660-89 produced approximately as many councilmen as held office in the Elizabethan period; J.R. Woodhead, *The Rulers of London, 1660-89* (1965).

2   There was no ordinance that forced officeholders to be councilmen or aldermen, but this has been concluded as the result of specific tests designed to discover just how many leading officeholders were also councilmen. Several select years were taken (1558-63, 1569, 1574, 1579, 1583, 1589, 1593, 1599 and 1603), during which all men positively identified as councilmen were put into one list — that is, those who served on committees of Common Council or the Court of Aldermen, or were sureties for bonds sealed under the City's seal. Then all men who were officeholders during those years were examined and classified in one of three ways: definitely a councilman because he also served on committees or stood bound for civic bonds; probably a councilman because he held more than one civic office; and third, the uncertain men who held only one office and were not committeemen or sureties. Because this selective test was made for a total of only thirteen of the forty-four years, some men in the probable or uncertain categories would have proven themselves councilmen in the other years. But even the results of testing in select years are quite convincing: 71% of hospital governors were definitely councilmen, 76% of auditors-general, 83% of hospital treasurers, and 91% of hospital auditors were also definitely councilmen. The percentages are higher for the latter officers because there were fewer of them over forty-four years, generally serving longer too, and it was therefore easier to have more information about them working in the select years. Counting the probable councilmen too shows that all the auditors-general and hospital auditors were councilmen, as were 98% of the hospital treasurers and 88% of hospital governors. In the later years of the reign it was common to have a few honorary governors, and to include the department heads, but with these exceptions I believe all hospital governors were councilmen.

3   For 1559-60, 81%; for 1582-3, 85%; for 1599-1600, 89%.

per cent because the replacement rate for hospital governors was higher than that among common councilmen. Governors were office-holders serving for short periods, often several short periods separated by longer intervals. Councilmen held a dignity more than an office and usually served continuously for long periods, often until their death. If 15 per cent of the council was new every year, which would be too high a figure, the total conciliar body during Queen Elizabeth's reign would have been about 1611. A more accurate estimate is 1107, found by calculating the average percentage of annual replacement on the Court of Aldermen (from Beaven) and applying that figure (9.6 per cent) to the council. This is still too high because men were sometimes replaced on the council by others who had previously been councilmen. Perhaps the closest total estimate would be between 1000 and 1050.

4

THE CITY'S JURISDICTION

The question of the City's jurisdiction has never been treated extensively. Such a study would have to discover the special arrangements that existed between the City and each of the liberties and suburbs. For the most part the authority of the aldermen and Common Council existed only within the twenty-six traditional wards. Three of those wards (Bridge Without in Southwark, Farringdon Without in the west and Portsoken in the east) lay entirely outside the walls of the City. Parts of three other wards (Aldersgate, Cripplegate, and Bishopsgate) extended north of the walls.[1] The London rulers had no authority in Westminster, which had twelve wards of its own governed by the dean of Westminster, a high steward, twelve burgesses, and twelve assistants.[2] In between the two cities, indeed even within the wards of London itself, there were many liberties that claimed various immunities from the aldermen's authority. Those of the Tower and St. Paul's were of sufficient age and authority to preclude disputes with the City on most points, but the land around the Tower was the subject of frequent disputes between the crown's officers at the Tower and the City authorities.[3] Rights of arrest within the churchyard of St. Paul's were not clear.[4] Another liberty was the precinct of St. Martin-le-Grand, governed by the dean and chapter of Westminster, which had been a problem to the City for several centuries. In the sixteenth century the precinct still claimed its residents could not be impressed into military service for the City.[5]

Much more serious problems existed in the suburbs, in the properties that formerly belonged to the monastic houses, and in such venerable enclaves as the Inns of Court and the Duchy of Lancaster lands between the City and Westminster.[6] The purchasers of monastic properties claimed the immunities enjoyed by the former owners, which, with the exception of the City's right to collect taxes and raise troops there, the

1 A useful reference map for London at this time is supplied with the Kingsford edition of Stow's *Survey*.
2 Statute 27 Eliz. I, c. 31 (1585) for details of its government.
3 *Remembrancia*, pp. 426 and note, 434 and *passim*.
4 Ibid. pp. 327-8.
5 Ibid. pp. 458-9. For some of the earlier disputes with St. Martin's see *Cal. Let.-Book K*, pp. 151-60.
6 For a discussion of the number and nature of these liberties see E.J. Davies, 'The Transformation of London', in *Tudor Studies Presented to A.F. Pollard*, ed. R.W. Seton-Watson (1924), pp. 287-314.

crown was prepared to allow them [1] The City's power to raise taxes and troops was frequently challenged. In March 1600 Alderman Humphrey Weld joined two men appointed by the Privy Council 'to take some reasonable course for the indifferent and equal assessments to be imposed upon the inhabitants of the Blackfriars to contribute rateably with the citizens of this City in all payments, as well for performance of Her Majesty's service hereafter as for the arrearages by them heretofore owing for the like service'.[2] Similar immunities from subsidies, troop levies, and the duties of watch and ward [3] in the City were claimed by royal officers living in the suburbs of London or in the City itself. The ruling laid down by the Privy Council was that royal servants were not exempt from charges or the responsibility to furnish troops; however, concerning watch and ward those servants who had to give personal attendance at some particular place could satisfy this obligation through a deputy. Other servants, the extraordinary ones who gave no personal attendance, were obligated to perform watch and ward.[4] This order met with continued resistance.[5]

A general difficulty presented by the liberties, whether they lay within a City ward or just beyond, and by the suburbs, was that they had their own traditions, and many had their own specific instruments of government.[6] Nor were their immunities and privileges framed in a consistent way, which would have simplified the City's dealings with them. The City's rights and responsibilities there were ambiguous at best. Such legal and traditional impediments to good government were made worse by the unwillingness of both the crown and the City to come to grips firmly with the problems presented by the liberties and suburbs. Thus while the charter of 6 James I (1608) extended the City's authority over Duke's Place in Trinity Parish near Aldgate, Great and Little St. Bartholomew's near Smithfield, Blackfriars, Whitefriars, and Coldharbour, these places were still exempt from paying fifteenths levied by Common Council, and from paying scot or serving in nightly watches. Blackfriars and Whitefriars obtained other

1 Pearl, *Puritan Revolution*, pp. 26-7. In chapter 1 of her book Professor Pearl gives a much more detailed description of the difficulties presented by the liberties than is attempted here; she also makes some penetrating remarks about the consequences of the City's and the crown's failure to come to terms with a growing London. See especially pp.37-44.

2 Rep. 25, fo. 60.

3 'Watch and ward' refers to the police power in the wards; it was in the hands of the citizens who served by rotation in the office of constable.

4 *APC*, xx. 256-9. The ruling was in February 1591.

5 *Remembrancia*, p. 25.

6 The City's relationship with Southwark has been explored in detail by David J. Johnson, *Southwark and the City* (1969).

special privileges.[1] For its part the City was anxious to raise revenue and troops in the suburbs without undertaking to incorporate them into the City, since these populous and extensive territories were burdensome to administrate. In the case of the 1608 charter the City did not come out very well.

The uniform authority of a single government was still lacking in these territories. The result was a vicious circle.[2] Because there was no single strong authority present, public order degenerated, over-crowding increased, industry operated without either City or livery company control, and aliens swarmed in freely. The worse the situation, the more unwilling the City was to become involved. Simultaneously, it was in the interests of many artisans, builders, and aliens especially not to have their suburbs incorporated.

But this did not mean that the City was completely at odds with the liberties and suburbs, for agreements could be made. In February 1601, for example, three senior aldermen (who were also justices of the peace) and four juniors met at the mayor's house in the City with the justices of Middlesex 'touching moneys to be collected for the building and making of two galleys for Her Majesty's service and the defense of this City'.[3] Significantly, reasons of national defense lay behind most co-operative efforts, and it was usually only for the same reasons that the Privy Council actively defended the City's claims to collect taxes and raise troops in the liberties and suburbs. The City also had some indirect jurisdictional authority outside the twenty-six wards. The mayor, recorder, and senior aldermen exercised a judicial supervision over London and Middlesex by virtue of being justices of oyer and terminer and gaol delivery. In charters of the early seventeenth century the aldermen's powers as justices were extended to many liberties. Furthermore the aldermen nominated two justices to serve for Middlesex and Surrey. Yet the City was satisfied with this marginal authority and declined to accept the crown's proposal in 1637 which would have made all the aldermen special justices for a number of the parishes and liberties of Middlesex and Surrey.[4] Relations between the liberties and

---

1 Birch, *Charters of London* (1887), pp. 144-5 and Pearl, pp. 31-2. Scot and lot referred to the traditional duties expected of every householder: cleaning the street in front of one's house, hanging out a lantern on a dark night, etc.; and serving various offices in the ward by rotation, like scavenger, beadle, and constable. One either performed these duties in person (bearing lot), or paid a sum (scot) that was used to employ permanent employees.

2 The problems of London's growth have been treated by other writers. See the works of Valerie Pearl, E.J. Davies and N.G. Brett-James, already cited.

3 Rep. 25, fo. 194.

4 Pearl, pp. 29-31.

the City, therefore, continued to be by special arrangement. Government in the liberties themselves was ineffectual because the backing of any strong authority was lacking.

5
THE BUREAUCRATS

Bridgemasters
William Draper, ironmonger, 1559-68
Robert Essington, leatherseller, 1559-69
Thomas Bates, haberdasher, 1568-86
John Randall, haberdasher, 1569-74
Robert Aske, goldsmith, 1574-89; a councilman
James Gonnell, stationer, 1586-94; a councilman
Thomas Ware, fishmonger, 1589-93; a notable councilman
Richard Denman, grocer, 1593- beyond 1603; a leading councilman
John Hall, clothier, 1594- beyond 1603; probably the councilman of 1589-93

Chamberlains
John Sturgeon, haberdasher, 1550-63
George Heton, merchant taylor, 1563-77; a councilman
John Mabbe, goldsmith, 1577-82; a notable councilman
Robert Brandon, goldsmith, 1583-91
Thomas Wilford, merchant taylor, 1591-1603; probably not the notable councilman

Common Serjeants
John Marshe, mercer, 1547-63; a councilman
Bernard Randolph, 1563-83
Thomas Kyrton, 1583-1601
Richard Wilbraham, 1601
Richard Wheler, 1601 - beyond 1603

Recorders
Ralph Cholmeley, 1553-63
Richard Onslow, 1563-6
Thomas Bromley, 1566-9
Thomas Wilbraham, 1569-71
William Fleetwood, 1571-92
Edward Coke, 1592
Edward Drew, 1592-4
Thomas Flemming, 1594-5
John Croke, 1595-1603

Remembrancers
Thomas Norton, grocer, 1571-84
Giles Fletcher, 1587-1605

Town Clerks
William Blackwell, 1540-70
Anthony Stapleton, 1570-4
William Sebright, 1574-1613.

INDEX

For additional offices not mentioned in the text or Index, see Appendix 2. The 'other common councilmen' (above, pp. 168-72) are not listed in the Index unless also mentioned in the text.